Roanoke River National Wildlife Refuge

Comprehensive Conservation Plan
&
Final
Environmental Impact Statement

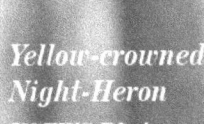

Yellow-crowned Night-Heron
USFWS Photo

Comprehensive Conservation Plans provide long-term guidance for management decisions; set forth goals, objectives, and strategies needed to accomplish refuge purposes; and identify the Fish and Wildlife Service's best estimate of future needs. These plans detail program planning levels that are sometimes substantially above current budget allocations and, as such, are primarily for Service strategic planning and program prioritization purposes. The plans do not constitute a commitment for staffing increases, operational and maintenance increases, or funding for future land acquisition.

Roanoke River National Wildlife Refuge

Comprehensive Conservation Plan

U.S. Department of the Interior
Fish and Wildlife Service
Southeast Region

October, 2005

Submitted by: //S// **Harvey Hill**   Date: 9/14/05

Harvey Hill, Refuge Manager
Roanoke River NWR

Concur: //S// **Pete Jerome**   Date: 9/29/05

Pete Jerome, Refuge Supervisor
Southeast Region

Concur: //S// **Jon Andrew**   Date: 9-29-05

Jon Andrew, Regional Chief
Southeast Region

Approved by: //S// **Cynthia Dohner**   Date: 9-30-05

Sam Hamilton, Regional Director
Southeast Region

**COMPREHENSIVE CONSERVATION PLAN
AND FINAL ENVIRONMENTAL IMPACT STATEMENT**

ROANOKE RIVER NATIONAL WILDLIFE REFUGE
Bertie County, North Carolina

U.S. Department of the Interior
Fish and Wildlife Service
Southeast Regional Office
1875 Century Boulevard
Atlanta, Georgia 30345

October 2005

TABLE OF CONTENTS

SECTION A. COMPREHENSIVE CONSERVATION PLAN AND FINAL ENVIRONMENTAL IMPACT STATEMENT

List of Figures

List of Tables

Executive Summary

The U.S. Fish and Wildlife Service has prepared this Comprehensive Conservation Plan and Final Environmental Impact Statement to guide the management of Roanoke River National Wildlife Refuge in Bertie County, North Carolina. The plan outlines programs and corresponding resource needs for the next 15 years, as mandated by the National Wildlife Refuge Improvement Act of 1997.

Before the Service began planning, it conducted a biological review of the refuge's wildlife and habitat management program and conducted public scoping meetings to solicit public opinion of the issues the plan should address. The biological review team was composed of biologists from federal and state agencies and nongovernmental organizations that have an interest in the refuge. The staff held public scoping meetings at four locations on four evenings. Another round of public meetings was held to solicit reaction to the proposed alternatives.

The management of flows in the Roanoke River by the U.S. Army Corps of Engineers for flood control and by a private power company for hydroelectric power generation is the major issue affecting the refuge. The managed flows extend the duration of flooding on refuge lands. The absence of a legal right-of-way to the refuge from the uplands limits public access. Extensive flooding limits administrative access for maintenance, biological surveys, and law enforcement. There is a need for more extensive biological surveys and monitoring and a demand for education and interpretive programs that cannot be met.

The Service developed and analyzed three alternatives. Alternative 1 is the status quo alternative. The staff does not currently actively manage habitat on the refuge. The staff surveys populations of neotropical migratory songbirds and the forest health and regeneration of bottomland hardwood forests. The refuge allows the six priority public use activities: hunting, fishing, wildlife observation, wildlife photography, and environmental education and interpretation. The staff conducts environmental education and interpretation on a request basis only. The zone law enforcement officer enforces regulations on the refuge and supervises the law enforcement officers on other area refuges. Six staff members are stationed in Windsor, North Carolina.

Alternative 2 proposes moderate program increases. The refuge would survey all habitat types, and develop and implement a management plan for all refuge habitats. The staff would survey most major wildlife groups on the refuge. The refuge would continue to allow the six priority public use activities, but would have the capacity to increase the number of opportunities. The staff would conduct regularly scheduled environmental education and interpretation programs. The Service would build a shop and equipment storage facility. There would be 11 staff members stationed at Roanoke River, including a law enforcement officer and public use specialist.

Alternative 3 proposes substantial program increases. The refuge would survey all habitat types, and develop and implement a management plan for all habitats on the refuge and on selected easements large enough to warrant consideration. The staff would survey a wide range of wildlife on the refuge. The refuge would increase further the number of public use opportunities. The Service would build a shop and equipment storage facility. There would be 22 staff members, including a law enforcement officer, public use specialist, media specialist, and technical specialists (e.g., hydrologist and entomologist.)

The staff selected Alternative 3 as the preferred alternative. It advances the refuge program considerably and outlines programs that would meet both the biological needs of refuge resources and needs of the public.

SECTION A. COMPREHENSIVE CONSERVATION PLAN AND FINAL ENVIRONMENTAL IMPACT STATEMENT

I. Background

INTRODUCTION

The U.S. Fish and Wildlife Service developed this Comprehensive Conservation Plan to provide a foundation for the management and use of Roanoke River National Wildlife Refuge in Bertie County, North Carolina. The plan is a working guide for the refuge's management programs and actions over the next 15 years.

The refuge is situated in the floodplain of the Roanoke River, the flows of which are managed for flood control by the U.S. Army Corps of Engineers and for hydroelectric power generation by a private power company. The timing, frequency, and duration of these managed flows are not similar to the natural flows under which the ecosystem evolved. The controlled flooding events often occur during the growing season, in contrast to natural flooding which occurred predominantly during the dormant season. The controlled events also occur for weeks in contrast to the natural flooding which rarely lasted more than a single week. The flows are being managed in such a way that they may have devastating effects on the overall health and diversity of the 200,000-acre bottomland hardwood ecosystem. The managed flows affect every aspect of refuge management, from biological monitoring to habitat management, maintenance, and public use.

Since the establishment of the refuge, the U.S. Fish and Wildlife Service has been engaged with stakeholders affected by the managed river flows. These stakeholders represent a variety of views on water management in the Roanoke River Valley. Their concerns include ecosystem integrity; the economic impact of recreational opportunities on the reservoirs; flood control; water supply; and hydroelectric power generation. Refuge staff and representatives from the Service's Ecological Services Office and Fisheries Coordination Office have been active participants in the development of a relicensing agreement with Dominion Power. Under the Technical Settlement Agreement issued by the Federal Energy Regulatory Commission to Dominion Power in 2004, Dominion Power has agreed to an adaptive management approach to address the impacts of hydroelectric power generation on downstream terrestrial and aquatic ecosystems. The first five years of the agreement term is a period of baseline data collection. After the initial five-year period, those impacts will be assessed and the flow releases will be adapted to minimize impacts.

Concurrently, the U.S. Army Corps of Engineers has been authorized to study its flood control operations on the Roanoke River under Section 216 of the Flood Control Act of 1970. Refuge staff and representatives from the Service's Ecological Services Office and Fisheries Coordination Office, other federal agencies, state agencies, and nongovernmental organizations are all active participants in the study. Several issues have been identified, including impacts on terrestrial wildlife and habitat; aquatic resources; channel geomorphology; sedimentation dynamics; water quality; and recreation on and below the reservoirs. The outcomes of these studies may result in a change of flood control operations. These changes may bring a more natural flow regime to the downstream ecosystem.

Over the next 15 years, the refuge staff will review this comprehensive conservation plan to consider any adaptations in releases for both hydroelectric power generation and flood control. The Service will continue to support a more natural river flow regime that will sustain healthy aquatic and terrestrial ecosystems.

The Service developed this plan in compliance with the National Wildlife Refuge System Improvement Act of 1997 and Part 602 (National Wildlife Refuge System Planning) of the Fish and Wildlife Service Manual. The actions described within this plan also meet the requirements of the National Environmental Policy Act of 1969. The refuge staff achieved compliance with this Act through the involvement of the public and the incorporation of an Environmental Impact Statement in this document, with a description of the alternatives considered and an analysis of the environmental consequences of the alternatives (Chapters III and IV). When fully implemented, this plan will strive to achieve the vision and purposes of Roanoke River National Wildlife Refuge.

The plan's overriding consideration is to carry out the purposes for which Congress established the refuge. Fish and wildlife are the first priority in refuge management, and the Service allows and encourages public use (wildlife-dependent recreation) as long as it is compatible with, or does not detract from, the refuge's mission and purposes.

A planning team prepared the plan. Members of the planning team included representatives from various Service programs, including the Divisions of Refuges; Fisheries; Ecological Services; Realty; and Migratory Birds. In developing the Draft Comprehensive Conservation Plan and Environmental Impact Statement, the planning team and refuge staff incorporated the input of local citizens and the general public through a series of stakeholder and public scoping meetings. Additional comments were then received from public review of the Draft Comprehensive Conservation Plan and Environmental Impact Statement, and have been incorporated in this final plan.

The Comprehensive Conservation Plan represents the Service's proposed alternative and is being put forward after considering three alternatives. After reviewing a wide range of public comments and management needs, the planning team developed these alternatives in an attempt to determine how to best meet the goals and objectives of Roanoke River National Wildlife Refuge. The proposed alternative is the Service's recommended course of action for future management of the refuge, and is the basis for this comprehensive conservation plan.

PURPOSE AND NEED FOR THE PLAN

The purpose of this comprehensive conservation plan is to identify the role that Roanoke River National Wildlife Refuge will play in supporting the mission of the National Wildlife Refuge System, and to provide guidance to the refuge's management programs and activities for the next 15 years. The plan will:

- provide a clear statement of direction for the future management of the refuge;
- provide refuge neighbors, visitors, and government officials with an understanding of the Fish and Wildlife Service's management actions on and around the refuge;
- ensure that the Service's management actions, including land protection and recreational and educational programs, are consistent with the mandates of the National Wildlife Refuge System Improvement Act of 1997;
- ensure that the management of the refuge is coordinated with federal, state, and county or parish plans; and
- provide a basis for the development of budget requests for the refuge's operational, maintenance, and capital improvement needs.

Perhaps the greatest need of the Service is to communicate with the public and include public participation in its efforts to carry out the mission of the National Wildlife Refuge System. Many agencies, organizations, institutions, businesses, and private citizens have developed relationships with the Service to advance the goals of the National Wildlife Refuge System. This plan supports the Partners in Flight Initiative, South Atlantic Coastal Plain Migratory Bird Conservation Plan, North American Waterfowl Management Plan, Western Hemisphere Shorebird Reserve Network, and National Wetlands Priority Conservation Plan.

PURPOSE AND NEED FOR THE ENVIRONMENTAL IMPACT STATEMENT

The purpose of the environmental impact statement for the plan is to determine and evaluate a range of reasonable management alternatives for Roanoke River National Wildlife Refuge. The staff generated each alternative with the potential to be fully developed into a final plan. The environmental impact statement also predicts and evaluates the biological, physical, and socioeconomic effects of implementing each alternative. From this range of alternatives, the Service identified the proposed management action.

In accordance with the guidelines of the National Environmental Policy Act, the Service identified a number of issues, concerns, and needs through discussions with the public, agency managers, and professionals. From these issues and concerns, the Service's planning team identified a range of three alternatives, evaluated the possible consequences of implementing each, and selected Alternative 3 as the preferred management action. In the opinion of the Service and the planning team, Alternative 3 is the best approach to guide the refuge's management direction.

To date, general guidance in the 1988 Habitat Preservation Proposal and the National Wildlife Administration Act of 1966 has guided refuge management. The National Wildlife Refuge System Improvement Act of 1997 requires that all national wildlife refuges have a comprehensive conservation plan in place within 15 years to meet the original purposes of the refuge and help fulfill the mission of the System to ensure integrated management.

DECISIONS TO BE MADE

The Service has identified and evaluated three management alternatives and considered comments from other agencies, organizations, and the public on the Draft Comprehensive Conservation Plan and Environmental Impact Statement for Roanoke River National Wildlife Refuge. The Service has included these comments, along with consideration of the refuge's purpose, the Service's mission, and other relevant factors in its decision to identify Alternative 3 as the preferred management alternative to guide the refuge for the next 15 years. The refuge will then implement the selected alternative, monitor the responses to management, and revise the plan as necessary

PLANNING STUDY AREA

Roanoke River National Wildlife Refuge is in northeast North Carolina, and starts less than one mile northwest of the mouth of the Roanoke River on the Albemarle Sound. Greenville and Rocky Mount, the nearest major cities, are located 50 miles southwest and west of the refuge, respectively. The major towns within the Roanoke River basin, moving downstream from the dam at Roanoke Rapids, include Roanoke Rapids, Weldon, Williamston, and Plymouth.

The planning study area for this environmental impact statement includes lands outside the existing refuge boundary that the Service is studying for inclusion in the National Wildlife Refuge System and/or partnership planning efforts. The Service presently owns and manages 20,978 acres of the 33,000 acres identified as lying within the refuge's approved acquisition boundary. The Service will seek to acquire, from willing sellers, the remaining acres. This environmental impact statement will identify management on refuge lands. The refuge staff will revise this plan to identify management of lands within the approved acquisition boundary and update the plan to reflect new lands as the Service acquires them.

OTHER RELEVANT ACTIVITIES AND PLANS

Along with the Service's legal mandates and initiatives, other planning activities directly influence the development of the comprehensive conservation plan. Other federal, state, and local agencies; local communities; nongovernmental organizations; and private individuals develop and coordinate planning initiatives to help restore habitats for fish and wildlife on and off public lands.

The Service is initiating cooperative partnerships in an effort to reduce the declining trend in biological diversity. Biological planning for species groups targeted in this plan reflects the North American Waterfowl Management Plan, which encompasses the Atlantic Coast Joint Venture and the joint venture between the North Carolina Wildlife Resources Commission and the Fish and Wildlife Service. The plan also reflects the provisions of the Partners in Flight Plan and the South Atlantic Migratory Bird Initiative.

The North American Waterfowl Management Plan of 1986 brings together international teams of biologists from private and government organizations from Canada and the United States. The partnerships, called Joint Ventures, are working to restore waterfowl and other migratory bird populations to the levels of the early 1970s by protecting about 6 million acres of priority wetland habitats from the Gulf of Mexico to the Canadian Arctic. The focus of the Atlantic Coast Joint Venture is on the middle and upper Atlantic coast. Within the Atlantic Coast Joint Venture is the joint venture formed between the North Carolina Wildlife Resources Commission, the Fish and Wildlife Service, and private conservation organizations. This joint venture has designated the Roanoke River system as its primary black duck focus area.

The South Atlantic Coastal Plain serves as primary migration habitat for migratory songbirds returning from Central and South America. It also provides wintering, breeding, and migration habitat for midcontinental wood duck and colonial bird populations. Restoration of migratory songbird populations is also a high priority of the Partners in Flight Plan.

The Partners in Flight Plan emphasizes land bird species as a priority for conservation. Habitat loss, population trends, and the vulnerability of species and habitats to threats are all factors used in the priority ranking of species. Further, biologists have identified focal species for each habitat type, from which population and habitat objectives and conservation actions will be determined. This list of focal species, objectives, and conservation actions will aid migratory bird management on the refuge.

THE U.S. FISH AND WILDLIFE SERVICE

The U.S. Fish and Wildlife Service is the primary federal agency responsible for the conservation, protection, and enhancement of the Nation's fish and wildlife populations and their habitats. Although the Service shares some conservation responsibilities with other federal, state, tribal, local, and private entities, it has specific trustee obligations for migratory birds, threatened and endangered species, anadromous fish, and certain marine mammals. In addition, the Service administers a national network of lands and waters for the management and protection of these resources.

As part of its mission, the Service manages more than 540 national wildlife refuges totaling over 93 million acres. These areas comprise the National Wildlife Refuge System, the world's largest collection of lands and waters specifically managed for fish and wildlife. The majority of these lands,

77 million acres, lie in Alaska. The remaining acres are spread across the other 49 states and several island territories.

NATIONAL WILDLIFE REFUGE SYSTEM

The mission of the National Wildlife Refuge System, as defined by the National Wildlife Refuge System Improvement Act of 1997, is:

"... to administer a national network of lands and waters for the conservation, management, and where appropriate, restoration of the fish, wildlife and plant resources and their habitats within the United States for the benefit of present and future generations of Americans."

The National Wildlife Refuge System Improvement Act of 1997 established, for the first time, a clear mission of wildlife conservation for the National Wildlife Refuge System. The Act states that the Service will manage each refuge to:

- fulfill the mission of the Refuge System;
- fulfill the individual purposes of each refuge;
- consider the needs of fish and wildlife first;
- fulfill the requirement of developing a Comprehensive Conservation Plan for each unit of the Refuge System, and fully involve the public in the preparation of these plans;
- maintain the biological integrity, diversity, and environmental health of the Refuge System; and
- recognize that wildlife-dependent recreation activities including hunting, fishing, wildlife observation, wildlife photography, and environmental education and interpretation are legitimate and priority public uses.

Following passage of the Act in 1997, the Service immediately began efforts to carry out the direction of the new legislation, including the preparation of comprehensive conservation plans for all refuges. The development of these plans is now ongoing nationally. Consistent with the Act, the Service is preparing all refuge comprehensive conservation plans in conjunction with public involvement, and is requiring each refuge to complete its plan within a 15-year schedule.

Approximately 37.5 million people visited the country's national wildlife refuges in 1998, mostly to observe wildlife in their natural habitats. As this visitation continues to grow, significant economic benefits are generated to the local communities that surround the refuges. Economists have reported that national wildlife refuge visitors contribute more than $400 million annually to the local economies. In addition, the National Survey of Fishing, Hunting, and Wildlife Associated Recreation reports that nearly 40 percent of the country's adults spent $101 billion on wildlife-related recreational pursuits in 1996 (U.S. Fish and Wildlife Service 1996).

Volunteerism continues to be a major contributor to the successes of the Refuge System. In 1998, volunteers contributed more than 1.5 million person-hours on the refuges nationwide, a service valued at more than $20.6 million.

The wildlife and habitat vision for national wildlife refuges stresses that wildlife comes first; that ecosystems, biodiversity, and wilderness are vital concepts in refuge management; that refuges must be healthy and their growth must be strategic; and that the Refuge System serves as a model for habitat management with broad participation from others.

A provision of the National Wildlife Refuge System Improvement Act of 1997, and subsequent agency policy, is that the Service shall ensure timely and effective cooperation and collaboration with other federal agencies and state fish and wildlife agencies during the course of acquiring and managing refuges. This cooperation is essential in providing the foundation for the protection and sustainability of fish and wildlife throughout the United States.

The North Carolina Wildlife Resources Commission is a state-partnering agency with the Service. It is charged with enforcement responsibilities for migratory birds and endangered species, as well as managing the state's natural resources. It also manages approximately 1.8 million acres of game lands in North Carolina, including 29,311 acres within the Roanoke River system.

The Commission coordinates the state's wildlife conservation program and provides public recreation opportunities, including an extensive hunting and fishing program, on several game lands and from several boat ramps located near Roanoke River National Wildlife Refuge. The Commission's participation and contribution throughout this comprehensive conservation planning process has been valuable. It is continuing its work with the Service to provide ongoing opportunities for an open dialogue with the public to improve the condition of fish and wildlife populations on the Roanoke River floodplain. Not only has the Commission participated in biological reviews, stakeholder meetings, and field reviews as part of the planning process, it is also an active partner in annual hunt coordination, planning, and various wildlife and habitat surveys. The Commission also assists the refuge staff in providing special wildlife observation opportunities. Roanoke River National Wildlife Refuge provides hunting opportunities for small game, deer, waterfowl, and wild turkey in cooperation with the Commission. A key part of the planning process is the integration of common mission objectives between the Service and the Commission.

SOUTH ATLANTIC COASTAL PLAIN ECOSYSTEM

OVERVIEW

Roanoke River National Wildlife Refuge lies within the South Atlantic Coastal Plain physiographic region (Figure 1). The South Atlantic Coastal Plain was once a 10-million-acre complex of forested wetlands and uplands, dunes, and marshes that extended from Florida to North Carolina. Historically, the extent and duration of seasonal flooding along the ecosystem's rivers fluctuated annually, recharging the South Atlantic Coastal Plain's aquatic systems and creating a rich diversity of dynamic habitats that supported a vast array of fish and wildlife resources.

Threats and Problems

Forest Loss and Fragmentation

The South Atlantic Coastal Plain has changed markedly over the last 100 years as civilization spread throughout the area. It has been estimated that land conversion has cleared 40 percent of the natural vegetation. The greatest changes to the landscape have been in the form of land clearing for agriculture and urban development (Hunter et al. 2001). Although these changes have allowed people to settle and earn a living in the area, they have had a tremendous effect on the biological diversity, biological integrity, and environmental health of the South Atlantic Coastal Plain. The changes have reduced vast areas of bottomland hardwood forests to forest fragments. These fragments range in size from very small tracts of limited functional value to a few large areas that have maintained many of the forest's original functions and values. Severe fragmentation has resulted in a significant decline in biological diversity and integrity. Species endemic to the South Atlantic Coastal Plain that have become extinct, threatened, or endangered include the red wolf, Bachman's warbler, Carolina parakeet, and passenger pigeon. The cerulean warbler is a candidate for listing as a federally threatened species. Table 1 provides a complete list of the threatened and endangered animals in North Carolina.

Breeding bird surveys show continuing declines in species and species populations. The avian species most adversely affected by fragmentation include those that are area-sensitive (dependent on large continuous blocks of hardwood forest); those that depend on forest interiors; those that depend on special habitat requirements such as mature forests or a particular food source; and/or those that depend on good water quality.

More than 300 species of breeding migratory songbirds occupy the region. Some of these species, including the Swainson's warbler, prothonotary warbler, swallow-tailed kite, wood thrush, and cerulean warbler, have declined significantly and need the benefits of large forested blocks to recover and sustain their existence.

Fragmentation has also brought the forest edge closer to the natural nesting sites of many forest interior-nesting birds. This structural alteration of the habitat has introduced the brown-headed cowbird into the nesting zones of forest-interior species. The brown-headed cowbird is a parasitic nester that lays eggs in the nests of other birds, rather than building a nest of its own. Nestling cowbirds are typically bigger and more aggressive and out-compete the host species. This results in poor reproductive success and declining populations of forest interior-nesting species that are forced to nest near forest edges.

Fragmentation of bottomland hardwood forests has left many of the remaining forested tracts surrounded by agricultural lands. Intensive agriculture has removed most of the forested corridors along sloughs that formerly connected the forest patches. The loss of connectivity between the remaining forested tracts hinders the movement of wildlife between tracts and reduces the functional values of many remaining smaller forest tracts. The lost connections also result in a loss of gene flow, further endangering the population of natural species. Restoring the connections to allow gene flow and reestablish travel corridors is particularly important for some wide-ranging species such as the black bear.

Figure 1. Roanoke River National Wildlife Refuge in the South Atlantic Coastal Plain Physiographic Area

Table 1. Threatened and endangered species of North Carolina.

Region	Status	Common name	Scientific Name
Coastal Plain	Endangered	Manatee, West Indian	*Trichechus manatus*
	Endangered	Sea Turtle, Hawksbill	*Eretmochelys imbricata*
	Endangered	Sea Turtle, Kemp's Ridley	*Lepidochelys kempii*
	Endangered	Sea Turtle, Leatherback	*Dermochelys coriacea*
	Endangered	Stork, Wood	*Mycteria americana*
	Endangered	Sturgeon, Shortnose	*Acipenser brevirostrum*
	Endangered	Tern, Roseate	*Sterna dougallii*
	Endangered	Whale, Finback	*Balaenoptera physalus*
	Endangered	Whale, Humpback	*Megaptera novaeangliae*
	Endangered	Whale, Right	*Balaena glacialis*
	Endangered	Whale, Sea	*Balaenoptera borealis*
	Endangered	Whale, Sperm	*Physeter catodon*
	Endangered	Wolf, Red	*Canis rufus*
	Endangered	Woodpecker, Red-cockaded	*Picoides borealis*
	Threatened	Alligator, American	*Alligator mississippiensis*
	Threatened	Eagle, Bald	*Haliaeetus leucocephalus*
	Threatened	Plover, Piping	*Charadrius melodus*
	Threatened	Sea Turtle, Green	*Chelonia mydas*
	Threatened	Sea Turtle, Loggerhead	*Caretta caretta*
	Threatened	Silverside, Waccamaw	*Menidia extensa*
	Endangered	Butterfly, Saint Francis' Satyr	*Neonympha mitchellii francisci*
Piedmont	Endangered	Heelsplitter, Carolina	*Lasmigona decorata*
	Endangered	Shiner, Cape Fear	*Notropsis mekistocholas*
	Endangered	Spinymussel, James	*Pleurobema collina*
	Endangered	Spinymussel, Tar River	*Elliptio steinstansana*
	Endangered	Wedgemussel, Dwarf	*Alasmidonta heterodon*
	Endangered	Bat, Gray	*Myotis grisescens*
Mountain	Endangered	Bat, Indiana	*Myotis sodalis*
	Endangered	Bat, Virginia Big-Eared	*Corynorhinus townsendii virginianus*
	Endangered	Elktoe, Appalachian	*Alasmidonta raveneliana*
	Endangered	Mussel, Oyster	*Epioblasma capsaeformis*
	Endangered	Pearlymussel, Littlewing	*Pegias fabula*
	Endangered	Spider, Spruce-Fir Moss	*Microhexura montivaga*
	Endangered	Squirrel, Carolina Northern Flying	*Glaucomys sabrinus coloratus*
	Threatened	Chub, Spotfin	*Cyprinella monacha*
	Threatened	Turtle, Bog	*Clemmys muhlenbergii*

Alterations to Hydrology

In addition to the loss of vast acreages of bottomland forested wetlands, significant alterations in the region's hydrology have occurred due to managed stream flows from flood control and hydroelectric power generation reservoirs; drainage ditches; river channel modifications; flood control levees; deforestation; and degradation to aquatic systems from excessive sedimentation, contaminants, and urban development.

The natural hydrology of a region connects forested wetlands and is indirectly responsible for the complexity and diversity of habitats through its effects on topography and soils. Natural resource managers recognize the importance of dynamic hydrology to forested wetlands and waterfowl-habitat relationships (Fredrickson and Heitmeyer 1988).

Instead of natural hydrology, large-scale man-made hydrological alterations have changed the spatial and temporal patterns of flooding throughout the entire South Atlantic Coastal Plain. In addition, these alterations have modified both the extent and duration of annual seasonal flooding. The alteration of this annual flooding regime has had an adverse effect on the forested wetlands and their associated wetland-dependent species. In view of the hydrologic changes, it is very difficult – if not impossible – to fully emulate and reconstruct the structure and functions of a natural wetland. Restoration of wetland functions is especially difficult since wetlands depend on a dynamic interface of hydrologic regimes to maintain water, vegetation, and animal complexes and processes (Mitsch and Gosselink 1993).

Siltation of Aquatic Ecosystems

Deforestation and hydrologic alteration have degraded aquatic systems, including lakes, rivers, sloughs and bayous. Clearing of bottomland hardwood forests has led to an accelerated accumulation of sediments and contaminants in aquatic systems. Sediment now fills many water bodies, greatly reducing their surface area and depth. Concurrently, the non-point source runoff of excess nutrients and contaminants is threatening the area's remaining aquatic resources. The Service lists six species of aquatic organisms as threatened and 12 species as endangered in North Carolina (Table 1).

Hydrologic alterations have basically eliminated the geomorphologic processes that created oxbow lakes, sloughs, and river meander scars. Consequently, the protection, conservation, and restoration of these aquatic resources are of added importance in light of the alterations associated with flood control and navigation.

Proliferation of Invasive Aquatic Plants

Compounding the problems faced by aquatic systems is the growing threat from invasive aquatic vegetation. Static water levels caused by the lack of annual flooding and reduced water depths resulting from excessive sedimentation have created conditions favorable for the establishment and proliferation of several species of invasive aquatic plants. Additionally, the introduction of exotic (nonnative) vegetation capable of aggressive growth is further threatening the viability of aquatic systems. These invasive aquatic species threaten the natural aquatic vegetation important to aquatic systems, and choke waterways to a degree that often prevents recreational use.

CONSERVATION PRIORITIES

The declines in the South Atlantic Coastal Plain's bottomland hardwood forests and their associated fish and wildlife resources have prompted the Service to designate this forest type as an area of special concern. A collaborative effort involving private, state, and federal conservation partners is now underway to implement a variety of tools to restore the functions and values of wetlands in the South Atlantic Coastal Plain. The goal is to prioritize and manage wetlands to most effectively maintain and possibly restore the biological diversity of the South Atlantic Coastal Plain. In addition, some areas are prioritized as focus areas for reforestation.

It is widely recognized, however, that much of the forested wetlands that have been cleared and converted to other uses in the South Atlantic Coastal Plain will not be reforested. Some areas would have lower value for reforestation and are targeted for intensive management for nonforest-dependent species, such as waterfowl and shorebirds. Through cooperative efforts, apportioning resources, and the focusing of available programs, the South Atlantic Coastal Plain's biological diversity can be improved.

Conservationists have initiated several coordinated efforts to set priorities and establish focus areas to counter the effects of hydrologic changes and forest fragmentation. The North American Waterfowl Management Plan, Atlantic Coast Joint Venture, was established in 1988 to help provide sufficient wintering waterfowl habitat throughout the Atlantic Coastal Plain.

One of the biggest challenges to the management and restoration efforts underway in the South Atlantic Coastal Plain, and one that affects refuges in particular, is the need to meet long-term management objectives that address comprehensive ecosystem needs. These needs include those of wintering migratory waterfowl, neotropical migratory birds, shorebirds, large mammals, and other wide-ranging species. Management for one species or species group often conflicts with the management objectives for another species or species group. The tendency is to pursue short-term priorities that frequently change as scientific knowledge expands and interests in special resources shift. Biologists must exercise caution to prevent the start-up of management and restoration actions that are difficult to reverse and fail to meet the long-term, comprehensive management needs of the ecosystem or a specific area within the ecosystem. An example might be a tendency to totally manage Roanoke River National Wildlife Refuge in an effort to provide habitat for many species of neotropical migratory songbirds that require a mature forest with a dense shrub understory. Such an approach may overlook the critical habitat needs of prairie warblers that do not tolerate mature forests, but instead require big gap openings.

The initial Atlantic Coast Joint Venture effort for waterfowl has expanded to establish breeding bird objectives for shorebirds and neotropical migratory forest-nesting birds. Partners in Flight has developed bird conservation plans to focus a number of private, state, and federal restoration programs into specific areas in an effort to provide maximum program benefits for neotropical migratory forest interior-nesting birds. The goal of this collaborative restoration effort is to provide islands or blocks of forested habitat in an otherwise highly fragmented landscape. The targeted block sizes range from 10,000 to 100,000 acres. Such areas are large enough to support viable populations of various suites of neotropical migratory songbirds. Of course, these areas will also support other species that depend on large forested blocks. Existing or proposed state wildlife management areas or national wildlife refuges anchor the plans. The expansion of forested blocks on public or private land enhances and supports these public lands.

Active management of croplands, moist-soil areas, and forested wetlands on both public and private land is necessary to meet the habitat goals of the Atlantic Coast Joint Venture (Reinecke and Baxter

1996). Effective management (i.e., vegetation manipulation and hydrology restoration) compensates for the spatial and temporal habitat changes that deforestation and hydrologic alterations have caused throughout the South Atlantic Coastal Plain. Appropriately managed, the Roanoke River National Wildlife Refuge will make a significant contribution to meeting the objectives of the Atlantic Coast Joint Venture. Setting habitat and species objectives from the perspective of the South Atlantic Coastal Plain is advantageous because it considers the overall landscape and enables managers to plan and provide habitat for a diversity of species throughout their range.

Although forest stand management is probably the best solution for restoring the vast forests that have been altered by commercial timber management, hydrology (flooding) drives the ecological system in the South Atlantic Coastal Plain. The plant and animal community throughout the South Atlantic Coastal Plain is dependent upon the hydrologic cycle. It is incumbent upon land managers to manage hydrology in an effort to restore the ecological diversity that once characterized the South Atlantic Coastal Plain. Land managers can plug canals and install water control structures in an effort to mimic historic flood cycles and meet wildlife habitat objectives. However, the best land management practices will not mitigate the continued disruption of the river's hydrologic regime to satisfy the needs of humans.

CHALLENGES

In order for Roanoke River National Wildlife Refuge to meet its multiple objectives of national, regional, and local scope – ranging from forest management to reducing forest fragmentation to providing for public use – the Service must fund and staff it well above current levels. Securing adequate funding and personnel, and successfully addressing the forested wetland alterations and hydrological functions, is the refuge's biggest challenge. In the interim, as needed funding and personnel become available, the refuge must concentrate on its highest priorities without committing irreversible actions that would preclude future implementation of the desired management programs.

THE REFUGE

LOCATION

Roanoke River National Wildlife Refuge is in Bertie County, North Carolina. The refuge is named for the Roanoke River, a 442-mile-long river with 9,875 square miles of drainage area in North Carolina and Virginia. The refuge's approved acquisition boundary lies in Bertie, Martin, and Halifax counties; the Service has only acquired land in Bertie County. The city of Plymouth (population 4,328) lies at the southeast end of the refuge. The city of Windsor (population 2,056) is 10 miles northeast of the refuge, and the city of Williamston (population 5,503) lies just southwest of the refuge (Figure 2). The refuge covers a total of 20,978 acres, and its southeastern end is at the outlet of the Roanoke River into Albemarle Sound. This region is part of the physiographic area known as the South Atlantic Coastal Plain and the Fish and Wildlife Service's administrative ecosystem known as the Roanoke-Tar-Neuse-Cape Fear Ecosystem.

INTRODUCTION AND HISTORY

The North Carolina Natural Heritage Program and the North Carolina Chapter of The Nature Conservancy jointly identified key tracts of the Roanoke River bottomlands and swamps that contained old-growth timber stands and unique populations of fish and wildlife resources (Lynch and Crawford 1980; Lynch 1981). In 1981, the Service identified approximately 145,000 acres in the Roanoke River floodplain supporting significant fish and wildlife resources worthy of protecting (USFWS 1981). In 1983, Frayer et al. indicated that in recent years forested wetland habitat losses have been occurring at a high rate on a national basis. During the 20-year period between the mid-1950s and 1970s, 92 percent of the national losses in forested wetlands occurred in the southeastern United States (Hefner and Brown 1984). The North American Waterfowl Management Plan, a 1986 cooperative agreement between the United States and Canada, noted significant declines in black duck populations over the previous 30 years. This plan identified the protection of 50,000 acres of black duck migration and wintering habitat along the east coast of the United States. It also identified concerns about the loss of wood duck breeding and wintering habitats and the need to maintain pre-breeding, migrating, and wintering habitat for mallards.

The Service, in 1985, focused on the potential of the Roanoke River bottomlands for enhancement of waterfowl habitat (USFWS 1985). In House Report 99-86, Part 1, filed in May 1985 and in the *Congressional Record* of October 14, 1986, the U.S. Congress identified the Roanoke River as a national priority under the Emergency Wetlands Resources Act (16 U.S.C. 3901 et seq.). The Act directed the Secretary of the Interior, in consultation with other federal agencies and state conservation agencies, to develop a national wetlands priority conservation plan to identify the types of wetlands and interests in wetlands that should be given priority with respect to federal and state acquisition. The Act cited the last large contiguous tracts of bottomland hardwoods, such as those of the Roanoke River in North Carolina and others, as examples of areas that should receive consideration for funding. Experts considered this wetland area of national significance to be the largest intact, and least disturbed, bottomland forest ecosystem remaining in the mid-Atlantic region (North Carolina Natural Heritage Program 1988).

The Category Concept Plan for Preservation of Black Duck Wintering Habitat specifically identified the protection of 25,000 acres of forested wetland habitat along the Roanoke River as the Service's top priority for this category in North Carolina (USFWS 1988). The Service identified approximately 30,000 acres that largely adjoin state lands and would further accomplish its fish and wildlife resource objectives. The Service prepared a Wildlife Habitat Preservation Proposal for the Roanoke River National Wildlife Refuge and Final Environmental Assessment in 1988 with an approved acquisition boundary of 33,000 acres. The Service issued a Finding of No Significant Impact on May 25, 1988, and established the refuge on August 10, 1989.

The proposed acquisitions qualified for funding under the Migratory Bird Conservation Act of 1929, as amended (16 U.S.C. 715-715R); the Migratory Bird Hunting and Conservation Stamp Act of March 18, 1934, as amended (16 U.S.C. 718-718H); and the Land and Water Conservation Fund Act of 1985 (16 U.S.C. 460d, 460e-4 to 460e-11). The Service dedicated the refuge on October 26, 1991.

The Service acquired the 2,782-acre Rainbow Tract in 1990; the 1,276-acre Askew Tract in 1991; the 3,748-acre Conine Island Tract, the 1,502-acre Company Swamp Tract, the 1,122-acre Hampton Swamp Tract, and the 2,000-acre Broadneck Tract in 1992; the Great Island, Goodman Island, and Sunken Marsh tracts (4,993 acres) and the 554-acre Rhodes Tract in 1997; and the 3,001-acre Town Swamp Tract in 2003 (Figure 2 and Appendix IV).

The Service acquired a Farmers Home Administration tract of 45 acres in fee title ownership in Nash County in 1992, and a tract of 129 acres in fee title in Sampson County in 1995.

The Service has acquired 98 easements with 75 landowners of 2,870 acres in 19 counties from the Farmers Home Administration, now the Farm Services Agency (Appendix IV).

Figure 2. Location and tracts of Roanoke River National Wildlife Refuge in Bertie County, North Carolina

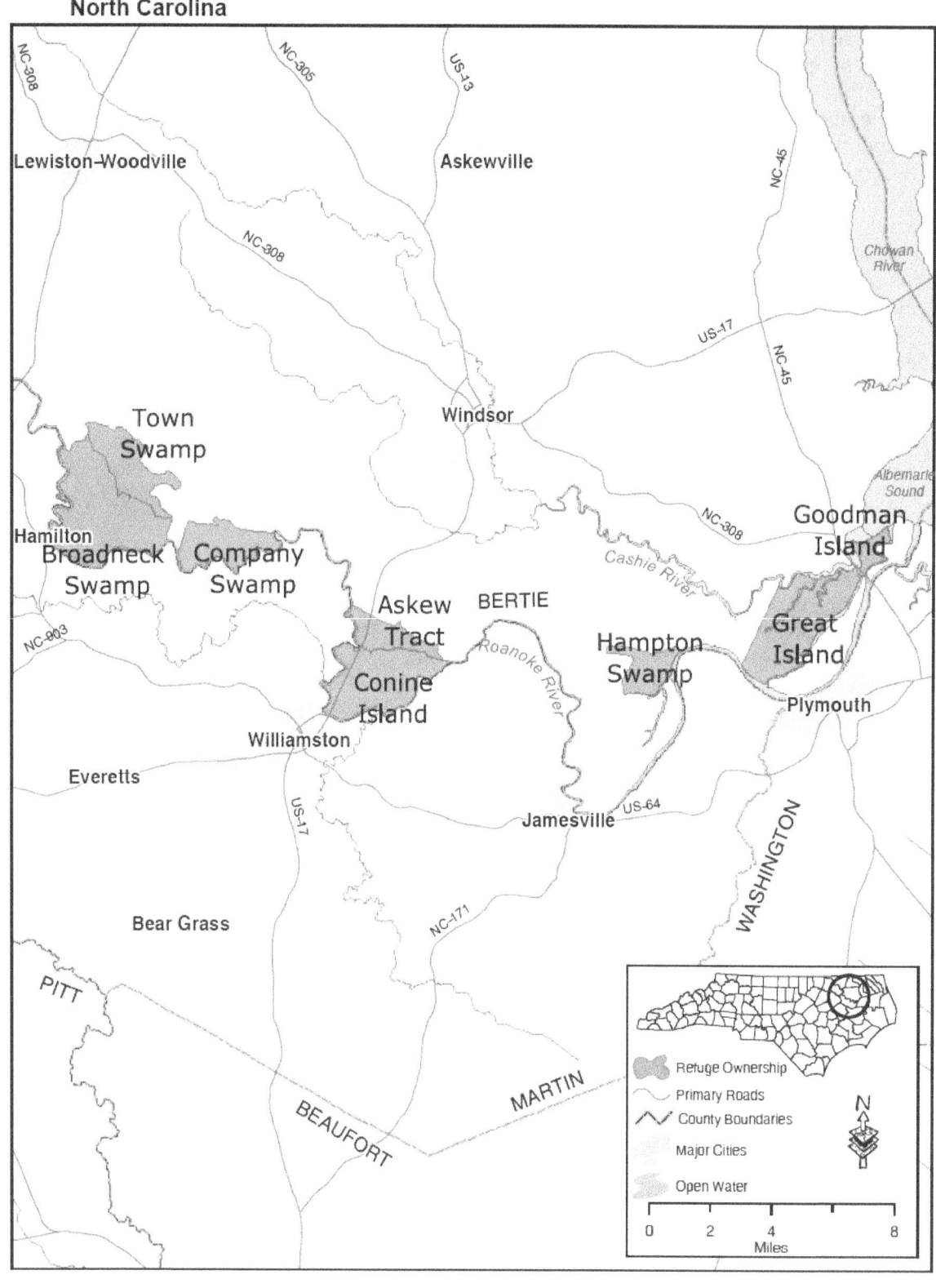

ADMINISTRATION

The refuge's administrative office is located in Windsor along the Cashie River. The refuge staff administers 20,978 acres of fee title land in Bertie County; two satellite fee title tracts acquired by the U.S. Department of Agriculture, Farm Services Agency (174 acres in two counties); and 98 conservation easements acquired by the Farm Services Agency (2,870 acres in 19 counties) throughout eastern North Carolina. The refuge's current staff includes a Project Leader, a Deputy Project Leader, a Wildlife Biologist, an Office Assistant, a Biological Science Technician, and an Engineering Equipment Operator.

PURPOSES AND ECOSYSTEM CONTEXT

The purpose of Roanoke River National Wildlife Refuge, as reflected in the refuge's authorizing legislation, is to protect and conserve migratory birds, and other wildlife resources through the protection of wetlands, in accordance with the following laws:

"...the conservation of wetlands of the Nation in order to maintain the public benefits they provide and to help fulfill international obligations contained in various migratory bird treaties and conventions..." (16 U.S.C., Sec. 3901(b), 100 Stat. 3583) (Emergency Wetlands Resources Act of 1986);

"...for use as an inviolate sanctuary, or for any other management purpose, for migratory birds..." (16 U.S.C. Sec. 664) (Migratory Bird Conservation Act of 1929);

"...for the development, advancement, management, conservation, and protection of fish and wildlife resources..." (6 U.S.C. Sec 742f(a)4); and

"...for the benefit of the United States Fish and Wildlife Service, in performing its activities and services..." (16 U.S.C. Sec. 742f(b)1) (Fish and Wildlife Act of 1956).

The Service's environmental assessment for the proposed establishment of the refuge in 1988 described the refuge's purpose and importance to migratory birds, particularly waterfowl:

> *To preserve wintering habitat for mallards, American black ducks, and wood ducks and production habitat for wood ducks to meet the habitat goals presented in the Ten-Year Waterfowl Habitat Acquisition Plan and the North American Waterfowl Management Plan.*

The Service further described the refuge purpose in the approval memorandum for the purchase of lands for the establishment of Roanoke River National Wildlife Refuge. The approval memorandum states that the primary reason for acquisition and inclusion of the area into the National Wildlife Refuge System was to preserve wintering habitat for mallards, American black ducks, wood ducks, and production habitat for wood ducks (U.S. Fish and Wildlife Service Southeast Region, Approval Memorandum 1988). The approval memorandum identified three objectives for which the area would be managed: to preserve an area that has traditional high use for wintering waterfowl; to provide additional waterfowl habitat through refuge management; and to establish a waterfowl sanctuary.

The North American Waterfowl Management Plan's Atlantic Coast Joint Venture office, working through a collaborative effort with private, state, and federal agencies, has established additional habitat objectives for the physiographic area.

REFUGE VISION STATEMENT

The vision for the refuge is as follows:

Roanoke River National Wildlife Refuge will protect, enhance, and manage high quality habitat for a diversity and abundance of migratory birds, fish, and other wildlife. Through new and existing partnerships, the refuge will foster and practice sound conservation in land management and river flow management to assure the physical and biological integrity of the Roanoke River floodplain.

The refuge will provide compatible wildlife-dependent public use opportunities, including environmental education, interpretation, and recreation. The refuge will provide increased opportunities to learn about the ecological and cultural importance of the Roanoke River floodplain. The refuge will become a national destination, and activities on the refuge will contribute to the local economy.

REFUGE GOALS

Wildlife, Fish, and Plant Populations: Protect, maintain, and enhance healthy and viable populations of indigenous migratory birds, wildlife, fish, and plants, including federal and state threatened and endangered species.

Habitat: Restore, maintain, and enhance the health and biodiversity of forested wetland habitats to ensure improved ecological productivity.

Public Use: Provide the public with safe, quality wildlife-dependent recreational and educational opportunities that focus on the wildlife and habitats of the refuge and the National Wildlife Refuge System. Continue to participate in local efforts to achieve a sustainable level of economic activity, including nature-based tourism.

Resource Protection: Protect refuge resources by limiting the adverse impacts of human activities and development.

Administration: Acquire and manage adequate funding, human resources, facilities, equipment, and infrastructure to accomplish the other refuge goals.

STEP-DOWN MANAGEMENT PLANS

A comprehensive conservation plan is a strategic plan that guides the future direction of the refuge. Before the staff can implement some of the strategies and projects, they must prepare or update detailed step-down management plans. To assist in preparing and implementing the step-down plans, the staff will develop partnerships with local agencies and organizations. The staff will develop these plans (Table 2) in accordance with the National Environmental Policy Act, which requires the identification and evaluation of alternatives and public review and involvement prior to their implementation.

Land Protection Plan (Develop), Draft Completion 2007: This plan will describe the land necessary to meet the needs identified by the Service and cooperating agencies and organizations for fish and wildlife resources in the Roanoke River Valley. It will also describe strategies to protect that land: fee simple acquisition, acquisition of easements, cooperative agreements with agencies and organizations, and agreements with private landowners.

Habitat Management Plan (Develop), Draft Completion 2008: This plan will describe the overall desired future habitat conditions needed to fulfill the refuge's purpose and objectives. The plan will include sections dealing with each habitat on the refuge. Procedures, techniques, strategies, and timetables for achieving desired future conditions will be incorporated into an overall plan.

Moist Soil/Water Management Plan (Update), Draft Completion 2007: This plan will describe the strategies and procedures (timing and duration of flooding and disturbance) for manipulating the refuge's water management units to meet habitat management objectives.

Forest Management Plan (Develop), Draft Completion 2007: This plan will describe strategies for meeting refuge forest management objectives. It will include direction on reforestation, wildlife habitat improvement, and harvest. Also, the plan will address scrub/shrub habitat management.

Fire Management Plan (Update), Draft Completion 2006: This plan will describe wild and prescribed fire management techniques that will be employed on the refuge. Wildfire control descriptions will include initial attack strategies and cooperative agreements with other agencies. There will be limited use of prescribed fire and its use will consist of hazardous fuel reductions and as a habitat management tool.

Road Plan (Develop), Draft Completion 2007: This plan will describe the layout of roads on the refuge, the anticipated improvements of each road, the method and timing of maintenance, and intended function of each road, e.g., public or administrative access.

Table 2. Roanoke River National Wildlife Refuge step-down management plans, arranged by issue sequence in the Goals and Objectives portion of the Comprehensive Conservation Plan.

Plan	Completion Date
Land Protection	2007
Habitat Management	2008
Moist Soil/Water Management	2007
Forest Management	2007
Fire Management	2006
Road	2007
Integrated Pest Management	2009
Nuisance Animal Control	2009
Exotic Plant Control	2009
Visitor Services	2007
Environmental Education	2007
Fishing	2006
Hunting and Trapping	2006
Sign	2006
Wildlife Inventory	2008
Law Enforcement	2006

Integrated Pest Management Plan (Develop and Update), Draft Completion 2009: This plan will address the complex issue of bringing exotic and nuisance plants and animals to a maintenance control level on the refuge. It will cover chemical pesticide use (aerial and ground application), mechanical eradication, and biological controls. The Nuisance/Exotic Animal and Plant control plans will be incorporated into this plan.

Nuisance Animal Management Plan (Update), Draft Completion 2009: This plan (as part of the Integrated Pest Management Plan) will describe survey, removal or control, and monitoring techniques for both terrestrial and aquatic nuisance and exotic animals (vertebrate and invertebrate). The plan will include feral swine, dogs, feral cats, and beaver control.

Exotic Plant Control Plan (Develop), Draft Completion 2009: This plan (as part of the Integrated Pest Management Plan) will describe survey, removal or control, and monitoring techniques for both terrestrial and aquatic nuisance and exotic plants.

Visitor Services Plan (Develop), Draft Completion 2007: This plan will describe the refuge's wildlife-dependent recreation, environmental education, and interpretation. Specific issues or items that will be addressed include facility requirements, site plans, and handicapped accessibility. The environmental education, fishing, hunting, and sign plans will be incorporated into this plan.

Environmental Education Plan *(Develop)*, Draft Completion 2007: This plan will reflect the objectives and strategies of the comprehensive conservation plan and address environmental education guidelines following Service standards.

Fishing Plan (Update), Draft Completion 2006: This plan (as part of the Visitor Services Plan) will address specific aspects of the refuge's fishing program. It will define season structures, fish areas, methods, handicapped accessibility, facilities needed, and refuge-specific regulations.

Hunting and Trapping Plan (Update), Draft Completion 2006: This plan (as part of the Visitor Services Plan) will address specific aspects of the refuge's hunting program. It will define species to be hunted/trapped, season structures, hunt areas, methods, all-terrain vehicle use, handicapped accessibility, facilities needed, and refuge-specific hunting regulations.

Sign Plan (Update), Draft Completion 2006: This plan (as part of the Visitor Services Plan) will describe the refuge's strategy for informing visitors via signage. It will incorporate Service guidelines.

Biological Inventory/Monitoring Plan (Develop), Draft Completion 2008: This plan will describe inventory and monitoring techniques and time frames. All plant communities and associations in the refuge, as well as all trust species (migratory birds, including songbirds, neotropical passerines, and waterfowl), listed species (federal and state threatened, endangered, and species of concern), and key resident species shall be inventoried and population trends will be monitored.

Law Enforcement Plan (Update), Draft Completion 2006: This plan will provide a reference to station policies, procedures, priorities, and programs concerning law enforcement.

LEGAL POLICY

A variety of international treaties, federal laws, and Presidential executive orders guide the administration of Roanoke River National Wildlife Refuge. The documents and acts listed in Appendix III contain management options under the refuge's establishing authority, the National

Wildlife Refuge System Administration Act of 1966, and the National Wildlife Refuge System Improvement Act of 1997 (the legal and policy guidance for the operation of national wildlife refuges).

THE PLANNING PROCESS

At initial planning meetings, the refuge and planning staff discussed strategies for developing the plan, identified their issues and concerns, and compiled a mailing list of likely interested government agencies, nongovernmental organizations, businesses, and individual citizens. The Service invited these agencies, organizations, businesses, and citizens to participate in two public scoping meetings on May 22 and 24, 2001, in Windsor and Halifax, North Carolina. The staff introduced attendees to the refuge and its planning process and asked them to identify their issues and concerns. The staff published announcements giving the locations, dates, and times for the public meetings in the *Federal Register* and in legal notices in local newspapers. The staff also sent press releases to local newspapers and public service announcements to television and radio stations. In addition, the planning staff placed 50 posters announcing the meetings in local post offices, local government buildings, and stores.

The Service expanded the planning team's identified issues and concerns to include those generated by the agencies, organizations, businesses, and citizens from the local community. These issues and concerns formed the basis for the development and comparison of the objectives in the different alternatives described in this environmental impact statement.

The refuge manager and planning staff presented the alternatives to the staff of the North Carolina Wildlife Resources Commission on March 20, 2002. The Commission staff gave their opinion of the alternatives and made suggestions for improving them.

The objectives were subjects of discussion at a second round of public meetings on April 9 and 11, 2002 in Windsor and Halifax, North Carolina. The planning staff again published announcements giving the locations, dates, and times for the public meetings as legal notices in local newspapers. They also sent press releases to local newspapers and public service announcements to television and radio stations. The staff placed 75 posters announcing the meetings in local post offices, local government buildings, and stores.

After considering and evaluating the issues, concerns, comments, and suggestions received from the aforementioned public meetings, the planning staff developed the Draft Comprehensive Conservation Plan and Environmental Impact Statement. This draft was completed and distributed to the public for review and comment from March 30 to July 18, 2005. A Notice of Availability for public review of the Draft Comprehensive Conservation Plan and Environmental Impact Statement was published in the *Federal Register* on March 30, 2005. Press releases and public service announcements were also sent to local newspapers and television and radio stations to inform the public of the availability of the draft for review and comment.

During this public review period, the refuge and planning staffs hosted two public forums on May 15 and 16, 2005. One was held at the Windsor, North Carolina, community building (the town in which the refuge headquarters is located); and the other was held at the Halifax County Agricultural Center (located near the northern end of the refuge's approved acquisition boundary). Each forum was held from 6:00 p.m. until 9:00 p.m. The forums started as an open house with the refuge staff available to discuss the draft plan and refuge operations with the audience. A 30-minute formal presentation on the draft plan was then made, followed by a facilitated discussion to solicit open-floor comments on the plan. A recorder wrote the comments on a flip chart, and the comments were then transcribed after the forums.

A total of 15 individuals submitted comments on the Draft Comprehensive Conservation Plan and Environmental Impact Statement, either in writing or at the two public forums. Some of these comments have been incorporated in this Comprehensive Conservation Plan and Final Environmental Impact Statement. A summary of the comments and the Service's responses to them are provided in Appendix XIII.

PLAN REVIEW AND REVISION

The staff will review this comprehensive conservation plan annually to determine the need for revision. A revision would occur if and when significant information becomes available, such as a change in ecological conditions or a major refuge expansion. Under the Technical Settlement Agreement issued by the Federal Energy Regulatory Commission to Dominion Power in 2004, Dominion Power has agreed to an adaptive management approach to address the impacts of hydropower generation on downstream terrestrial and aquatic ecosystems. The first five years of the agreement term is a period of baseline data collection. After the initial five-year period, those impacts will be assessed and flow releases will be adapted to minimize impacts.

Concurrently, the U.S. Army Corps of Engineers has been authorized to study its flood control operations on the Roanoke River under Section 216 of the Flood Control Act of 1970. This study may also result in a change of floodwater releases on the downstream ecosystem. Over the next 15 years, the staff will consider those adaptations in its annual reviews of this comprehensive conservation plan.

The staff will augment the final plan by developing detailed step-down management plans to address the completion of specific strategies in support of the refuge's goals and objectives. Revisions to the comprehensive conservation plan and the step-down management plans will be subject to public review and compliance with the National Environmental Policy Act.

PLANNING ISSUES AND CONCERNS

The input of local citizens and public agencies, the team members' knowledge of the area, and the resource needs identified by the refuge staff and biological review team all contributed to the issues and concerns addressed in the plan. The Fish and Wildlife Service assembled a planning team (see Table 25, Chapter V) to evaluate the resource needs. The team then developed a list of goals, objectives, and strategies to shape the management of the refuge for the next 15 years.

These issues provided the basis for developing the refuge's alternative management objectives and strategies. These issues played a role in determining the desired future conditions for the refuge and were considered in the preparation of this long-term comprehensive conservation plan. The issues and concerns are described below. They are of local, regional, and national significance and reflect similar issues that were, in part, identified by the public at the planning meetings.

HYDROLOGY

Roanoke River Surface Hydrology

The Roanoke River's surface hydrology dominates management of the refuge and affects all of its resources. The flows of the river are managed by dam operators upstream of the refuge, primarily for flood control and hydroelectric power generation. This managed flow regime has resulted in a highly altered system with which the floodplain ecosystem did not evolve. Presently, the dam operators release flows in a way that reduces the magnitude of short-duration floods by creating long-duration moderate floods in the spring and summer months (Figure 3). In other words, areas that once flooded may never flood, and areas that do flood are flooded for a much longer period of time. Prolonged flooding of the floodplain during the wrong time of year has caused the river's water quality to deteriorate, resulting in waters with low dissolved oxygen levels draining back into the river. This is of special concern when fish eggs and fry are present in the river during the late spring and summer. At this life stage, low levels of dissolved oxygen will kill the eggs and fry. These flows also affect aquatic resources by minimizing floodplain spawning habitat in the spring, eliminating the exposure of spawning and resting habitat around bars in the summer, and saturating the banks and promoting bank erosion.

The managed flows also affect terrestrial resources by inhibiting plant regeneration and natural plant successional stages, and the actual killing of viable hardwoods. The flows flood nests and foraging habitat of birds that nest on or near the ground, and artificially disperse other wildlife populations. There are also concerns with the quality of the water being released from the reservoirs behind the dams. In summary, although there is little documentation of the effects of managed river flows on the Roanoke River ecosystem, documented science supports the conclusion that managed flow regimes have disrupted and are continuing to disrupt the normal evolutionary ecological successional processes of floodplains, and will significantly alter or destroy the ecological balances normally associated with free-flowing, hardwood river bottom floodplain systems over time (Beasley and Hightower 2000; Boon et al. 1992; Collier et al. 1996; Fontaine and Bartell 1983; Hunt 1988; Jackson and Marmulla 1999; Ligon et al. 1995; Merona et al. 2001; Petts 1984; Poff and Hart 2002; Pringle et al. 2000; Ruane et al. 1986; Trush et al. 2000; Vaughn and Taylor 1999).

Global Warming and Sea Level Rise

The downstream end of the refuge is at sea level. Seasonally flooded bald cypress and swamp tupelo trees cover the majority of the refuge. Scientists predict that sea levels along the North Carolina coast will rise from 2 to 3 feet in the next 100 years due to global warming. That rise in water levels will change the types of vegetative cover on the refuge. The grass-dominated freshwater marshes that occupy the fringe of the riverbanks will expand into areas currently covered by bald cypress and swamp tupelo trees. Bald cypress and swamp tupelo forests will expand into areas currently occupied by bottomland hardwood forests.

As the habitats change, the wildlife species that inhabit those habitats will also change. Colonial nesting birds such as herons and egrets that currently utilize tall trees along the river will lose their roost sites as trees die and fall. New candidate roost trees further upslope will be separated from open water by freshwater marshes. Cavity-nesting waterfowl, songbirds, and mammals will lose their cavities as the trees they currently use fall, but other trees further upslope will replace them as cavity trees. The freshwater marshes that will expand into the former bald cypress - swamp tupelo forests will provide habitat for species of songbirds and waterfowl not currently inhabiting the refuge.

Drainage

Before the refuge became established, previous land managers dug drainage ditches to facilitate timber harvest and access for hunting. These canals still exist on the refuge today. They effectively lower the water table, draining subsurface water during periods of low water. They allow an increased rate of surface water flow from the river to flood areas behind the natural river levees at moderate river flows. This drainage affects the refuge's plant community by providing habitat for

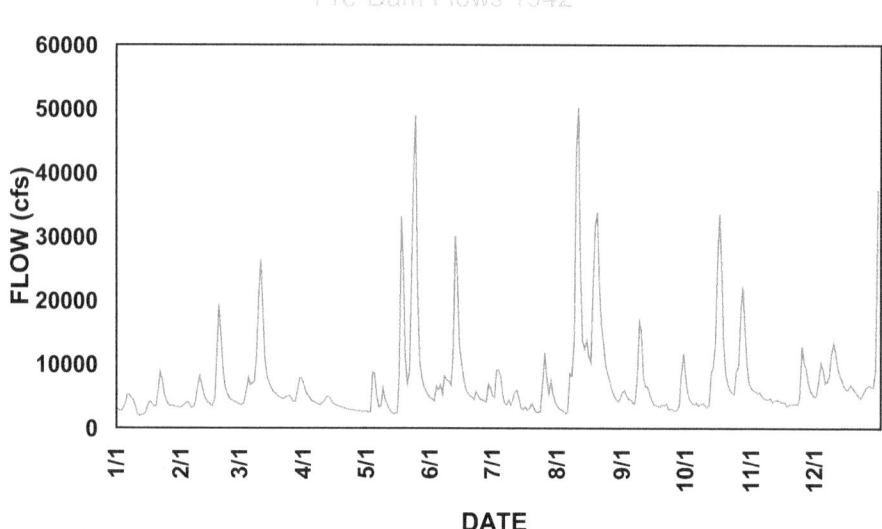

Pre-Dam Flows 1942

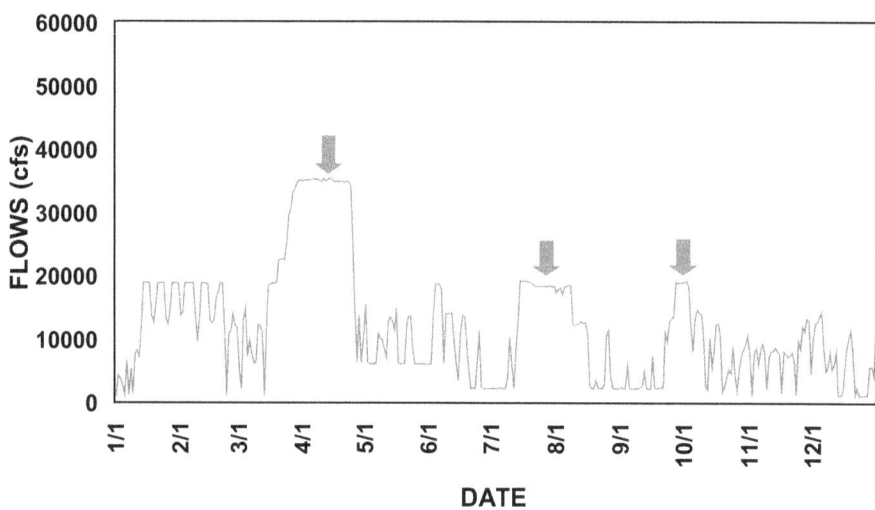

Post-Dam Flows- 1975

species adapted to better drainage close to the canals and on the tops of spoil banks. Flooding of areas behind natural river levees during the growing season inhibits plant regeneration and favors species that are better adapted to more frequent flooding than would have occurred otherwise.

The combination of managed stream flows and drainage canals in the bottomland forests exposes the forests to more frequent flooding and draining, as documented on the Roanoke River National Wildlife Refuge.

FISH AND WILDLIFE POPULATIONS

Threatened and Endangered Species

Recovery and protection of threatened and endangered plants and animals is an important responsibility delegated to the Service and a priority of the National Wildlife Refuge System. Two threatened or endangered animals are thought to use (or could use) Roanoke River National Wildlife Refuge: the bald eagle (federally threatened) and shortnose sturgeon (federally endangered).

Bald eagles have historically nested on lands now included in the Roanoke River National Wildlife Refuge. While eagles are not currently nesting on the refuge, they do nest in adjacent counties and travel the river corridor. Eight eagles are currently nesting along the Roanoke River below the dam at Roanoke Rapids. The refuge's habitat protection and management activities provide suitable habitat for nesting eagles, and as recovery progresses it is likely that the bald eagle will nest within refuge boundaries.

Shortnose sturgeon historically occurred in the river. The North Carolina Wildlife Resources Commission caught a shortnose sturgeon in a gill net in the western Albemarle Sound in 1998. The refuge can support shortnose sturgeon recovery efforts by protecting and managing riverine habitat and providing technical assistance to other Service divisions or resource management agencies.

Waterfowl

The scoping process identified the management of all refuge forestland for waterfowl as an issue. The refuge's waterfowl objectives guide operation and management actions. In order to meet the refuge's waterfowl purpose, the refuge must maintain the forest to meet waterfowl habitat needs and provide sufficient resting and feeding areas for waterfowl.

Staff of the U.S. Fish and Wildlife Service and cooperating agencies and organizations conducted a Biological Review of Roanoke River National Wildlife Refuge in 1999 and 2000 as part of the comprehensive conservation planning process. They identified objectives and strategies to enhance waterfowl habitat.

Neotropical Migratory Birds

Neotropical migratory birds present special management concerns. There are 35 breeding species found along the Roanoke River. Providing habitat (i.e., interior forest) for these birds is one of the refuge's major objectives. Strategic forest management compatible with the refuge's waterfowl habitat objectives would contribute to the interior forest needs of neotropical migratory birds. Staff of the U.S. Fish and Wildlife Service and cooperating agencies and organizations conducted a Biological Review of Roanoke River National Wildlife Refuge in 1999 and 2000 as part of the comprehensive conservation planning process. They identified objectives and strategies needed to meet the minimum feeding and nesting habitat requirements of neotropical migratory birds. Neotropical migratory birds are also a major focus of the refuge's wildlife observation program, as many birders visit the refuge to observe them.

Data Needs

Wildlife data collection on the refuge has focused on neotropical migratory birds in one habitat. Cooperating federal and state agencies, nongovernmental organizations, and the public have all encouraged the Service to continue that data collection and expand it to include all the wildlife species on the refuge and the effects of managed river flows, refuge management, and public use on the diversity and health of the wildlife.

HABITATS

Bottomland Hardwood Management

The refuge was established to protect and manage the forest in the Roanoke River floodplain. Fishing and hunting are traditional parts of the area's culture, and forest management is seen as a first step toward maintaining the opportunities for hunting (primarily for white-tailed deer). In addition, forest areas provide habitat for neotropical migratory bird populations and the associated public use. Beaver pond management is a significant issue in maintaining forest tracts.

Roanoke River National Wildlife Refuge is near several large forested tracts in the South Atlantic Coastal Plain Physiographic Zone. Maintenance and stabilization of the area's forested wetland patches is an important goal of cooperative private-state-federal partnerships under the North American Waterfowl Management Plan, Partners in Flight, and the Atlantic Coast Joint Venture. These partnerships recommend the protection and management of forested patches in the following quantities and sizes: 10 patches over 100,000 acres; 15 patches over 20,000 acres; 7 patches over 10,000 acres; and 30 patches over 6,000 acres. With strategic management, the refuge can provide significant amounts of interior forest with the proper overstory and understory conditions, restored hydrology, and managed beaver ponds.

Data Needs

Data collection on the refuge has focused on the reproduction and health of bottomland hardwoods. Cooperating federal and state agencies, nongovernmental organizations, and the public have all encouraged the Service to continue that data collection and expand it to include all the habitats on the refuge and the effects of managed river flows, refuge management, and public use on the diversity and condition of the habitats.

PUBLIC USE

Visitor Services and Education

The refuge is located in Bertie County (2000 population 19,773) within 10 miles of the county seat of Windsor, North Carolina (population 2,056). Several local initiatives work to promote nature-based tourism in northeastern North Carolina. Two nonprofit groups, Partnership for the Sounds and Roanoke River Partners, promote ecotourism in several rural counties in the region that have an abundance of natural resources to attract tourists, but are dominated by wetlands that limit traditional economic development. A few commercial businesses have interests in guiding canoeing and angling adventures. The refuge is an important link to the other natural areas that together make these experiences possible. Carefully selected and managed staff, programs, and facilities will provide the wildlife-dependent environmental education, interpretation, and recreational opportunities that refuge visitors expect.

Hunting

Hunting and fishing are integral parts of rural North Carolina culture. It is not surprising that there is a considerable state and local interest in expanding hunting opportunities. The initial strategy must be to maintain the quality of hunting at existing levels. Any additional hunting opportunities will be dependent on providing safe, quality experiences that are compatible with the purposes for which the Service established the refuge. However, hunting opportunities would be made available to a greater number of people over a larger land base through the refuge's continuation of a land acquisition program.

Fishing

Under current conditions, the refuge cannot expand the area available for fishing opportunities without compromising the safety of the public. One possible alternative is to develop safe access to bank fishing areas.

Refuge Access

In general, lack of access, both interior and exterior, limits some public uses on the refuge. No all-weather roads or trails exist.

The managed flow regime and floodplain hydrology have limited and will continue to limit road access, regardless of construction type or location. Future road access improvements will be appropriately sensitive to the refuge's floodplain hydrology and ecology. Vehicular access to the Conine Island and Askew tracts is available via U.S. Highway 13/17. Private lands between state highways and refuge access roads limit public vehicular access to other refuge tracts. Presently, these refuge tracts are only accessible from the river. The general lack of improved access to the refuge does not limit travel by foot or canoe, however. Development of seasonal habitat management roads following acquisition of rights-of-way through some private holdings will provide improved seasonal public access. The Service maintains 15 miles of roads and trails that exist within the refuge. Floodplain hydrology and seasonal weather limit vehicular access to most of the refuge. Roads that run through sloughs will remain seasonal.

Farm Services Agency Fee Title Tract Access

The refuge staff manages two Farm Services Agency fee title tracts large enough to provide public use opportunities. One tract, located in Sampson County, is part of North Carolina's State Game Lands program, and is open to public hunting managed by the State of North Carolina. Public access is limited. Future refuge land acquisition could provide public access and increased compatible public use opportunities on these tracts.

GENERAL ADMINISTRATION

Funding and Staffing

Funding has been insufficient to support refuge programs. Inadequate staff and facilities have prevented the refuge from realizing its purpose and management objectives. The refuge is not meeting its wildlife habitat objectives; conducts too few wildlife inventories; has few public use facilities; has incomplete habitat/wildlife management plans; provides little environmental education, interpretation, or wildlife observation opportunities; and has limited public access.

Cultural Resources

Cultural resources are present on Roanoke River National Wildlife Refuge. Although the number of archaeological investigations has been limited, two archaeological sites have been located (Phelps 1982; Kanaski 2002). The staff must conduct management activities so as to avoid compromising sensitive sites.

Members of the federally recognized Tuscarora Native American tribe live on a reservation in Lewiston, Niagara County, north of Buffalo, New York. The Service will coordinate any cultural resource investigations involving Native American sites with the Tuscarora tribe pursuant to the National Historic Preservation Act of 1966, as amended.

Land Acquisition and Forest Fragmentation

Congress established the refuge to protect forested areas (bottomland hardwood forests) important to migratory birds, especially wintering and nesting waterfowl. Since the refuge's establishment, conservationists have realized its value as breeding habitat for neotropical migratory songbirds, many of which require contiguous blocks of several thousand acres of forest. A number of state and federal agencies and nongovernmental organizations are undertaking a concerted effort to protect those contiguous blocks. They have identified the 190,000 acres of the lower Roanoke River floodplain as an area that should be protected by some means as wildlife management areas, working farms, and forests. The Service is a partner in this effort.

The refuge's current acquisition boundary reflects the importance of protecting and managing the Roanoke River's forested corridor. Many private properties lie between the forests owned by government agencies and nongovernmental organizations in the Roanoke River Valley, but they are outside the refuge acquisition boundary. The refuge has an approved preliminary project proposal that outlines 44,730 additional acres of high priority habitat that the Service should consider protecting. Such properties are important links in connecting the conservation areas and providing a continuous forested riparian corridor along the river. To maintain the potential to protect these lands, the Service must have the authority to manage and protect (through acquisition of fee title interest or conservation easements) the habitat between the refuge's current acquisition boundary and other protected natural resource areas.

Law Enforcement and Refuge Regulations

In the past, the refuge has enforced applicable laws and regulations through the use of two dual-function law enforcement officers. Those officers are no longer on the refuge staff. Currently, the refuge depends on one zone law enforcement officer to enforce laws and regulations, and the amount of time that can be devoted to this effort is limited. This is particularly evident during the hunting season, when the law enforcement workload is at its highest. The refuge must rely on full-time state law enforcement officers to assist the zone law enforcement officer. Their workload limits the amount of time they can spend on the refuge.

Other Resource Protection

Other threats to refuge resources require closer monitoring and management. Pest plants and animals and wildlife disease are all concerns to which the refuge should be paying closer attention.

II. Affected Environment

GEOGRAPHIC ECOSYSTEM CONTEXT

The refuge is one of the 10 national wildlife refuges in eastern North Carolina. Those 10 national wildlife refuges - Alligator River, Cedar Island, Currituck, Great Dismal Swamp, Mackay Island, Mattamuskeet, Pea Island, Pocosin Lakes, Swanquarter, and Roanoke River; and the Back Bay National Wildlife Refuge in Virginia - are all in the watersheds of the Roanoke, Tar, Neuse, and Cape Fear Rivers, which the Fish and Wildlife Service classifies as Ecosystem Unit #34.

LOCATION

The refuge ownership is in the lower portion of the watershed and extends from below the Fall Zone near Hamilton in Bertie County, North Carolina, downstream to the Albemarle Sound in Bertie County, North Carolina. Presently, the refuge is divided into four distinct areas below the fall zone: (1) Broadneck Swamp/Town Swamp (upper middle part of the acquisition boundary); (2) Company Swamp (upper middle); (3) Askew-Conine (lower middle); (4) Hampton Swamp (lower) and; Great/Goodman Islands (lower).

PHYSICAL ENVIRONMENT

CLIMATE

Since the flow of air over North Carolina is predominantly from west to east, the continental influence is much greater than the ocean or marine influence. Therefore, the state experiences a fairly large variation in temperature from winter to summer.

The Gulf Stream current flows only a short distance off the North Carolina coast. One might think this "river" of warm water would have a profound effect on the climate. However, the prevalence of westerly winds limits its direct effects.

Lows usually reform along the coast as "Cape Hatteras lows" and then move north along the coast. Winter's low-pressure storms are usually more intense because of the large north-to-south contrasts.

Winter storms bring prolonged periods of steady rain and are responsible for most of the winter precipitation. The forms of precipitation in spring begin to change from these steady rains to occasional thunderstorms. The Gulf of Mexico's warm, moist air produces warm, humid weather throughout the summer, when rainfall comes from occasional thunderstorms. Autumn, North Carolina's driest season, is to many people the most pleasant with its many clear, warm days and cool nights with little rain. This weather usually lasts until November.

Impacts of occasional hurricanes in Bertie and Martin counties are secondary; the storms usually pass off the coast east of the area. The most recent hurricanes that scored direct hits were Floyd in 1999 and Isabel in 2003. Most North Carolina tornadoes occur in the Piedmont and the interior of the coastal plain, which spares Bertie and Martin counties. However, tornadoes have touched down three times since 1992, causing damage to refuge lands and, in one case, maintenance facilities.

The average annual precipitation the past 45 years was 48.88 inches, and the average snowfall was 6.3 inches. Rainfall is evenly distributed throughout the year; the average monthly rainfall ranges from 2.75 in November to 5.87 in July.

Of the total annual precipitation, about 27 inches usually falls in April through September. The growing season for most crops falls within this period. In two years out of ten, the rainfall in April through September is less than 22 inches. The heaviest one-day rainfall during the period of record was 14.35 inches at Lewiston on September16, 1999. Thunderstorms occur on about 45 days each year.

The average seasonal snowfall is about 6 inches. The greatest snow depth at any one time during the period of record was 14 inches. On an average of three days, at least one inch of snow is on the ground. The number of such days varies greatly from year-to-year.

The average relative humidity in mid-afternoon is about 50 percent. Humidity is higher at night, and the average at dawn is about 85 percent. The sun shines 60 percent of the time in summer and 55 percent in winter. The prevailing wind is from the southeast. Average wind speed is highest, 9 miles per hour, in spring.

The average daily maximum temperature from 1958-1981 was 72 degrees Fahrenheit, and the average daily minimum was 46.8 degrees.

In winter the average temperature is 42 degrees, and the average daily minimum temperature is 30 degrees. The lowest temperature on record, which occurred at Lewiston on January 13, l962, is -1 degree. In summer the average temperature is 76 degrees, and the average daily maximum is 88. The highest recorded temperature, which occurred on August 1, 1980, is 105 degrees.

The last freezing temperature in spring is: one year in 10, May 5; two years in 10, April 29; and five years in 10, April 16. The first freezing temperature in the fall is: one year in 10, October 8; two years in 10, October 13; and five years in 10, October 21.

GEOLOGY

Pliocene and lower Pleistocene sediments in the Carolinas were deposited in several distinct basins believed to be the result of structural downwarping, possibly due to reactivation of older fault systems. These depocenters were the loci of marine embayments and are bounded by arches over which less sedimentation has occurred. The major Pliocene-Pleistocene depocenter in North Carolina, the Albemarle embayment, occupied most of northeastern North Carolina and extended into southeastern Virginia (Ward et al. 1991).

The Roanoke-Albemarle system can be divided into three distinctive parts: upper Roanoke River, lower Roanoke River, and Albemarle Sound estuarine system. The upper Roanoke River (above the Roanoke Rapids Dam) constitutes the major portion of the river drainage system (87 percent) and is located within the Piedmont Province. The lower Roanoke River basin (below the Roanoke Rapids Dam to about 5 miles northeast of Plymouth) constitutes a much smaller portion of the river drainage basin (13 percent) and is within the Coastal Plain Province. The Roanoke River drains into the western end of the Albemarle Sound.

The Coastal Plain Province lies east of the Piedmont Province. The Piedmont begins at the "Fall Line," which is a broad transition zone where the crystalline rocks of the Piedmont (i.e., the igneous and metamorphic rocks that cause the rapids in the Roanoke River at Roanoke Rapids) become buried by the marine sediments of the Coastal Plain. The Mush Island Tract, the tract of the acquisition boundary furthest upstream, is immediately downstream from the "Fall Line" or in the western edge of the Coastal Plain.

Thin beds of Quaternary sediments were deposited on the surface of the Coastal Plain during the past three million years (Riggs and Belknap 1988). This Quaternary history and the resulting surface veneer of unconsolidated sediments directly dictates the general characteristics of the Coastal Plain, including the regional morphology and character of the drainage systems and flooded estuaries, soil types, and potential land use. Quaternary sediments were deposited by the coastal system, which rapidly migrated back and forth across the Coastal Plain-Continental Shelf as the sea level fluctuated in response to repeated episodes of glaciation and deglaciation. Within this rapidly changing coastal system, extremely varied sediments, including gravel, sands, clays, and peat in all possible combinations, were deposited in river, estuarine, barrier island, and continental shelf environments. The Quaternary sediments range from a few meters in thickness in places along the lower Roanoke River up to 70 meters in the outer Albemarle area (Riggs et al., in prep.). The Quaternary history continues today.

MINERALS

Sand is the only mineral resource occurring in economic quantities. Two sand pits are adjacent to the refuge's Askew tract north boundary in Bertie County. There is a private sand pit west of U.S. Highway 13/17, and the North Carolina Department of Transportation operates a sand pit east of U.S. Highway 13/17.

On refuge lands the Service owns all mineral rights on the Broadneck, Rhodes, Company Swamp, and Conine Island tracts. The Nature Conservancy has retained the mineral rights on Hampton Swamp. An unknown party reserved oil and mineral rights on Great and Goodman Islands. Ownership of oil and mineral rights on the Askew tract is unknown; additional deed research needs to be done.

ARCHAEOLOGICAL RESOURCES

Two archaeological sites are documented on the refuge (Phelps 1982; Kanaski 2002). Both sites are located partially in the river. Due to chronic bank sloughing, it is unknown whether one of the sites still exists and how much longer the second site will remain intact.

SOILS

Annual floods over the centuries have overtopped the riverbanks, dropping suspended sediments from upriver to form the levees and ridges of the floodplain. The coarser, heavier sediments fall out closest to the river, forming the natural levees immediately adjacent to the river channel, while the finer, lighter sediments (clays) gradually settle in the slack water areas ponded behind the levees. These sediments are supplemented each year by humus from abundant leaf litter decay, resulting in deep, rich soils.

The presence of the three reservoirs upstream has reduced the amount of sediment deposition in recent years. Soil types identified from the Roanoke River floodplain include Altavista, Augusta, Bibb*, Chewacla, Conetoe, Congaree, Dorovan*, various Hapludults, Roanoke*, Una*, Wahee, Wehadkee*, and Wickham. Soils with an asterisk are listed as hydric in "Hydric Soils of the United States" (USDA, Soil Conservation Service 1985). Hydric soils are "soils that in their undrained condition are saturated, flooded or ponded long enough during the growing season to develop anaerobic conditions that favor the growth and regeneration of hydrophytic (water-loving) vegetation" (USDA, Soil Conservation Service 1985). (See Figure 4 for the hydric and non-hydric soil locations of the Roanoke River floodplain area.)

Soils of the refuge floodplains are predominately of the Wehadkee and Chewacla series, which are nearly level, poorly drained (high water table 6 to 12 inches below the surface), and somewhat poorly drained (high water table 12 to 18 inches below the surface) and have a loamy surface layer and subsoil. The soils from North Carolina Highway 11/42 downstream to and including Conine Island and the Askew Tract are frequently flooded Wehadkee loams on the lowest elevations and frequently flooded Chewacla loams on the natural levees and hardwood flats. The soil in the Devil's Gut area is also the frequently flooded Chewacla loam. The soil on Great and Goodman Islands is the frequently flooded Dorovan mucky peat. Frequently flooded soils are those that flood at least once every two years.

HYDROLOGY

The refuge consists entirely of Roanoke River wetlands. These wetlands are in the coastal plain province or lower portion of the Roanoke River system that begins in the Blue Ridge Mountains of central Virginia and drains 9,875 square miles. Water is the driving force of the Roanoke River Refuge's bottomland hardwood communities. Water forms and maintains the floodplain by transporting and redistributing sediments. It provides seasonal access for aquatic organisms to the floodplain and transports nutrients and detritus across the floodplain and to estuarine areas. Sources of water to the Roanoke River system include precipitation and runoff, and the groundwater that originates from them.

In addition to the Roanoke River, the lower portion streams included in the system that drain, run through, flood, or potentially affect refuge lands are (from upstream to downstream): Indian Creek; three unnamed river levee breeches in the Broadneck Swamp; Black Gut; one unnamed river levee breach in Company Swamp; Coniott Creek; one unnamed river levee breach in Askew Tract; Conoho Creek; one unnamed river levee breach on Conine Island; Conine Creek; Sweetwater Creek; Spellers Creek; Devil's Gut; Gardner Creek; Cashie River; Broad Creek; Grennell Creek; Middle River; and Eastmost River.

Patterns of water flow within alluvial systems such as the Roanoke are distinctly seasonal when unregulated. Highest flows generally occur as a result of winter-spring rains. Lowest flows usually occur during the late summer and fall months. Peaks in the flow may occur at any time due to extreme storms such as hurricanes. The magnitude of flooding at any site along the lower basin is a function of the location, as well as river discharge (Wharton et al. 1982). Discharge peaks are usually higher in the narrower, upper portions of alluvial rivers and attenuate as the waters reach the broader, flatter floodplain.

The Roanoke River exhibits the seasonal cycles described above; however, the flow within the system is greatly regulated by three upstream impoundments. The net effect of the cumulative operation of these reservoirs is to reduce the peaks but extend the duration of flooding in the lower basin and to cause rapid fluctuations in both discharge and temperature immediately below Roanoke Rapids Reservoir. The result is that higher elevation areas that once flooded now rarely flood, and those lower elevation areas that do flood do so for a longer period.

Figure 4. Hydric and Non-hydric Soils of Roanoke River Floodplain Area

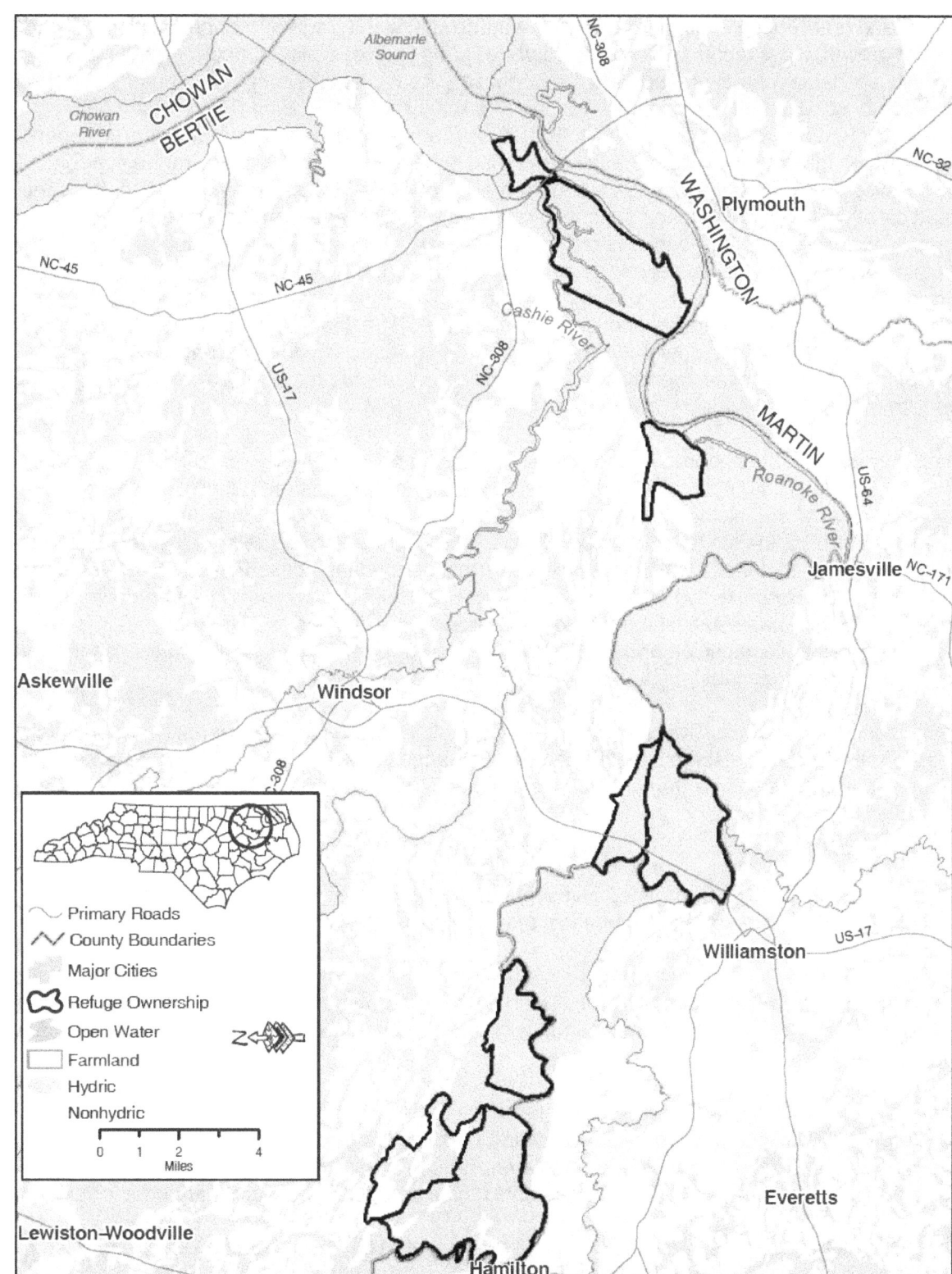

Organisms that depend on alluvial river systems for life requisites have co-evolved with the seasonal fluctuations inherent in these systems. Winter and spring flooding provides accessibility and creates seasonal and reproduction habitat for fish and waterfowl, which forage and depend on the abundant emergent growth, mast (acorns), and macroinvertebrates. Accessibility to and foraging upon seasonally available macroinvertebrates are necessary for wintering waterfowl to ensure that they are in satisfactory condition for successful breeding after their return migration (Fredrickson 1980; Drobney 1982, 1984; Rundle and Sayre 1983). Fish production in such systems not only depends upon access to this macroinvertebrate prey, but also is dependent upon access to the floodplain for breeding sites (Bryan and Connor 1981; Wharton et al. 1981). Biologists have documented species such as carp, white catfish, spotted sunfish, pirate perch, fliers, yellow and brown bullheads, warmouth, hickory shad, blue-backed herring, alewife, and chain pickerel as breeding on the floodplain, which subsequently serves as nursery habitat for their larvae and juveniles. The altered flow regime on the river during the spawning season could negatively impact spawning and nursery habitat of the species enumerated above. Annual drying of the floodplain is also critical to maintaining the system's integrity and health. Drydown is necessary for adequate aeration and growth of tree roots, tree seed germination and sapling establishment, and growth of emergent plants in order to maintain the system's vegetation.

Deviation from historical patterns and magnitudes of seasonal discharge create imbalances within the ecosystem. Petts (1984) noted that downstream changes due to upstream impoundments can occur to both the physical and biological components of the river, floodplain, estuary, and delta. Such changes may disrupt the life history cycles of organisms that co-evolved with the system. Some evidence suggests that the lower basin is experiencing such imbalances. Prolonged duration of flooding within the Roanoke system may eliminate the normal seasonal pattern of drydown and prevent germination and establishment of young hardwoods, resulting in a gradual shift in the system's vegetative composition and eliminating an important resource from both an economic and wildlife management standpoint (Dr. Russ Lee, personal communication).

The decline in the Roanoke River's striped bass population may have been partially attributable to the discharge resulting from reservoir-regulated flows. Changes in seasonal discharge patterns may result in less-than-adequate attractant flows; attractant flows which are too high; discharges during spawning which flush eggs and larvae onto the floodplain; discharges which are insufficient for suspending eggs and larvae; or combinations of these conditions. Hydropower peaking operations that cause rapid hourly changes also may cause disruptions in spawning activity. A multiagency Roanoke River Water Flow Committee investigated the flow issues surrounding the decrease in Roanoke River striped bass. The committee developed a river flow regime to enhance conditions for striped bass spring spawning.

Specifically, the combination of managed stream flows and drainage canals in bottomland forests exposes the forests to more frequent flooding and draining on the Roanoke River National Wildlife Refuge.

The lower Roanoke River has three stream classifications: (1) Roanoke Rapids Dam downstream to North Carolina Highway 48 - Class WS3; (2) North Carolina Highway 48 to River Mile 18 at Jamesville - Class C; and (3) River Mile 18 to river mouth - Class CSw (C Swamp). Each classification has separate standards. Appendix I contains the classification standards for each.

Groundwater is in sequence of sand, clay, and limestone that lie under Bertie County and becomes thicker from west to east. These beds are about 400 feet thick in the west and increase to about 1,900 feet in thickness in the east. The upper sandy aquifer makes up an average of about 100 feet of these deposits. The limestone aquifer is in the southeastern part of the county and is only a few inches thick. The lower sandy aquifer makes up the rest of the deposits. In the western third of the county, these deposits contain only fresh water in all but a few areas. In the center of the county, the depth to brackish water is about 600 feet. The depth decreases toward the east to a depth of less than 300 feet in the vicinity of the Chowan River estuary.

FLUVIAL GEOMORPHOLOGY

Water not only plays a major role in determining what and how the flora and fauna is distributed over the floodplain, but is also the driving force in shaping the river channel and its banks. The altered flow regime on the river has disrupted the natural rhythmic up-and-down movement of the river within its channel. Flow regulation results in sustained higher than normal low flows and the elimination of high peak flows. These sustained low flows have a stage elevation relatively high on the banks that affect bank morphology. The prolonged stage contributes to extensive undercutting and bank failure. Eroding banks are particularly evident along the middle reaches of the river along the refuge's Broadneck and Company Swamp tracts and surrounding area. Refuge levee habitat erodes at a high rate during these prolonged flows. River levee habitat contains the highest diversity of plant and wildlife along the river. Stands of river cane provide nesting habitat for high priority neotropical birds (Swainson's warbler and Kentucky warbler), which are common along these levees. Eroding levees methodically reduce the amount of cane (habitat) for these important species. In addition, the undercutting facilitates the relatively rapid felling of large canopy trees into the river. These trees are a key component in providing suitable nesting habitat for the rare cerulean warblers present in this reach.

WATER QUALITY

There are 29 National Pollution Discharge Elimination System (NPDES) permitted sites on the Roanoke River between the Roanoke Rapids Dam and Plymouth. The sites vary from small domestic sewage treatment systems to pulp/paper mills. Eight involve domestic sewage systems for cities and towns, the largest being Roanoke Rapids. The Cashie River has six NPDES-permitted sites. Several NPDES sites discharge into waters adjacent to or directly upstream from refuge lands/waters. Some of the largest and their NPDES permit numbers are: International Paper, NC0057657; Roanoke Rapids Sewage Discharge/Roanoke Rapids Waste Water Treatment Plant, NC0024201; Weldon Waste Water Treatment Plant, NC0025721; Hamilton Waste Water Treatment Plant, NC0044776; Williamston Waste Water Treatment Plant, NC0020044; United Organics, NC0068187; Plymouth Waste Water Treatment Plant, NC0020028; and Weyerhaeuser Company/Plymouth Plant, NC0000680.

In 1990 the North Carolina State Health Director, Dr. Ronald H. Levine, issued dioxin-related health advisories concerning the consumption of fish from several North Carolina streams including the Roanoke River and Welch Creek. The health advisories varied depending on the location. Tests showed a dioxin contamination of 37.5 parts per trillion in fish from Welch Creek. The state suggests advisories on fish with 3-30 parts per trillion of dioxin and no consumption above 30 parts per trillion. Therefore, the state bans the consumption of fish from Welch Creek. The advisory suggests a limit of one meal per month on fish from the Roanoke River below the Roanoke Rapids Dam. The state has advised pregnant women and nursing mothers not to consume any fish from the Roanoke River. The state has assigned good-fair bioclassifications from Lewiston-Woodville to below Williamston based on benthic macroinvertebrate data, the biological community in the Roanoke River. The state has listed a 28.5-mile stretch of river from Williamston down to the Albemarle Sound as impaired waters due to the fish consumption advisory and dioxin levels.

Since the 1950s, the Corps of Engineers has managed the flows on the Roanoke River as a flood control project. Since the 1960s, Dominion Generation has further managed the flows with two hydroelectric projects. The managed flow regime currently in place sometimes causes dissolved oxygen levels to fall below the state standard of 5 milligrams/liter on the lower Roanoke River. These conditions may occur during prolonged periods of low flow or after floodwaters impinged in the extensive wooded wetlands adjacent to the Roanoke River lose dissolved oxygen and flow back into the river. Preliminary investigations conducted by Dominion Generation and the Service also suggest that hydropower peaking operations may contribute to wetland inundation, further impacting dissolved oxygen levels in the Roanoke River.

On April 1, 1998, the U.S. Geological Survey established five stations to monitor water quality continuously along the Roanoke River. The Survey operates the stations and records pH, dissolved oxygen, percent of dissolved oxygen, water temperature, and specific conductivity every 15 minutes. These stations have documented numerous episodes of hypoxic conditions on the Roanoke River, some of which lasted for days and weeks. Data collected by the Weyerhaeuser Company near Plymouth have documented periods of high salinity and low dissolved oxygen associated with reverse flows in the Roanoke River. Because of natural and manmade alterations to the flow of the Roanoke River, coupled with existing inputs of oxygen-consuming wastes, the river is unable to accommodate further loads of oxygen-consuming materials and still maintain water quality standards.

AIR QUALITY

Fires and paper pulp mills are the only significant source of air quality degradation in the region. State law mandates that no source of air pollution shall cause any listed ambient air quality standard (Section .0400) to be exceeded or contribute to a violation of any listed ambient air quality standard except as allowed by Rules .0531 or .0532 (.0401[c], NCAC, Title 15A, Subchapter 2D - Air Pollution Control Requirements, North Carolina Department of Environment and Natural Resources).

Subchapter 2D lists ambient air quality standards for sulfur oxides (measured as sulfur dioxide), total suspended particulates, carbon monoxide, ozone, hydrocarbons, nitrogen dioxide, lead, and particulate matter. Section .0508 enumerates control of particulates from pulp and paper mills. Section 0.0520 (7) indicates that fires purposely set to forest lands for forest management practices acceptable to the North Carolina Division of Forestry and the Environmental Management Commission are permissible if not prohibited by ordinances and regulations of governmental entities having jurisdiction. The regulation also includes a disclaimer that addresses certain potential liabilities of burning even though permissible.

Pulp and paper mills on each end of the approved refuge acquisition boundary may have a negative impact on air quality. There are two paper pulp mills below the dams at Roanoke Rapids. One mill operated by International Paper Corporation is located 3-4 miles below the Roanoke Rapids Dam (approximately 5 miles upstream or northwest of Mush Island). The Weyerhaeuser Company owns and operates the other mill in Plymouth, North Carolina, one-half mile south of Great Island.

VISUAL RESOURCES

The Roanoke River Refuge is part of an extensive bottomland hardwood conservation initiative within the river basin's coastal plain reach. The bottomland hardwood forests are the largest intact and least disturbed of their type remaining in the mid-Atlantic region. Visitors to the refuge have the opportunity to experience the solitude, wildness, uninterrupted quiet, and spirit of adventure with compass and map while observing the natural processes on the floodplain. The casual observer will see large expanses of cypress-gum swamps dominated by tupelo gum and an occasional monarch cypress tree. During the growing season, the swamps are a living cathedral, alive with neotropical songbirds, wading birds, beaver, mink, otter, and other species. Between the cypress-gum swamps and sloughs are hardwood flats and ridges. Presently, red maple, sweetgum, green ash, and American elm dominate many of the flats and ridges. The oak/hickory component is still present, but is not dominant due to past timber practices and the managed flow regime within the system.

From the river, one will see a well-established levee in the upper and middle reaches of the river. Further on down below Williamston, the levee disappears and cypress-gum forests dominate the lower reach. Where the levee is present, there are unstable banks with large trees, stands of river cane, and chunks of riverbank sloughing into the river at what appears to be an accelerated rate. The levee forest is mature with sycamore, cottonwood, sweetgum, and sugarberry present as dominant species. Bird diversity is highest on the levee habitat.

Development along the river has been minimal due to the river's expansive active floodplain. There are no wilderness resources present on the coastal plain reach of the Roanoke River. However, some refuge lands have potential for designation as research natural areas, in particular Rainbow slough on the Broadneck tract, and the Company Swamp, Conine Island, Great Island, and Goodman Island tracts.

BIOLOGICAL ENVIRONMENT

VEGETATIVE COMMUNITIES

The Roanoke River is a typical southeastern United States alluvial system that has formed forested swamps in the Coastal Plain region (Figure 5). From Weldon to Scotland Neck, the Roanoke River floodplain is relatively narrow with some locations only a mile wide. The natural levees and ridges alternate with sloughs and backswamps in rapid succession. The floodplain becomes flatter and broader in the middle section. Widths of 2 to 3 miles, with 1,000-acre cypress-gum backswamps, are not uncommon. The continued presence of levees and ridges makes the middle section the most diverse and productive. The river is essentially at sea level below Jamesville and broad expanses of cypress-gum swamp as much as 5 miles wide dominate.

There are no documented occurrences of plant species from the Federal Endangered Species List on the refuge. The North Carolina Division of Natural Heritage has described 15 natural communities in the floodplain on the basis of vegetation and physical characteristics (Lynch 1981), and 10 of these communities occur on the refuge. The National Wetlands Inventory described the entire refuge as a palustrine, forested wetland with deciduous or broad-leafed deciduous vegetation and a water regime ranging from temporarily flooded to semipermanently flooded (Cowardin et al. 1979). Schafale and Weakley (1990) identify six natural communities within the refuge boundary:

- Coastal plain levee forest (brownwater subtype)
- Cypress-gum swamp (blackwater subtype)
- Cypress-gum swamp (brownwater subtype)
- Coastal plain bottomland hardwoods (brownwater subtype)
- Coastal plain semipermanent impoundment and mesic mixed hardwood forest (coastal plain subtype)

Figure 5. Vegetative habitat types of Roanoke River National Wildlife Refuge.

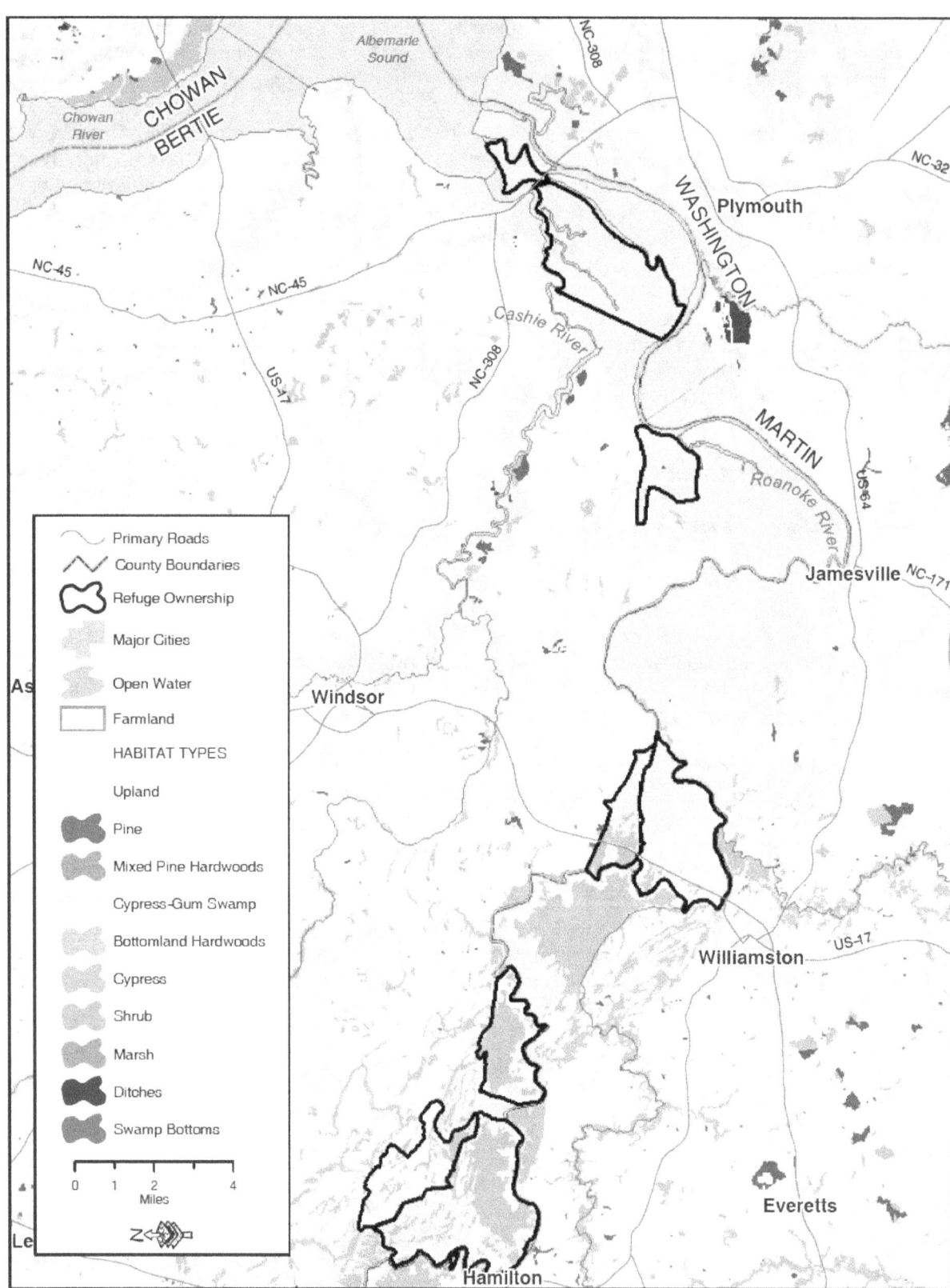

Coastal plain levee forests (brownwater subtype). This forest type occurs on the natural levees parallel to the river and its major creeks. It is prominent on refuge lands located upstream of Williamston and is still distinguishable as far downstream as Conine Island. The dominant canopy species of this bottomland type are sugarberry, sycamore, and green ash. Other species on the levees include cherrybark oak, eastern cottonwood, water hickory, sycamore, black walnut, American elm, and sweetgum. Boxelder dominates the subcanopy. The dominant shrubs include spicebush, pawpaw, and buckeye with a complete ground cover of mixed grasses, sedges, and rivercane.

Coastal plain bottomland hardwoods (brownwater subtype). Alluvial flats, low ridges, and high ridges occur on refuge lands located in the river's upper middle section as far down as Conine Island. Bottomland hardwoods occur on slightly higher ridges or in second bottoms formed by the migrating river channel. They usually occur on parallel ridges interspersed with fingers of cypress-gum sloughs or filled-in ancient river channels. A variety of oaks including cherrybark, swamp chestnut, laurel, and willow dominate these communities. Other hardwoods present include bitternut hickory, green ash, and sweetgum. The understory consists of ironwood and American and deciduous holly. The ground cover is sparse to dense and includes grasses, sedges, giant river cane, and false stinging nettle.

Cypress-gum swamps (brownwater subtype). The cypress-tupelo swamps occur in the river's upper middle to middle section at the Broadneck, Company, and Conine/Askew tracts and at the river's mouth on Goodman Island. They are areas of low elevation (backswamps landward of the natural levees, sloughs, and lower areas of the ridge and swale system) where the seasonal floodwaters may become trapped for long periods. In some areas the water table annually remains at or near the surface. Bald cypress and tupelo gum dominate this type, which has a shrub layer of Carolina water ash and very little ground cover. Logging has removed most of the mature cypress. In the logged areas, tupelo gum is the dominant tree species.

Cypress-gum swamps (blackwater subtype). Cypress-gum flats and swamp pocosin forests occur below Jamesville on the refuge's Hampton Swamp and Great Island Tracts. There is no distinguishable river levee feature found on these tracts. Two prominent blackwater creeks fork into Great Island from the Cashie River. The dominant tree is water tupelo; however, cypress and red maple are also prevalent. Water ash, sweet bay, black alder, and tag alder provide the understory. Loggers high-graded the cypress; however, nobody knows what species are present on the interior portions of theses tracts, particularly around Great Island.

Mesic mixed hardwood forests (coastal plain subtype). These communities flooded occasionally before construction of the dams, but now rarely or never flood. Found on the high ridges of Broadneck Swamp, the species present that distinguish these ridges as mesic mixed hardwood forests are American beech, American holly, shagbark hickory, and loblolly pine. Shrubs include dogwood, ironwood, blueberry, and gallberry. The ground cover consists of mixed grasses and sedges.

FIRE IN BOTTOMLAND HARDWOODS

Fire management would play a limited role in maintaining the bottomland hardwood forests of the Roanoke River. The vegetative species present would not likely tolerate a moderate to heavy fire. Moist-soil conditions along with sparse ground cover would prevent a significant fire from destroying this habitat. The upland tree species would be more tolerant of fire, but fire is not essential in maintaining this forest community. Due to the limited acreage the Service currently manages, it would be difficult to incorporate fire into the refuge's forest management plan.

Birds. After an absence of many years, the threatened bald eagle recently returned to nest across the river from the Goodman Island Tract. Eight eagles are currently nesting along the Roanoke River below the dam at Roanoke Rapids. Several species listed as high priority by the Service and/or listed by the State of North Carolina as rare and of special concern include the Swainson's warbler, Kentucky warbler, wood thrush, prothonotary warbler, Mississippi kite, and cerulean warbler. At least 219 species of birds, including 88 breeding species (33 neotropical and 55 resident) utilize the Roanoke River floodplain (Lynch and Crawford 1980). The area supports the highest density of nesting birds, especially songbirds, anywhere in North Carolina (LeGrand 1994). The refuge project area supports at least five active heron rookeries. The Conine Island rookery, containing great blue herons, great egrets, and anhingas, is the largest inland heron rookery in the state. The American Bird Conservancy recognizes it as a continentally important bird place. The Company Swamp Tract contains at least two great egret rookeries, and the Broadneck Tract has a yellow-crowned night heron rookery. The red-shouldered hawk and barred owl are characteristic raptor species found in the wooded swamps and bottomland hardwoods. (See Table 3 for the known ranges of priority birds at Roanoke River National Wildlife Refuge.)

Wintering and migrating waterfowl make extensive use of the refuge's wetlands. Principal species include the mallard, wood duck, black duck, and wigeon. Waterfowl use on the refuge and surrounding wetlands is dependent on beaver ponds and/or backswamp flooding. The degree and duration of backswamp flooding is dependent upon basin rainfall and upriver reservoir dam releases.

The Roanoke River floodplain provides habitat for a significant portion of the three most commonly harvested duck species in North Carolina. Studies (U.S. Fish and Wildlife Service 1983) have shown the importance of wooded wetlands to wintering waterfowl as prime sources of cover and food, providing supplemental dietary needs prior to spring migration, mating, and nesting. Migratory mallards, American black ducks, and some wood ducks use the bottomland hardwoods and cypress-gum swamps primarily in the fall and winter months. They often feed in shallow water, and for migration and pre-breeding activities they supplement this with the high protein foods found in the wooded floodplain, including acorns; beechnuts; the seeds of buttonbush, bald cypress and tupelo gum; insects; and the abundance of aquatic invertebrates such as snails, crustaceans, and insects (Bellrose 1976). Other wood ducks move into the area in the late winter and spring to nest in cavities in the standing timber along the river, blackwater streams, sloughs, and beaver ponds.

The bottomland hardwood habitat along the Roanoke River supports one of the largest natural populations of wild turkey in North Carolina, with densities exceeding 15 birds per square mile in parts of the area (North Carolina Wildlife Resources Commission, unpublished data). The ancient river ridges and terraces provide excellent food and cover for feeding and nesting turkeys (McClanahan 1979). Woodcock and bobwhite quail also occur sporadically along the river (Barick and Critcher 1975).

Table 3. Known ranges of priority birds at Roanoke River National Wildlife Refuge.

SPECIES	HABITAT	BREEDING RANGE	WINTER RANGE
NEOTROPICAL MIGRATORY SONGBIRDS			
Cerulean Warbler	Deciduous Forests	Minnesota - New York South to Gulf Coast	South America
Prothonotary Warbler	Riverine Swamps	Minnesota - New York South to Gulf Coast	Central and South America
Swainson's Warbler	Forested Swamps	Oklahoma - Maryland South to Gulf Coast	Jamaica and Mexico
Kentucky Warbler	Deciduous Forests	Nebraska - Ohio South to Gulf Coast	Mexico and Central America
Wood Thrush	Bottomland Forests	South Dakota - Maine South to Gulf Coast	Mexico – Central America
RAPTORS			
Mississippi Kite	Bottomland Forests	Kansas - North Carolina South to Gulf Coast	South America
Red-shouldered Hawk	Bottomland Forests	North Dakota – Maine South to Gulf Coast	Oklahoma - New York South to Mexico
Barred Owl	Forested Swamps	North Dakota - Maine South to Gulf Coast	North Dakota-Maine South to Gulf Coast
COLONIAL NESTING BIRDS			
Great Blue Heron	Bottomland Forests	North Dakota - Maine South to Gulf Coast	Southern United States
Yellow-crowned Night Heron	Swamps	Missouri - Maine South to Gulf Coast	Florida and South
Great Egret	Bottomland Forests	Tennessee - New York South to Gulf Coast	South Carolina – Texas
Anhinga	Bottomland Forests	North Carolina - Texas South to Brazil	Southern U.S. – South America
WATERFOWL			
Wood Duck	Bottomland Forests	Throughout the United States and southern Canada	North Carolina – Kansas and South
Black Duck	Bottomland Forests and Coastal Marshes	Canada to Illinois and North Carolina	Eastern United States

Mammals. The combination of hard and soft mast-producing trees and the availability of cover habitat provides for high mammal populations. The North Carolina Wildlife Resources Commission classifies the Roanoke River floodplain as high density white-tailed deer habitat, with density estimates ranging as high as 24.3 animals per square kilometer (62.4/square mile) in some areas (Osborne 1981). Likewise, a remnant population of black bear occurs along the lower river in one of the few remaining expanses of habitat for this species in this part of the state (U.S. Fish and Wildlife Service 1981). In addition to the availability of food, these bears probably take advantage of the abundance of large old trees for winter denning sites. Gray squirrels and marsh rabbits are abundant. Furbearers include raccoon, mink, muskrat, otter, fox, bobcat, beaver, and opossum (Barick and Critcher 1975). Two bats occur that are federal species of concern: Rafinesque's big-eared bat and southeastern myotis. Both bat species utilize hollow bald cypress trees as roost sites.

Reptiles and Amphibians. Representative floodplain amphibians and reptiles include the southern leopard frog, green tree frog, southern dusky salamander, black rat snake, eastern cottonmouth, yellow-bellied turtle, snapping turtle, and five-lined skink (Maki et al. 1980). Tinkle (1959) found that narrow long levees were indispensable for the egg-laying of many amphibious snakes and reptiles.

Fish. The Roanoke River and its tributaries provide excellent habitat for many fish species. The North Carolina Wildlife Resources Commission classifies the Roanoke River between Williamston and the Roanoke Rapids dam as a carp-catfish stream (Fish 1968). It classified Coniott Creek, which forms the northeast boundary of the Broadneck Swamp, as a redfin-warmouth tributary (Carnes 1965). The Commission also classified stations within the Roanoke as carp-catfish, and determined Conoho Creek to be a redfin-warmouth stream.

The Roanoke River and its associated floodplain wetlands are especially critical to anadromous species (Johnson et al. 1981; Hassler et al. 1981). Roanoke River anadromous fish include the striped bass, blueback herring, alewife, hickory shad, and American shad. The river from above the Mush Island Tract and downstream to Broadneck Tract provides critical spawning habitat for a highly significant population of striped bass. The life cycle of this population has co-evolved with the Roanoke River to the point where spawning adults, eggs, larvae, and juveniles are all dependent upon the presence of appropriate parameters within the system. Adult striped bass migrate to historical upstream spawning grounds attracted by springtime freshwater inputs from the upstream watershed. Developing eggs require moderate river flows for transport downstream (Rulifson et al. 1992a). The transport is too slow under low flow conditions, and under high flow conditions water flushes eggs over the levees onto the floodplain and out into the Sound, where the chances of successful hatch and survival are minimal.

Within a few days after hatching, the new striped bass larvae must feed where the highest nutrients occur. This is optimal under moderate flow conditions in the Roanoke River delta. High spring water flows flush nutrients and detritus from the swamps within the refuge acquisition boundary and from other floodplain sites into the Roanoke River, thus establishing conditions required for optimal development of phytoplankton and zooplankton communities used as a food base for the young larvae in the critical areas of the Roanoke River delta (Rulifson 1992). As larvae mature into juveniles and move eastward into nursery areas in the Sound, the river continues to influence their well-being and development by moderating salinity regimes appropriate for their growth and development. The river reach through the refuge serves a critical function in linking the life cycle stages and in ensuring the survival of given year classes (Rulifson et al. 1992b). In addition, 12 to 13 species of native mussels are present in the system.

Hickory shad and blueback herring utilize the floodplain for spawning and nursery habitat (Peters et al. 1998). The North Carolina Wildlife Resources Commission and refuge staff have documented striped bass on the floodplain feeding on herring and shad. The floodplain is also important to a number of resident, nonmigratory species as foraging, nursery and spawning habitat.

INSECTS AND DISEASES

In recent years, the forest tent caterpillar has caused widespread defoliation on the floodplain. It is not clear whether this defoliation is natural or the result of the altered flow regime. One current hypothesis is that prolonged flooding from the altered flow regime is adversely impacting a parasitic wasp that preys on the forest tent caterpillar. This parasitic wasp spends part of its life cycle in the ground. Prolonged flooding kills the wasp so that it can no longer serve as a check on the populations of forest tent caterpillar. This may account for the large defoliation outbreaks that resource managers have observed in the last decade.

The gypsy moth is now well established as far south as northeastern North Carolina. The North Carolina Division of Plant Industry and USDA Forest Service closely monitor gypsy moth populations using pheromone traps located throughout the Roanoke River floodplain, including refuge lands. When they detect large-scale outbreaks, they use integrated pest management techniques to suppress the outbreak, but not necessarily eliminate the species from the area. In 1999, they treated the Devil's Gut Preserve for gypsy moth. This is of significance to the Service, because refuge lands are just above Conine Island and below Hampton Swamp in the Devil's Gut Preserve.

EXOTIC ORGANISMS

Four exotic organisms exist within the river system and are presently impacting or have the potential to impact refuge lands. They are the Asian clam (*Corbicula fluminea*), common carp (*Cyprinus carpio*), nutria (*Myocaster coypus*), and the gypsy moth (*Lymantria dispar*).

THREATENED AND ENDANGERED SPECIES

After an absence of many years, the threatened bald eagle recently returned to nest across the river from the Goodman Island Tract and on a tributary near Jamesville. Eight bald eagles are currently nesting along the Roanoke River below the dam at Roanoke Rapids.

The status of the federally endangered shortnose sturgeon in the Roanoke River is unclear. In 1998, an adult male shortnose sturgeon was captured in a North Carolina Wildlife Resource Commission gill net set in the Western Albemarle Sound. This is the second documented catch of this species since 1985. The Service has not documented any other federally threatened or endangered species on or adjacent to refuge lands.

When planning and implementing management actions, the refuge staff will give primary consideration to the status and habitat requirements of the species listed in Table 4.

SOCIOECONOMIC CONDITIONS AND LAND USE

Roanoke River National Wildlife Refuge lies in Bertie County. However, the part of the Roanoke River Valley with large bottomland hardwood forest contiguous with the refuge also includes land in Martin, Halifax, Northampton, and Washington counties. Residents from these counties are the most frequent visitors to the refuge. The refuge affects the environment, society, and economy of these counties more than any other area. In planning and implementing refuge activities, the refuge staff must consider the social and economic conditions of the counties. Land use in the communities influences the water and air quality in the Roanoke River and on the refuge. The relative availability of open space will affect the availability of land for wildlife habitat, both on and off the refuge. The land protection step-down plan will also consider lands in Martin, Halifax, Northampton, and Washington counties.

Table 4. Species of concern on the Roanoke River National Wildlife Refuge.

Species/Feature	Status	Habitat		
		River	Bottomland Hardwood	River Levee
Shortnose Sturgeon	FL	X	X	
Bald Eagle	FL	X	X	X
Rafinesque's Big-eared Bat	FSC		X	
Southeastern Myotis	FSC		X	
Chowanoke Crayfish	FSC	X		
Cerulean Warbler	FSC			X
Atlantic Sturgeon	SC	X		
Hickory Shad	SC	X	X	
Alewife	SC	X	X	
Blue-backed Herring	SC	X	X	
Striped Bass	SC	X	X	
Swainson's Warbler	SC			X
Mississippi Kite	SC		X	X
Yellow-crowned Night Heron	SC		X	
Wood Duck	SC	X	X	
Rookeries	SC	X	X	
Black Duck	SC	X	X	
Status: FL=Federally listed; FSC=Federal Species of Concern; SL=State listed; SC=Species of Management Concern.				

Traditionally, the area has not been at the forefront of economic growth or development in the State of North Carolina, and historically unemployment has been higher than the state average. Instead, much of the economic and social life of the area centers on tourism on the barrier islands of the Outer Banks, 100 miles east of Bertie County; the city of Greenville, 50 miles south of the refuge; and the city of Rocky Mount, 50 miles southeast of the refuge.

The area is predominantly rural. Hunting and recreational fishing are popular pastimes. Farming, commercial fishing, and forestry are important elements of the economy.
The largest towns in the area and their 2000 populations are Windsor (2,056) in Bertie County; Williamston (5,503) in Martin County; Plymouth (4,328) in Washington County; Roanoke Rapids (16,600) in Halifax County; and Garysburg (1,254) in Northampton County. Windsor, Williamston, and Plymouth are also county seats. Jackson is the county seat of Northampton County with a 2000 population of 695 (Northampton County Chamber of Commerce 2002a). Halifax is the county seat of Halifax County with a 2000 population of 327 (Roanoke Valley Chamber of Commerce 2002).

DEMOGRAPHICS

The area's counties are primarily rural and their populations are generally equal to what they were earlier in the century (U.S. Census Bureau 2000).

The population is diverse, with equal numbers of white and black residents and representatives of Hispanic, Asian, and Native American origin. Three thousand members of the Haliwa-Saponi Indian tribe reside in Northampton County (U.S. Census Bureau 2000). In 2000, the median family income was far below the state average of $35,320. The poverty and unemployment rates were well above the state average of 12.6 percent (U.S. Census Bureau 2000). The percentage of high school and college graduates is well below the state averages. The homeownership rate is above the state average. The number of persons per household is approximately the same as the state average (U.S. Census Bureau 2000) (Table 5).

LAND USE

The area has had a long history of timber production and active logging. Sixty percent of the area is still forested and 30 percent is still farmed. The farms are decreasing in numbers and total area, but increasing in size per farm. Gross receipts are decreasing and the operations are diversifying from crops only to hogs and chickens grown in large confinement facilities. The primary crops are cotton, corn, soybeans, and wheat (USDA, Census of Agriculture 2002) (Table 6 and Appendix VII).

FORESTRY

Timber has always been a source of income for the lower Roanoke River Valley. However, much of the timber was cleared for the cultivation of cotton and other crops. Today, the area is approximately 57 percent forested, comparable to the rest of the northern coastal plain of North Carolina which is 53 percent forested. Most of the forest is loblolly pine; however, oak-gum-cypress and oak-hickory stands are also common (USDA Forest Service 2003) (Table 7).

In 2000, private landowners were the largest forest owner, followed by the forest industry. Federal, state, county, and local governments owned less than three percent (USDA Forest Service 2003). In 1990, the value of timber sold was $26.4 million. The payroll from forest products was $9.9 million of the $62.3 million from all manufactured products (USDA Forest Service 1991).

EMPLOYMENT

Manufacturing and agriculture are the largest employers in the lower Roanoke River Valley (U.S. Department of Commerce, County Business Patterns 2000). Perdue Farms, Weyerhaeuser, International Paper, and Georgia Pacific are the largest employers (Table 8) (North Carolina Department of Economic Security Commission 1999).

OUTDOOR RECREATION

Fish and wildlife resources have had a profound effect on recreation in the area. Bertie, Martin, Halifax, Northampton, and Washington counties have always had an abundance of fish and game due to the diversity of lands and waters. Early in the twentieth century, sportsmen's clubs were created in the area for the purpose of protecting game and wildlife. Later, as part of a comprehensive wildlife management program, Roanoke River National Wildlife Refuge was created to preserve and restore habitat for native wildlife and migratory birds (U.S. Fish and Wildlife Service 1981). The North Carolina Wildlife Resources Commission manages the Roanoke River Wetlands and Martin County Game Land to provide hunting opportunities in the area.

Table 5. Demographic data for the Lower Roanoke River Valley.

Data	County					
	Bertie	Martin	Washington	Northampton	Halifax	North Carolina
2000 Population	19,733	25,593	13,732	21,980	56,703	8 million
Population Change 1990-2000	-3%	+2%	-2%	-1%	-1%	+21.4%
Long Term Population Change	2000 same as 1900	2000 same as 1940	2000 same as 1960	2000 same as 1910	2000 same as 1940	+100% since 1950
Percent White	35.9	52.5	48.3	39.1	42.6	72.1
Percent Black	62.3	45.4	48.9	59.4	52.6	21.6
Percent Hispanic	1.0	2.1	2.3	0.7	1.0	4.7
Percent Native American	0.4	0.3	0.1	0.3	0.5	1.2
Percent Asian	0.4	0.2	0.3	0.1	0.3	1.4
Median Family Income	$22,816	$26,053	$22,726	$24,218	$24,741	$35,320
Percent Poverty Rate	22.9	20.1	20.5	23.1	23.6	12.6
Unemployment Rate	8.4	7.2	7.9	11.1	11.2	6.7
Percent High School Graduates	54.0	55.0	59.0	47.0	50.0	56.0
Percent College Graduates	8.0	9.0	8.0	14.0	8.0	14.0
Home Ownership	74.9	71.8	73.6	77	67	69.4
Persons per Household	2.53	2,53	2.52	2.44	2.51	2.49

Table 6. Land use data for the Lower Roanoke River Valley.

	County				
	Bertie	**Martin**	**Washington**	**Northampton**	**Halifax**
2000 Acres Forested	304,900	177,200	84,200	188,000	254,900
Percent Forested	68	60	38	55	55
Acres Cropland	92,982	77,823	100,388	95,809	103,929
Percent Cropland	21	27	47	28	22
2002 Acres in Farms	142,552	110,677	114,423	150,666	194,651
1997 Acres in Farms	154,338	115,202	107,280	160,464	185,382
Trend in Farmland	-7%	-4%	+7%	-6%	+5%
2002 Size of Farms	432	363	593	459	512
1997 Size of Farms	416	296	528	469	547
Trend in Farm Size	+4%	+23%	+12%	-6%	-6%
Value of Products (2002-1997)	$85 million (-23%)	$40 million (-36%)	$46 million (-31%)	$61 million (-34%)	$64 million (+34%)
Value of Products per Farm, 2002	$257,692	$130,792	$239,113	$187,090	$169,659
Value of Products per Farm, 1997	$298,986	$161,846	$332,784	$269,673	$286,794
Trend in Value per Farm	-14%	-19%	-28%	-31%	-41%
Important Crops	Cotton Corn Peanuts Hogs Chickens	Cotton Peanuts Soybeans Hogs Chickens	Soybeans Corn Cotton Hogs Chickens	Cotton Peanuts Soybeans Hogs Chickens	Cotton Peanuts Soybeans Hogs Chickens

Table 7. Forestry data for the Lower Roanoke River Valley in 2000.

	County				
	Bertie	**Martin**	**Washington**	**Northampton**	**Halifax**
Major Cover Types					
Loblolly Pine	38%	33%	41%	42%	32%
Oak-Gum-Cypress	26%	31%	19%	8%	19%
Oak-Hickory	17%	22%	19%	26%	32%
Ownership					
Private	76%	66%	54%	85%	80%
Industry	18%	24%	27%	14%	19%
Government	6%	10%	19%	1%	1%
Economic Impact					
Timber Value	$26.4 million	$14.5 million	$10.8 million	$17.0 million	$22.1 million
Manufactured Products	$62.3 million	$157.4 million	$5.7 million	$25.1 million	$118.3 million
Payroll	$9.9 million	$3.5 million	$3.3 million	$12.6 million	$48.4 million

Table 8. Employment data for the Lower Roanoke River Valley.

	County				
	Bertie	**Martin**	**Washington**	**Northampton**	**Halifax**
Annual Payroll	$103.1 million	$115.8 million	$132.5 million	$67.9 million	$34.1 million
Employees	5,388	5,743	4,543	4,500	16,500
Major Employer	Perdue	Weyerhaeuser	Weyerhaeuser	Georgia Pacific	International Paper
Employees	2,690	1,000	300	200	612
Major Employing Sectors	Manufacturing Agriculture Health Care Retail Trade Wholesale	Retail Trade Manufacturing Agriculture Health Care Hotel & Food	Agriculture Manufacturing Retail Trade Health Care Hotel & Food	Agriculture Manufacturing Health Care Wholesale Retail Trade	Manufacturing Retail Trade Health Care Hotel & Food Agriculture

Recreation in the area is also dependent on the water in the Roanoke River and the Albemarle Sound. Boat ramps provide access to the river and sound. Numerous outfitters provide boats and guided tours. The North Carolina Division of Parks and Recreation and the Roanoke River Partners, a nongovernmental organization, actively promote ecotourism. The North Carolina Coastal Plain Paddle Trails Guide lists a trail along the Roanoke River through the refuge; the tributaries Broad Creek and Cow Creek in Bertie County adjacent to the refuge; and Conoho Creek, Spellers Creek, and Devil's Gut in Martin County on the south side of the river adjacent to the refuge (North Carolina Division of Parks and Recreation 2001). The Roanoke River Partners have built and are maintaining camping platforms along the lower reaches of the river below Williamston. Future plans include adding platforms or designating camping areas along the middle and upper reaches of the river from Williamston to Weldon.

The State of North Carolina owns the Roanoke River Wetlands Game Land for wildlife management and hunting opportunities. The town of Windsor also has the Cashie Wetlands Walk, a raised boardwalk through the wetlands along the Cashie River. The Partnership for the Sounds, a nongovernmental organization that promotes sustainable economic development, operates the Roanoke-Cashie River Center in Windsor to educate the public about the natural heritage of the area that developed along the rivers (Tetterton 1998).

Other nature-based recreation areas include Moratock Park in Martin County; Pettigrew State Park, Bachelor Bay State Game Land, and Pocosin Lakes National Wildlife Refuge in Washington County; Lake Gaston in Northampton County; and Medoc Mountain State Park and Roanoke Canal Trail in Halifax County (Tetterton 1998).

Many of the area's festivals focus on natural resources, such as the Cashie River Festival in Windsor, Bertie County; the Jamesville Herring Festival in Martin County; Riverfest in Plymouth, Washington County; and Rockfish Run in Weldon, Halifax County (Tetterton 1998).

OUTDOOR RECREATION ECONOMICS

Fish and wildlife are the focus of the refuge, but they are also important to the local economy. First, a considerable commercial fishery is present in both the Roanoke River and the Albemarle Sound. Striped bass, alewife, blueback herring, and catfish are the major species harvested, and American shad are also important. Secondly, hunting and fishing are economically important to local businesses, both directly as the local population spends money and indirectly as an attraction that draws sportsmen from outside the county.

Unfortunately, a general lack of regard for the preservation of fish and wildlife resources, combined with the construction of hydropower generation dams and wetland clearing and draining, has led to the loss of valuable fishery spawning grounds and the loss of habitat for many wildlife species. In the attempt to protect and restore some of these resources, Roanoke River National Wildlife Refuge serves an important role, not only by providing habitat for diverse plant and wildlife species, but also as a place where people can go to enjoy these resources, either through observation or more directly through hunting and fishing.

A survey of wildlife-dependent recreationists in North Carolina, conducted by the Service in 2001, documented an average expenditure of $69 per day by anglers; $74 per day by hunters; and $199 per day for wildlife observers and photographers (U.S. Fish and Wildlife Service 2001).

The Partnership for the Sounds performed a study of the economic impacts of their facilities and found that the average visitor spent $108 per visit, with a range of $63.70 to $332.55 per day

(Vogelsang 2001). A similar study of visitors at the Chincoteague National Wildlife Refuge in Virginia showed a range of expenditures from $62 to $101 per day (U.S. Environmental Protection Agency 1997).

A study on birdwatchers commissioned by the State of New Jersey demonstrated that the average visitor to the shorebird migration spent $130 per day (New Jersey Department of Environmental Protection 2000). Birdwatchers on eight national wildlife refuges in New Jersey reported a range of expenditures from $25 to $41 per day (Kerlinger 1994).

Ecotourists on Dauphin Island, Alabama, spent an average of $60 per visitor per day (Kerlinger 1999).

Birdwatchers on High Island, Texas, reported an average expenditure of $46 per day, and nonresidents reported $693 per trip (Eubanks et al. 1993). The average visitor to the Great Texas Coastal Birding Trail spent $78 per day (Eubanks and Stoll 1999).

Studies at the Santa Ana National Wildlife Refuge in south Texas demonstrated a range of expenditures from $88 to $145 per day on nature-based tourist activities. The Laguna Atascosa National Wildlife Refuge in south Texas reported a range of $83 to $117 per day (U.S. Environmental Protection Agency 1997).

Bird watchers to the Salton Sea National Wildlife Refuge in California spent an average of $57 per day (National Audubon Society 1998).

When improved access, facilities, and staffing are added, Roanoke River National Wildlife Refuge can play an important role in the economic life of the community. Ecotourism, hunting, fishing, wildlife observation and photography, and environmental interpretation are increasingly being seen as lucrative industries. As the population increases and the number of places left to enjoy wildlife decreases, the refuge may become even more important to the local community. It can benefit the community directly by providing recreational opportunities for the local population, and indirectly by attracting tourists from outside the county to generate additional dollars to the local economy.

TOURISM

Tourism in the area is based on the area's cultural and natural attractions. Boat ramps provide access to the river and sound. Numerous outfitters provide boats and guided tours. The county seats have historic districts featuring old homes and limited development along the Roanoke River. Bertie County features the Hope Plantation, a restored plantation house and homestead. The town of Windsor operates the Livermon Recreational Park and Zoo (Tetterton 1998).

Other cultural attractions include Fort Branch in Martin County; Port O' Plymouth Roanoke River Museum and Somerset Place in Washington County; Northampton County Museum in Jackson; and the Roanoke Canal, Chockoyotte Aqueduct, Lakeland Arts Center, and Canal Arts Center in Halifax County (Tetterton 1998).

Cultural resource events that attract tourists include the Spring Tour of Historic Homes and Buildings and the Open House at Hope Plantation in Bertie County; the Fort Branch Living History and Battle Reenactment and the Native American Heritage Festival and Pow Wow in Martin County; the Civil War Living History Weekend, Somerset Homecoming, Indian Heritage Week, and Living History Day in Washington County; and Halifax Day in Halifax County (Tetterton 1998).

With improved access, Roanoke River National Wildlife Refuge could serve as an additional attraction to tourists visiting the area. If the refuge had better roads and more facilities, tourists might stay longer in the area to enjoy the opportunities provided for wildlife-dependent recreation and interpretation. The result would be more income for the local economy.

TRANSPORTATION

In the early days, the area's residents relied on water transportation. The rivers and streams that crisscross the counties served as a means for transportation, trade, and communication between almost every community in the area. Some of the important waterways were the Roanoke, Chowan, and Cashie rivers. While today these waterways are no longer necessary for most of the transportation needs within the area, they are still important as sources of income and for recreation.

U.S. Highway 64 runs east and west through the southern edge of the area and connects population centers in central North Carolina and Interstate 95 to the Outer Banks on the eastern coast. U.S. Highway 17/13 runs north and south through the center of the area and connects U.S. Highway 64 with population centers in southeastern Virginia. A number of smaller roads connect the various communities in the area.

Roanoke River National Wildlife Refuge can be reached via U.S. Highway 17/13. All roads within the refuge are unpaved, single-lane, and not suitable for standard passenger vehicles. Although road access is limited, public access to the refuge on foot is unlimited.

CULTURAL ENVIRONMENT

Bertie County is a rural county in predominantly rural northeastern North Carolina. Cultural opportunities in the immediate area are limited to the history-based facilities outlined in the Tourism section; theater at local high schools; and music and art at local fairs and festivals. The city of Greenville, North Carolina and East Carolina University, located 50 miles south of the refuge, offer the nearest opportunities for large theatrical or musical performances. Norfolk, Virginia, located 70 miles to the northeast, has the area's largest art museums and venues for the performing arts.

RECREATIONAL USES OF THE REFUGE

HUNTING

Hunting and fishing are the primary recreational activities conducted in the Roanoke River project area. The refuge administers a well-developed hunt program in cooperation with the State of North Carolina as part of a Joint Venture Partnership, which was entered into by the state and the Fish and Wildlife Service when Congress established the refuge. In addition to the appropriate licenses, a special permit is necessary when hunting on state or refuge lands on the Roanoke River. The Service offers several types of hunting opportunities, which include a bow and arrow either-sex deer hunt; a muzzleloader either-sex deer hunt; a shotgun/rifle either-sex deer hunt; small game hunts; turkey hunts; youth turkey hunt; and waterfowl hunt. The current numbers of annual hunter use days are 2,000 for deer hunters with archery; 1,000 for deer hunters with muzzleloaders; 3,750 for deer hunters with modern guns; 1,000 for small game hunters; 200 for waterfowl hunters; and 530 for turkey hunters.

FISHING

The refuge's backswamps and river tributaries are not open to fishing. However, the refuge allows anglers to walk across the Conine Island Tract from U.S. Highway 13/17 to gain fishing access to the Roanoke River and Conine Creek, unless a permitted hunt is underway. The refuge staff estimates that these two locations currently bring in 3,000 annual angler use days.

ENVIRONMENTAL EDUCATION

The refuge does not have a developed environmental education program. The staff has taken college-level students, local community leaders, congressional staff, and teacher workshop groups out on the refuge to teach them about the bottomland hardwood forest ecosystem and flow issues on the river. Approximately 50 students use the refuge annually.

INTERPRETATION

The refuge has developed a three-quarter-mile interpretive trail, east off the northbound lanes of U.S. Highway 13/17. At the head of the trail is an interpretive kiosk that describes the Service's ecosystem approach to management and the ecology of the river's bottomland hardwood forests. The trail and kiosk are part of the Charles Kuralt Trail system, which connects the 11 national wildlife refuges in the Roanoke-Tar-Neuse-Cape Fear ecosystem in northeastern North Carolina and southeastern Virginia. Through a series of stops along the trail that are described in a brochure, visitors can learn about the ecology of a bottomland hardwood forest. The trail has plaques that identify and describe various species of trees. In addition, the refuge has hosted annual bird tours during the spring migrations and on International Migratory Bird Day. About 200 visitors annually use the refuge for interpretation.

WILDLIFE OBSERVATION

The refuge's three-quarter mile interpretative trail, part of the Charles Kuralt Trail, is the only area formally designated for wildlife observation. However, visitors can observe wildlife on the refuge's 22 miles of old logging trails at any time when no hunting is being conducted on the refuge. In addition, boating on the river provides opportunities to observe wildlife. Approximately 2,000 annual visitors currently use the refuge for wildlife observation.

WILDLIFE PHOTOGRAPHY

Although no photography blinds are available for public use, refuge visitors can photograph wildlife in areas not restricted to access during normal visitation hours. Currently, about 100 visitors annually pursue wildlife photography on the refuge.

OTHER RECREATIONAL ACTIVITIES

At high water, refuge regulations permit canoeing in the backswamps. A few local residents canoe the swamps, and one outfitter guides groups on the river and its floodplain.

REFUGE INFRASTRUCTURE

ROADS AND TRAILS

Old logging roads and trails formerly used by hunting clubs make up the refuge's road and trail system. Access to refuge lands, except the Conine Island and Askew tracts, is by boat only. The Conine Island and Askew tracts can be accessed via U.S. Highway 13/17 or from the Roanoke River.

The refuge maintains the logging roads as grassy trails. The staff mows them once a year. There are approximately 15 miles of roads on refuge lands (Figures 6 and 7).

The Charles Kuralt Trail was established by the Service and the Coastal Wildlife Refuge Society in honor of the late CBS News journalist Charles Kuralt for the recognition he brought to the National Wildlife Refuge System. It links together 11 national wildlife refuges and one national fish hatchery in the Roanoke-Tar-Neuse-Cape Fear ecosystem. The Roanoke River National Wildlife Refuge component of the trail presently consists of a three-quarter-mile, handicapped-accessible gravel trail located on Conine Island with access from U.S. Highway 13/17.

Presently, only the refuge staff has vehicular access to the Company and Broadneck Swamp tracts from upland sites. No public vehicular access is available except to Town Swamp during hunts. Improvements (redesigned or hydrologically-sensitive roads with gravel) have been made to approximately two miles of the Company Swamp road and one mile of Break of Dam road on the Broadneck Tract. Additional improvements are planned and their funding is pending.

UTILITY CORRIDORS AND DISTRIBUTION

Dominion Generation Power Company has two power transmission rights-of-way across refuge lands. One is on Company Swamp and the other is on Hampton Swamp. Crews from Dominion Generation mow and/or spray the woody debris with wetland-compatible chemicals under the Company Swamp corridor every two to four years.

COMMUNICATIONS SYSTEM

The refuge's communications system currently consists of mobile radios with no base station. Cellular phones are used for communication between the field and office.

SOLID WASTE COLLECTION AND DISPOSAL

Presently, there is no solid waste collection and disposal on refuge lands. Primitive camping by hunters is permitted with no solid waste disposal protocol in place.

Figure 6. Current Visitor Facilities at the Roanoke River National Wildlife Refuge (Askew and Conine Island Tracts).

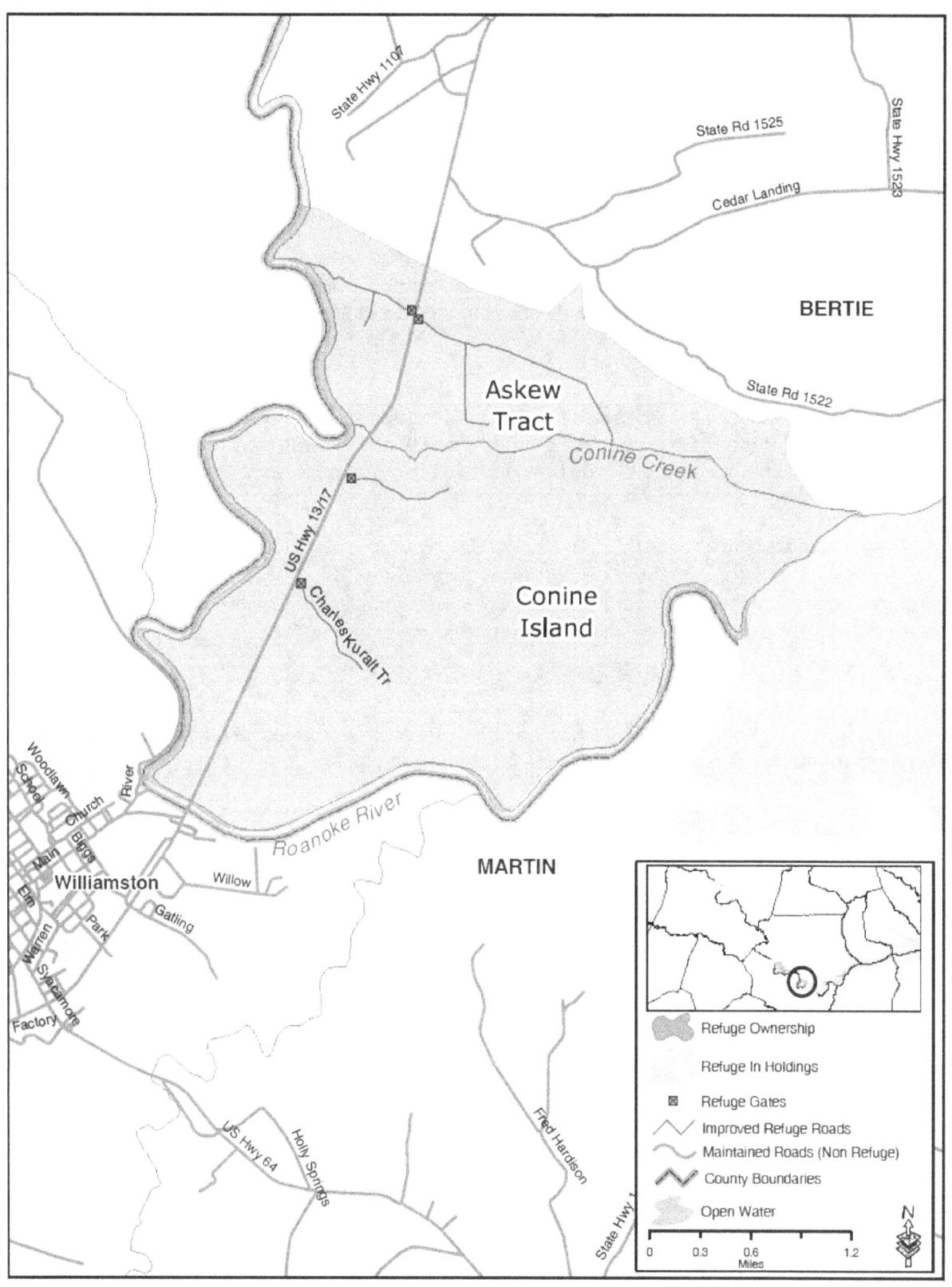

Figure 7. Current Visitor Facilities at the Roanoke River National Wildlife Refuge (Company Swamp, Broadneck Swamp, Town Swamp Tracts),

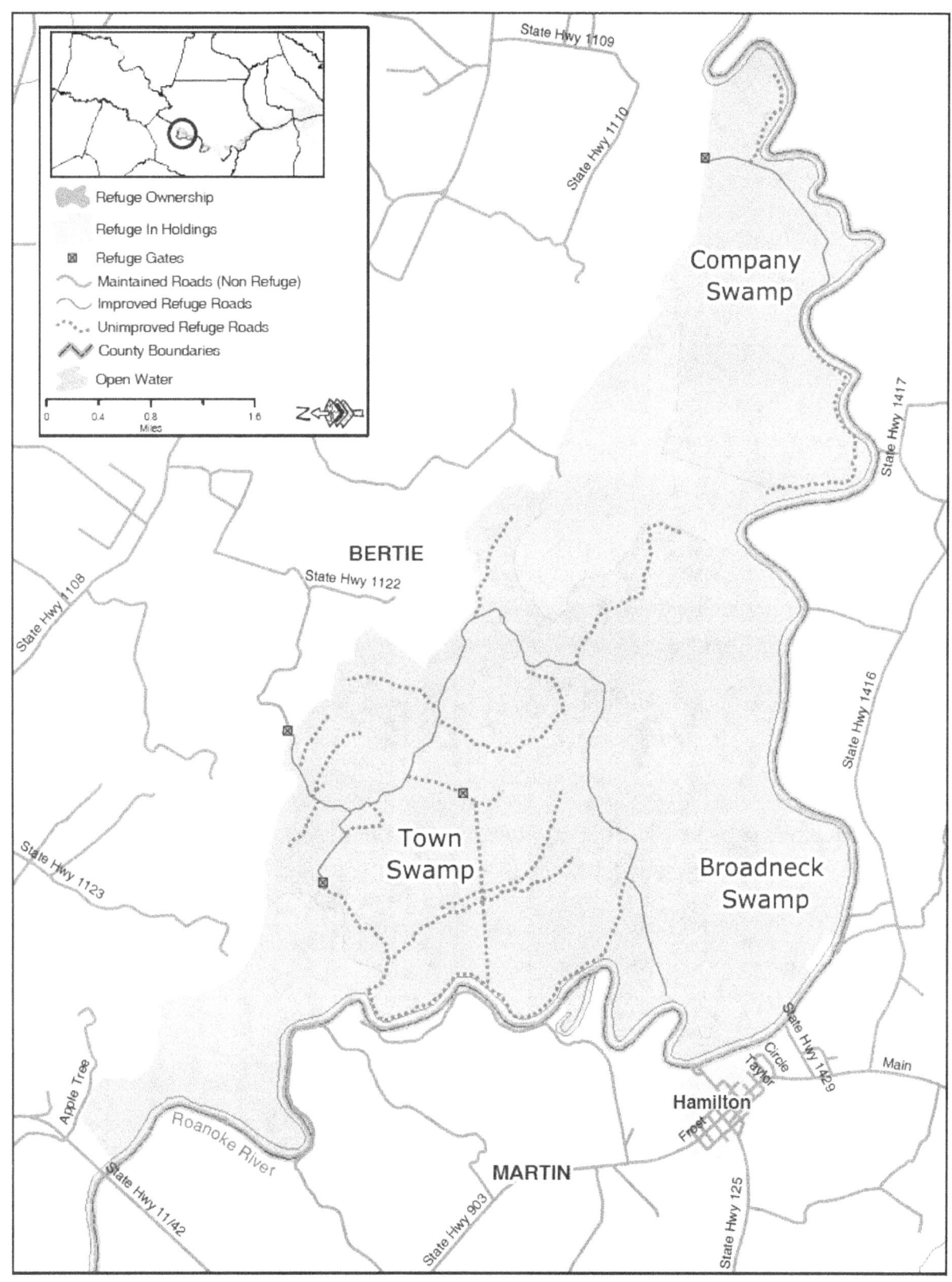

III. ALTERNATIVES

FORMULATION OF ALTERNATIVES

Management alternatives are different approaches or combinations of management objectives and strategies designed to achieve the refuge purpose, vision, and the goals identified in the comprehensive conservation plan; the priorities and goals of the Roanoke-Tar-Neuse-Cape Fear Ecosystem Team; the mission of the National Wildlife Refuge System; and the mission of the Fish and Wildlife Service. Alternatives are formulated to address the significant issues, concerns, and problems identified by the Service and during public scoping.

The three alternatives identified and evaluated represent different approaches to provide permanent protection, restoration and management of the refuge's fish, wildlife, plants, habitats and other resources. A major consideration in the formulation of the alternatives is the ability to obtain sufficient proprietary interest in lands to facilitate a physical and biological connection of bottomland hardwood forests, and to restore the functions and values of wetlands.

Refuge managers assessed the biological conditions and analyzed the external relationships affecting the refuge. This information contributed to the development of goals and objectives and, in turn, helped to formulate the alternatives. As a result, each alternative presents different sets of objectives for reaching refuge goals. Each alternative was evaluated based on how much progress it would make and how it would address the identified issues related to fish and wildlife populations, habitats, land protection and conservation, education and visitor services, and refuge administration.

The staff designed all of the management alternatives for the area within the current approved acquisition boundary of 33,000 acres. This plan will be revised as the Service acquires land within the approved acquisition boundary. Acquisition of a larger area beyond the existing boundary will require the development of a land protection plan outside of this plan.

DESCRIPTION OF MANAGEMENT ALTERNATIVES

Serving as a basis for each alternative, the staff developed goals and sets of objectives to achieve the refuge's purpose and the mission of the National Wildlife Refuge System. Objectives are desired conditions or outcomes that are grouped into sets and, for this planning effort, consolidated into three alternatives. These alternatives represent a range of different approaches for managing the refuge over a 15-year time frame. The three preliminary alternatives are summarized below.

ALTERNATIVE 1 - NO ACTION

Under this alternative, the Service will protect, maintain, restore, and enhance 20,978 acres of refuge lands for resident wildlife, waterfowl, migratory nongame birds, and threatened and endangered species. The refuge would develop and implement management programs with little baseline biological information. The refuge would direct all management actions towards achieving the refuge's primary purposes (i.e., preserving migratory and breeding habitat for neotropical songbirds; providing production habitat for wood ducks; and helping to meet the habitat conservation goals of the North American Waterfowl Management Plan), while contributing to other national, regional, and state goals to protect and restore neotropical breeding bird, wood duck, wintering American black duck and other waterfowl, colonial nesting bird, and anadromous fish populations.

The staff would limit surveys to breeding neotropical migratory songbirds on 40 levee plots, 5 forest health plots, and 100 regeneration plots. The only habitat management would be maintaining wood duck boxes.

The Service would maintain the current level of wildlife-dependent recreation activities (e.g., hunting, fishing, wildlife observation, and interpretation) and environmental education opportunities. The refuge would continue quality hunting programs on 8,480 hunter use days consistent with sound biological principles. It would permit fishing for 3,000 angler use days along the banks of the Roanoke River and Conine Creek. The refuge would provide no wildlife observation sites/platforms or interpretive kiosks. There is no protocol in place for handling sanitary waste. It would maintain existing facilities to support wildlife observation for 5,000 visitors and wildlife photography for 500 visitors. The staff would conduct environmental education programs for 50 students, provide interpretive opportunities for 1,000 visitors, and target outreach efforts to 500 people on a reactive basis (i.e., only on request). The refuge would make no improvements to exterior or interior access roads. Administrative roads would be available for hiking to support wildlife-dependent recreation to the extent that these opportunities do not interfere significantly with or detract from the achievement of wildlife conservation.

Under this alternative, the refuge would continue to seek acquisition of all properties from willing sellers within the present acquisition boundary (Figure 8). Lands acquired as part of the refuge would be available for compatible public wildlife-dependent recreation and environmental education opportunities. Purchases from willing sellers would be the preferred option to expand conservation efforts in the acquisition area. Other important land protection options include outreach and partnerships with adjacent landowners, hunt clubs, and the Natural Resources Conservation Service through conservation easements, cooperative agreements, and federal programs such as the Wetlands Reserve Program. These land conservation options would promote the linkage of bottomland hardwood forest tracts and contribute to overall natural resource conservation within the acquisition area.

The staff would protect cultural resources by requesting investigations as they plan construction and management operations. They would control pest animals and plants as they encounter them, but without a comprehensive management plan. They would monitor water quality at two sites as time permits. The zone law enforcement officer would enforce refuge regulations during the hunting season and as time allows outside of the hunting season.

The staff would manage refuge facilities and property to minimum Service standards to ensure the safety of employees and staff. Communications on the refuge would remain limited, without adequate radio or cell phone coverage. The number of refuge staff would remain at six; annual volunteer hours would remain at 1,500.

Figure 8. Existing acquisition boundary expansion, Roanoke River National Wildlife Refuge.

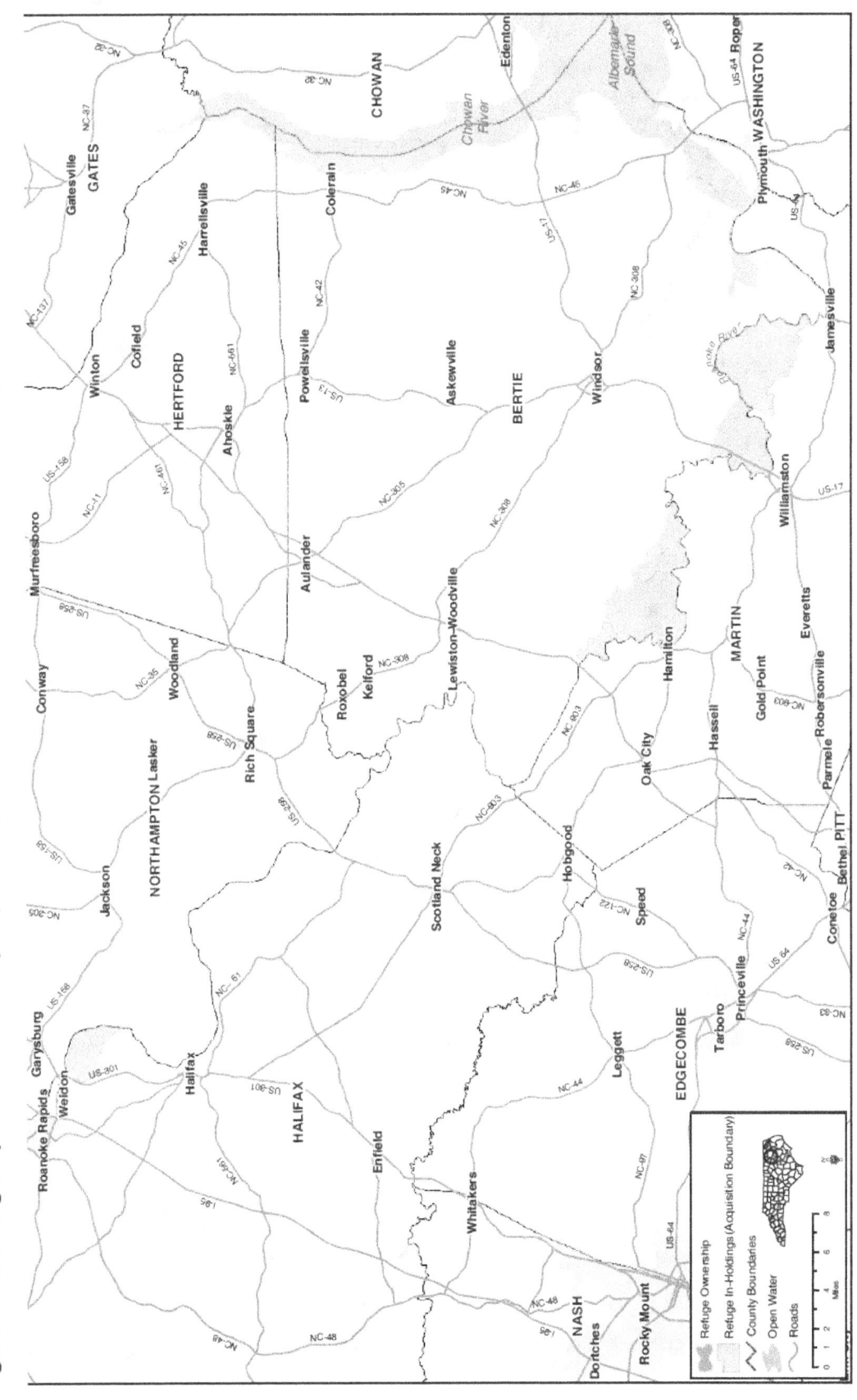

This alternative would develop and implement a program to manage and restore the refuge's forest and hydrology in support of migratory birds and other wildlife, and improve the public use program to better support the six priority public uses (hunting, fishing, wildlife observation, wildlife photography, and environmental education and interpretation). This alternative would also add staff, equipment, and facilities to support the programs. Under this alternative, the Service will protect, maintain, restore, and enhance 20,978 acres of refuge lands for resident wildlife, waterfowl, migratory nongame birds, and threatened and endangered species.

The staff would initiate extensive wildlife and plant censuses and inventory activities to obtain the biological information needed to implement management programs on the refuge. They would direct all refuge management actions toward achieving the refuge's primary purposes (i.e., preserving migratory and breeding habitat for neotropical migratory songbirds; providing production habitat for wood ducks; and helping to meet the habitat conservation goals of the North American Waterfowl Management Plan), while contributing to other national, regional, and state goals to protect and restore neotropical breeding bird, wood duck, wintering American black duck and other waterfowl, colonial nesting bird, and anadromous fish populations. The staff would expand its surveys for breeding neotropical migratory songbirds from 40 to 60 levee plots; add three forest health plots on a reference site off the refuge to the five on the refuge; and add 60 regeneration plots on a reference site off the refuge to the 100 regeneration plots on the refuge. The staff would implement active habitat management through forest stand management, and water level manipulations in beaver ponds and artificial drainage ditches designed to provide a diverse complex of habitats that meet the foraging, resting, and breeding requirements for a variety of species.

The Service would increase opportunities for wildlife-dependent recreation activities (hunting, fishing, wildlife observation, wildlife photography, environmental education and interpretation). It would make improvements to interior and exterior access roads to provide seasonal vehicular access to a broad segment of the public. Administrative roads would be available as hiking trails to support wildlife-dependent recreation to the extent that these opportunities do not interfere significantly with or detract from the achievement of wildlife conservation. The refuge would provide wildlife observation sites/platforms and interpretive kiosks. The refuge would institute a protocol for handling sanitary waste. It would continue a quality hunting program for 8,480 hunter use days consistent with sound biological principles. The staff would promote fishing along the banks of the Roanoke River to increase the use from 3,000 to 4,000 angler use days. They would plan environmental education programs for 500 students, interpretive programs for 3,000 visitors, and an outreach program to reach 1,000 people on a regular basis, and promote them extensively. They would schedule six annual tours, build and maintain three new kiosks, and develop printed interpretive materials. They would maintain the new and existing facilities to increase opportunities for wildlife observation from 5,000 to 10,000 visitors and wildlife photography from 500 to 1,000 visitors.

Under this alternative, the refuge would continue to seek acquisition of all properties from willing sellers within the present acquisition boundary (Figure 8). Lands acquired as part of the refuge would be available for compatible public wildlife-dependent recreation and environmental education opportunities. Purchases from willing sellers would be the preferred option to expand conservation efforts in the acquisition area. Other important land protection options include outreach and partnerships with adjacent landowners, hunt clubs, and the Natural Resources Conservation Service through conservation easements, cooperative agreements, and federal programs such as the Wetlands Reserve Program. These land conservation options would promote the linkage of bottomland hardwood forest tracts and contribute to overall natural resource conservation within the acquisition area.

The staff would protect cultural resources by requesting investigations as they plan construction and management operations. They would develop integrated pest management plans to control pest animals and plants and control them as they reach threshold levels. They would monitor water quality at four sites. A full-time law enforcement officer would enforce refuge regulations year-round and be proactive with outreach efforts focused on law enforcement.

The staff would manage refuge facilities and property to Service standards to ensure the safety of employees and staff, and efficiency of the operation. Communications would improve with a refuge radio system. The number of refuge staff would increase to 11; and annual volunteer hours would increase to 5,000 with more recruitment efforts.

ALTERNATIVE 3 - COMPREHENSIVE PROGRAM IMPROVEMENT

This alternative would develop and implement a program to manage and restore the refuge's forest and hydrology in support of migratory birds and other wildlife, and improve the public use program to better support the six priority public uses (hunting, fishing, wildlife observation, wildlife photography, and environmental education and interpretation). This alternative would also add staff, equipment, and facilities to support the programs. Under this alternative, the Service will protect, maintain, restore, and enhance 20,978 acres of refuge lands for resident wildlife, waterfowl, migratory nongame birds, and threatened and endangered species.

The staff would initiate extensive wildlife and plant censuses and inventory activities to obtain the biological information needed to implement management programs on the refuge. They would broaden refuge management actions beyond achieving the refuge's primary purposes (i.e., preserving migratory and breeding habitat for neotropical migratory songbirds; providing production habitat for wood ducks; and helping to meet the habitat conservation goals of the North American Waterfowl Management Plan), while contributing to other national, regional, and state goals to protect and restore neotropical breeding bird, wood duck, wintering American black duck and other waterfowl, colonial nesting bird, and anadromous fish populations.

The staff would expand its surveys for breeding neotropical migratory songbirds from 40 to 60 levee plots, add three forest health plots on a reference site off the refuge to the five on the refuge, and add 60 regeneration plots on a reference site off the refuge to the 100 regeneration plots on the refuge. They would also survey breeding birds on 40 interior swamp plots. They would add a survey of nonbreeding birds on 100 plots, a study of invertebrates on the refuge and off the refuge on a reference site, and data collection on the deer herd. The staff would implement active habitat management through forest stand management, and water level manipulations in beaver ponds and artificial drainage ditches designed to provide a diverse complex of habitats that meets the foraging, resting, and breeding requirements for a variety of species.

The Service would increase opportunities for wildlife-dependent recreation activities (hunting, fishing, wildlife observation, wildlife photography, and environmental education and interpretation. It would make improvements to interior or exterior access roads to provide seasonal vehicular access to a broad segment of the public. Administrative roads would be available as hiking trails to support wildlife-dependent recreation to the extent that these opportunities do not interfere significantly with or detract from the achievement of wildlife conservation. The refuge would provide wildlife observation sites/platforms and interpretive kiosks. The refuge would institute a protocol for handling sanitary waste. It would increase the quality hunting program to 8,680 hunter use days consistent with sound biological principles. The staff would promote fishing along the banks of the Roanoke River to increase use from 3,000 to 5,000 angler use days. They would plan environmental education programs for 500 students, interpretive programs for 3,000 visitors, and an outreach program to reach 1,000 people on a regular basis and promote them extensively. They would schedule six annual tours, build and maintain three new kiosks, and develop printed interpretive materials. They would maintain the new and existing facilities to increase opportunities for wildlife observation from 5,000 to 10,000 visitors and wildlife photography from 500 to 1,000 visitors. A new media relations specialist would develop regular programs for radio and print media.

Under this alternative, the refuge would continue to seek acquisition of all properties from willing sellers within the present acquisition boundary (Figure 8). Lands acquired as part of the refuge would be available for compatible public wildlife-dependent recreation and environmental education opportunities. Purchases from willing sellers would be the preferred option to expand conservation efforts in the acquisition area. Other important land protection options include outreach and partnerships with adjacent landowners, hunt clubs, and the Natural Resources Conservation Service through conservation easements, cooperative agreements, and federal programs such as the Wetlands Reserve Program. These land conservation options would promote the linkage of bottomland hardwood forest tracts and contribute to overall natural resource conservation within the acquisition area.

The staff would protect cultural resources by having a comprehensive inventory of the refuge performed and requesting investigations as they plan construction and management operations. They would develop integrated pest management plans to control pest animals and plants and control them as they reach threshold levels. They would monitor water quality at four sites. A full-time law enforcement officer would enforce refuge regulations year-round and be proactive with outreach efforts focused on law enforcement.

The staff would manage refuge facilities and property to Service standards to ensure the safety of employees and staff, maximize the efficiency of the operation, and meet all refuge needs. Communications would improve with a refuge radio system. The number of refuge staff would increase to 22; and annual volunteer hours would increase to 10,000 with more recruitment efforts.

PREFERRED ALTERNATIVE

The refuge staff selected Alternative 3 as the preferred alternative for managing Roanoke River National Wildlife Refuge over the next 15 years. The next section – the Comprehensive Conservation Plan – includes the goals, objectives, and strategies listed for Alternative 3.

Implementing the proposed alternative would result in better habitat management and increased public use opportunities, while meeting the refuge's primary purpose of protecting habitat for migratory birds. Specific results will include increased songbird and wood duck use and production; enhanced habitat and increased protection for other forest interior-dependent wildlife; enhanced resident wildlife populations; optimum wetland conditions within a managed flow situation; and greater opportunities for a variety of compatible wildlife-dependent recreational and environmental education activities.

An overriding concern reflected in this plan is that wildlife conservation is the first priority in refuge management. The Service allows public uses if they are compatible and appropriate with wildlife and habitat conservation. The refuge will emphasize wildlife-dependent public uses (e.g., hunting, fishing, wildlife observation, wildlife photography, and environmental education and interpretation).

COMPREHENSIVE CONSERVATION PLAN

Under this alternative, the Service will protect, maintain, restore, and enhance refuge lands for resident wildlife, waterfowl, migratory nongame birds, and threatened and endangered species. The refuge staff will initiate extensive wildlife and plant census and inventory activities to develop the baseline biological information needed to implement management programs on the refuge.

The refuge will direct all management actions toward achieving the refuge's primary purposes: (1) preserving nesting and migratory habitat for neotropical migratory songbirds; (2) providing production habitat for wood ducks; and (3) helping to meet the habitat conservation goals of the North American Waterfowl Management Plan. In addition, the staff will manage the refuge to contribute to other national, regional, and state goals for protecting and restoring populations of wildlife.

The refuge will implement active habitat management through forest management and beaver pond management designed to provide a historically diverse complex of habitats that meet the foraging, resting, and breeding requirements for a variety of species.

Under this alternative, the refuge would continue to seek acquisition of all willing seller inholdings within the present acquisition boundary. Lands acquired as part of the refuge would be available for compatible wildlife-dependent recreation and environmental education.

Acquisition from willing sellers would be one option used to improve conservation efforts in the expansion area. Equally important options include outreach programs and partnerships with adjacent landowners and hunting clubs to use conservation easements, cooperative agreements, and federal programs such as the Wetland Reserve Program to link bottomland hardwood forest tracts and to provide wildlife, soil, and water conservation benefits.

During the 15-year life of this plan, the refuge will develop and implement a forest management plan, designed to create spatially and specifically diverse bottomland hardwood forest (with little negative effect to avian fauna objectives).

The refuge will provide opportunities for high quality wildlife-dependent recreation (hunting, fishing, wildlife observation, wildlife photography, and environmental education and interpretation) activities. The staff will make improvements to the refuge's interior and exterior access roads to provide seasonal vehicular access to a broad segment of the public. They will permit hiking use to support wildlife-dependent recreation to the extent that these opportunities do not significantly interfere or detract from the achievement of wildlife conservation. The refuge will provide wildlife observation sites and platforms; interpretive trails, boardwalks, and kiosks; and restrooms at specific sites to allow for fully accessible environmental education and interpretation opportunities. The staff will provide quality fishing and hunting programs, consistent with sound biological principles with sufficient focus on migratory bird needs for sanctuary, loafing, feeding, and courting requirements. The refuge will permit fishing along the banks of the river, its tributaries, and acquired water bodies. The staff will develop and implement an environmental education plan, incorporating an aggressive and proactive promotion of both on- and off-site programs.

GOALS, OBJECTIVES, AND STRATEGIES

The goals, objectives, and strategies addressed below are the Service's response to the issues, concerns, and needs expressed by the planning team, the refuge staff, and the public. These goals, objectives, and strategies reflect the Service's commitment to achieve the mandates of the National Wildlife Refuge System Improvement Act of 1997, the mission of the National Wildlife Refuge System, the North American Waterfowl Management Plan, and the purpose and vision for Roanoke River National Wildlife Refuge. Depending upon the availability of funds and staff, the Service intends to accomplish these goals, objectives, and strategies during the next 15 years.

ALTERNATIVE 3 - PREFERRED ALTERNATIVE

GOAL 1. FISH AND WILDLIFE POPULATIONS

Protect, maintain, and enhance healthy and viable populations of indigenous migratory birds, wildlife, fish, and plants, including federal and state threatened and endangered species.

Discussion: Water is the driving force in the bottomland hardwood forest systems found along the Roanoke River. After years of carving away and depositing sediments, a forest system exists that supports a diverse wildlife community. The system continues to change with water dictating the degree and direction of future change. The forest system that exists today evolved with a very flashy, run-of-river flow regime. The decision to deviate from this type of flow regime to permit hydroelectric power and flood control activities may have irreversible consequences for the wildlife found within the floodplain. It is believed the managed flow regime on the Roanoke River has disrupted the natural dynamics of the system in a way that may be affecting the abundance and distribution of the fish and wildlife species found on the refuge. Prolonged flooding during the spring, which is the breeding season for most wildlife species, may be having adverse impacts on the overall species diversity and abundance found on the refuge, threatening the viability of some species. Surveys and studies of fish and wildlife populations are designed in a way to document whether managed river flows are impacting the recruitment, distribution, and survivorship of species within a given animal group. Surveys and studies are also designed to document occurrence and learn more about species habitat associations. Standardized census and survey techniques will be employed when conducting surveys and all data will be compiled into databases. This information is critical to formulating actions for all other refuge programs. All data will be shared with appropriate state and federal partners in an effort to further ecosystem management. Species will be managed as populations rather than individuals. Threatened and endangered species will be protected and managed toward recovery. All population management activities will strive to protect, maintain, and enhance species diversity in the broad context of the refuge and/or Roanoke River floodplain. This alternative allows for sufficient monitoring of fish and wildlife populations found on the refuge and will enable the staff to work towards achieving the stated goal.

Objective 1: Colonial Nesting Birds

Survey nesting population and location of colonial nesting birds from the ground annually and from the air every three years, and the status of the yellow-crowned night heron rookery annually. Conduct ground surveys of Conine Island rookery annually to confirm species composition of nesting population.

Discussion: The largest inland heron rookery in North Carolina exists on the refuge (estimated 2,500 nests in 1997 Conine Island rookery) in addition to several smaller rookeries. Great blue heron, great egret, and anhinga are also nesting in these rookeries. There is also a well-established yellow-crowned night heron rookery located on the refuge that is impacted by the managed flow regime. Prolonged flooding in the spring prevents yellow-crowned night herons from being able to forage in the vicinity of the rookery. Refuge staff has observed abandonment and low productivity in years when prolonged flooding has occurred in the spring. This plan allows for sufficient monitoring of rookeries found on the refuge.

Strategies:

- Conduct aerial survey of refuge rookeries every three years to determine nesting population and location of new rookeries.

- Determine the productivity and presence or absence of yellow-crowned night herons in Rainbow Slough annually.

- Conduct ground surveys of Conine Island rookery annually to confirm species composition of nesting population.

- Record opportunistic observations of colonial nesting birds annually.

- Recruit agencies, universities, and organizations to perform studies and investigations to determine the impacts of a managed flow regime on colonial nesting birds on the refuge.

- Cooperate with the Corps of Engineers, hydroelectric power company, the North Carolina Department of Environment and Natural Resources, and The Nature Conservancy to examine the impacts of managed flow regimes on the behavior and productivity of colonial nesting birds.

- Comply with Service obligations in the Federal Energy Regulatory Commission license to address the impact that hydroelectric power generation has on the lower Roanoke River ecosystem.

- Continue to actively participate in the Corps of Engineers' Section 216 study to examine the impacts of flow regimes on the behavior and productivity of colonial nesting birds.

Objective 2: Fish

Protect and promote self-sustaining populations of anadromous and resident fish populations that use the refuge and adjacent waters for the benefit of the ecosystem and the public continuously. Inventory refuge floodplain fishes on a five-year cycle.

Discussion: Fish are an important component of the food chain within the Roanoke River system. Various species of mammals and birds rely on both resident and anadromous fish as a food source. Refuge lands have been shown to provide spawning and nursery habitat for some anadromous species during the spring. A combination of a managed flow regime on the river and breaches in the levee from past logging efforts may adversely impact the spawning and nursery habitat of fish. This plan will allow for surveys of anadromous fish species every five years.

Strategies:

- Document presence, movement and reproductive condition of anadromous fish utilizing the floodplain between the five-year inventory cycle as time permits.

- Inventory refuge floodplain fishes on a five-year cycle.

- Recruit agencies, universities, and organizations to perform studies and investigations on the refuge to determine the impacts of a managed flow regime on fish.

- Cooperate with the Corps of Engineers, hydroelectric power company, the North Carolina Department of Environment and Natural Resources, and The Nature Conservancy to continuously examine the impacts of managed flow regimes on the diversity, abundance, and productivity of anadromous fish.

- Comply with Service obligations in the Federal Energy Regulatory Commission license that address the impact of hydroelectric power generation on the lower Roanoke River ecosystem.

- Continue to actively participate in the Corps of Engineers' Section 216 study to examine the impacts of flow regimes on the behavior and productivity of fish.

Objective 3: Invertebrate Species

Note observations of invertebrate species as opportunities occur.

Discussion: Invertebrate species are a critical component of the food chain within a bottomland system with all forms of wildlife depending on them in some way. The abundance and diversity of invertebrates is a good indicator of the ecological condition of a bottomland system. It is believed that the managed flow regime on the Roanoke River may have adverse impacts on key invertebrate species. Studies will focus on looking at how water quality and quantity affect indicator invertebrate species such as the crayfish. This plan allows for monitoring invertebrate species and determining the impacts a managed flow regime has on invertebrate populations.

Strategies:

- Record observations of invertebrate occurrences and behavior as opportunities occur between the five-year monitoring cycle.

- Establish invertebrate monitoring protocol within five years and monitor invertebrate populations within 10 years.

- Initiate a study sampling invertebrates on the floodplain and compare to a floodplain with unmanaged flows within 15 years.

- Recruit agencies, universities, and organizations to perform studies and investigations on the refuge to determine the impacts of a managed flow regime on invertebrates.

- Cooperate with the Corps of Engineers, hydroelectric power company, the North Carolina Department of Environment and Natural Resources, and The Nature Conservancy to examine the impacts of managed flow regimes on the diversity, abundance, and productivity of invertebrates.

- Comply with Service obligations in the Federal Energy Regulatory Commission license that address the impact of hydroelectric power generation on the lower Roanoke River ecosystem.

- Continue to actively participate in the Corps of Engineers' Section 216 study to examine the impacts of flow regimes on the behavior and productivity of invertebrates.

Objective 4: Mammals

Manage large and small mammal populations continuously to achieve habitat management objectives and stable relationships between flora and fauna.

Discussion: The high productivity within the bottomland system allows for a diverse small and large mammal population to be present. White-tailed deer, beaver, and raccoon can reach population levels that adversely affect ecosystem functions. Beaver are present in high numbers and have and continue to cause deterioration and loss of bottomland hardwoods throughout the refuge either by tree removal or holding water in areas for long periods of time, causing flood- intolerant trees to die. The beavers provide habitat for waterfowl, but also destroy habitat for many other species groups. The staff must carefully assess the impact of beavers, establish a tolerable threshold population, and develop a plan to manage the population and extent of flooding caused by beaver ponds and their impacts to forest and wildlife resources.

Health checks of refuge deer herds in 2001 indicate that the deer population is in fair condition; however, data collected suggests that deer are too plentiful for the resources available. Deer often forage in agriculture fields that provide an artificially high supply of food within traveling distance of the refuge. During years when non-edible crops are planted in place of corn, soybeans, or peanuts, the artificially high population of crop-fed deer end up overbrowsing the limited native vegetation found within the bottomland forests. The deer become stressed nutritionally, reducing their fitness and causing them to be susceptible to disease. The Service will assess the herd health based on abomasal parasite counts; the Service will initiate more intensive data collection on deer herd health if the abomasal parasite counts indicate the need to do so.

Little is known about the impacts, if any, the exotic nutria is having on native furbearers. It is theorized that since the nutria and muskrat occupy similar niches, the nutria may actually be displacing muskrats.

The managed flow regime may impact the abundance and diversity of small mammals ranging from gray squirrels to shrews due to their inability to relocate quickly and find sufficient food resources during periods of prolonged flooding. It is believed that the diversity, distribution, and abundance of this mammal group are being adversely affected by the managed flow regime.

The four-lane U.S. Highway 13/17 bisects the Conine Island and Askew tracts of the refuge for approximately 3.5 miles. Every year mammals such as beaver, mink, fox, squirrel, raccoon and opossum are killed along this stretch of the highway. The refuge staff is interested in initiating a survey to tabulate numbers, species, and time of year the mammals are killed.

This plan allows for sufficient monitoring of mammals found on the refuge and any impacts the managed flow regime has on small mammals, and begins a mammal road kill survey.

Strategies:

- Manage white-tailed deer populations through public hunting.

- Note observations of mammals as opportunities occur.

- Conduct abomasal parasite count from white-tailed deer every five years.

- Develop and implement beaver management plan within five years that will establish a threshold for the beaver population and manage the extent of flooded areas behind dams.

- Qualify the relationship between the exotic nutria and indigenous furbearer populations within 10 years.

- Conduct baseline surveys of small mammals, including bats, within 10 years.

- Participate in northeastern North Carolina refuge study of black bear population within five years.

- Initiate refuge U.S. Highway 13/17 right-of-way survey of road-killed mammals within 15 years.

- Recruit agencies, universities, and organizations to perform studies and investigations on the refuge to determine the impacts of a managed flow regime on the distribution and productivity of mammals.

- Cooperate with the Corps of Engineers, hydroelectric power company, the North Carolina Department of Environment and Natural Resources, and The Nature Conservancy to examine the impacts of managed flow regimes on the diversity, abundance, and productivity of mammals.

- Comply with Service obligations in the Federal Energy Regulatory Commission license that address the impact of hydroelectric power generation on the lower Roanoke River ecosystem.

- Continue to actively participate in the Corps of Engineers' Section 216 study to examine the impacts of flow regimes on the behavior and productivity of mammals.

Objective 5: Neotropical Migratory Songbirds

Provide nesting, foraging, and resting habitat for about 33 species of breeding neotropical migratory songbirds continuously. Provide foraging and resting habitat for about 40 species of nonbreeding neotropical migratory songbirds continuously. Increase efforts to monitor trends of breeding birds and expand to monitoring nonbreeding birds on levee habitat and expand surveys to interior swamp habitat. Increase survey frequency of cerulean warblers on a limited stretch of the river and the coastal plain reach of the Roanoke River to once every three years.

Discussion: The refuge provides nesting habitat for several species of neotropical migratory birds that are designated as high priority species in the Partners in Flight Plan for the South Atlantic Coastal Plain Physiographic Region. This plan provides for extensive surveys of breeding neotropical migratory songbirds on levee habitat. Because the greatest diversity of species and several high priority species are found on the levees, emphasis is being placed on this habitat type. A number of high priority species are also found in the interior sections of the cypress/tupelo swamps. This plan will expand surveys to this habitat type. Point count surveys will enable refuge staff to document trends of species diversity and abundance over time and any impacts prolonged spring floods may have on species populations. Monitoring efforts will be expanded to determine the species occurrence and population trends of nonbreeding birds. The cerulean warbler is a species that has shown significant decline throughout its range since the 1970s. A disjunct population is present on the coastal plain reach of the Roanoke River, with a pocket of individuals found on and in the vicinity of refuge lands; a 20-mile stretch of river on the Broadneck and Company Swamp Units. Due to the status of this species, special surveys are conducted for the cerulean warbler. This plan will provide for frequent monitoring of the cerulean warbler population along the Roanoke River. As funds from grants become available, or partners express an interest in conducting research on the refuge, more intensive surveys will be conducted.

Strategies:

- Increase efforts to monitor trends of breeding bird populations on 40 established levee plots to 60 levee plots using point count techniques annually.

- Establish and conduct annual monitoring of breeding bird population trends on 40 interior swamp point count plots.

- Conduct point count surveys of nonbreeding birds on the 60 levee and 40 interior swamp plots annually.

- Monitor trends of cerulean warbler population on 20 miles of the Roanoke River in the Broadneck and Company Swamp sections annually.

- Monitor trends of cerulean warbler population on the lower 130 miles of the Roanoke River once every three years.

- Recruit agencies, universities, and organizations to perform studies and investigations on the refuge to determine the impacts of a managed flow regime on the distribution and productivity of breeding migratory bird species.

- Cooperate with the Corps of Engineers, hydroelectric power company, the North Carolina Department of Environment and Natural Resources, and The Nature Conservancy to examine the impacts of managed flow regimes on the diversity, abundance, and productivity of neotropical migratory songbirds.

- Comply with Service obligations in the Federal Energy Regulatory Commission license that address the impact of hydroelectric power generation on the lower Roanoke River ecosystem.

- Continue to actively participate in the Corps of Engineers' Section 216 study to examine the impacts of flow regimes on the behavior and productivity of neotropical migratory songbirds.

Objective 6: Raptors

Monitor osprey population in the western Albemarle Sound annually.

Discussion: Ideal habitat for osprey and bald eagle is present near the mouth of the Roanoke River and into Bachelor's Bay (western portion of Albemarle Sound). The bountiful supply of fish in this area throughout the spring and summer offers a limitless supply of food for osprey and bald eagle. With the gradual rise in sea level, cypress trees are now surrounded by water providing ideal nesting sites. Ospreys also commonly use the channel markers located in the Roanoke River and Bay as nesting sites. Monitoring osprey productivity is one way resource managers can detect whether chemical contaminants are a problem in the system. In addition, banding young osprey chicks will allow biologists to learn more about the life history of the species. Bald eagles tend to be solitary nesters and prefer more isolated nesting sites, such as monarch pine or cypress trees. The North Carolina Wildlife Resources Commission conducts annual aerial surveys of bald eagles during the spring to determine the number of active nests.

The four-lane U.S. Highway 13/17 bisects the Conine Island and Askew tracts of the refuge for approximately 3.5 miles. Every year several barred owls and occasionally hawks are killed along this stretch of the highway. The refuge staff is interested in initiating a survey to tabulate numbers, species, and time of year the raptors are killed. This plan provides for annual productivity checks and banding of osprey nesting at the mouth of the Roanoke River and western Albemarle Sound, and within 10 years begins to survey the number of road-killed raptors along the U.S. Highway 13/17 corridor within the refuge.

Strategies:

- Band osprey in conjunction with productivity surveys in Bachelor's Bay annually.

- Conduct opportunistic productivity survey of bald eagle nests in conjunction with other surveys.

- Initiate refuge U.S. Highway 13/17 right-of-way survey of road-killed raptors within 10 years.

- Document presence of Mississippi kite nests and conduct population surveys of Mississippi kites annually.

- Recruit agencies, universities, and organizations to perform studies and investigations on the refuge to determine the impacts of a managed flow regime on the distribution and productivity of raptors.

- Cooperate with the Corps of Engineers, hydroelectric power company, the North Carolina Department of Environment and Natural Resources, and The Nature Conservancy to examine the impacts of managed flow regimes on the diversity, abundance, and productivity of raptors.

- Comply with Service obligations in the Federal Energy Regulatory Commission license that address the impact of hydroelectric power generation on the lower Roanoke River ecosystem.

- Continue to actively participate in the Corps of Engineers' Section 216 study to examine the impacts of flow regimes on the behavior and productivity of raptors.

Objective 7: Reptiles and Amphibians

Protect and conserve populations of amphibians and reptiles.

Discussion: Reptiles and amphibians are abundant and functionally important in bottomland communities and are significant components of their ecosystem. Many species of herpetofauna are wide-ranging and may serve as key indicator species in evaluating the environmental health of an ecosystem. The managed flow regime on the river can adversely impact species diversity and population levels of reptiles and amphibians on the refuge. This plan provides limited effort toward understanding the dynamics of the herpetofauna found on the refuge.

Strategies:

- Document observations of species occurrence, behavior, and location as opportunities present themselves.

- Establish protocol and initiate survey of herpetofauna within 10 years.

- Monitor population trends every five years.

- Recruit agencies, universities, and organizations to perform studies and investigations on the refuge to determine the impacts of a managed flow regime on the herpetofauna within the refuge.

- Cooperate with the Corps of Engineers, hydroelectric power company, the North Carolina Department of Environment and Natural Resources, and The Nature Conservancy to examine the impacts of managed flow regimes on the diversity, abundance, and productivity of reptiles and amphibians.

- Comply with Service obligations in the Federal Energy Regulatory Commission license that address the impact of hydroelectric power generation on the lower Roanoke River ecosystem.

- Continue to actively participate in the Corps of Engineers' Section 216 study to examine the impacts of flow regimes on the behavior and productivity of reptiles and amphibians on the refuge.

Objective 8: Waterfowl

Monitor populations of wood ducks and wintering waterfowl and cooperate with partners to maintain and restore habitat continuously.

Discussion: The wood duck and hooded merganser are the primary waterfowl species that breed in the bottomland forests in the Roanoke River system. This plan provides an increased monitoring effort on the productivity of local wood ducks and hooded mergansers near the mouth of the Roanoke River and in sloughs located on the refuge. The Roanoke River bottomlands also provide wintering habitat for migratory waterfowl such as the mallard, American black duck, American wigeon, and blue-winged teal. This plan provides for establishing and conducting wintering waterfowl surveys on the river and in forested habitat within five years. As funds from grants become available or partners express an interest in conducting research on the refuge, more intensive surveys will be conducted.

Strategies:

- Collect productivity data on 100 wood duck boxes three times a year.

- Conduct summer banding program of wood ducks to meet regional banding quotas established by the U.S. Fish and Wildlife Service Office of Migratory Birds.

- Establish and conduct wintering waterfowl surveys on the river and in forested habitat within five years.

- Establish protocol for and conduct natural cavity monitoring for wood duck nesting by 2008.

- Cooperate with partners and apply for funding under the North American Wetlands Conservation Act to restore and enhance resident and wintering waterfowl habitat.

- Recruit agencies, universities, and organizations to perform studies and investigations on the refuge to determine the impacts of a managed flow regime on the distribution and productivity of waterfowl.

- Cooperate with the Corps of Engineers, hydroelectric power company, the North Carolina Department of Environment and Natural Resources, and The Nature Conservancy to examine the impacts of managed flow regimes on the diversity, abundance, and productivity of waterfowl.

- Comply with Service obligations in the Federal Energy Regulatory Commission license that address the impact of hydroelectric power generation on waterfowl in the lower Roanoke River ecosystem.

- Continue to actively participate in the Corps of Engineers' Section 216 study to examine the impacts of flow regimes on the behavior and productivity of waterfowl on the refuge.

Table 9. Projects supporting wildlife strategies.

Strategy	Projects
Personnel Projects	
Conduct surveys, monitoring, studies, and investigations.	Utilize existing wildlife biologist and biological technician. Recruit, hire, and train new biological technicians (RONS 91022 and 00004), and hydrologist (RONS 00006).
Encourage universities, other agencies, and organizations to conduct surveys, monitoring, studies, and investigations.	Utilize existing manager, assistant manager, and wildlife biologist.
Administer public hunts to manage deer population.	Utilize existing manager, assistant manager, and zone law enforcement officer. Hire a new Refuge law enforcement officer (RONS 05001).
Protect wildlife.	Utilize existing zone law enforcement officer. Hire a new Refuge law enforcement officer (RONS 05001).
Manage budget, contracts, personnel, and property.	Utilize existing refuge manager, assistant manager, and office assistant. Recruit, hire, and train new office assistant (RONS 00010).
Apply for flexible funds and other grants.	Utilize existing manager, assistant manager, and wildlife biologist.
Maintain equipment and administrative roads.	Utilize the existing equipment operator. Recruit, hire, and train a new wage grade supervisor (RONS 00013), three new equipment operators (RONS 97037,00008 and 00009) and three new maintenance workers (RONS 00012, and 00014, and 00015).
Financial Management Projects	
Ensure budget integrity.	Manage budget, contracts, personnel, and property.
Secure adequate funding to operate refuge.	Prepare annual budget requests and maintain the Refuge Operation Needs System (RONS) and Service Asset Maintenance Management Systems (SAMMS). Apply for grants to finance studies and investigations. Apply for grants to construct new wood duck boxes. Request addition to base funding (RONS 00003). Request funding for studies on impact of flooding on wildlife (RONS 97033 and 05001).
Equipment Projects	
Maintain and replace equipment to survey and protect wildlife.	Replace equipment (various MMS projects).
Facility Projects	
Maintain, rehabilitate, and restore facilities to facilitate surveys and protection of wildlife.	Rehabilitate roads and restore wetlands (various MMS projects).

GOAL 2. HABITATS

Restore, maintain, and enhance the health and biodiversity of bottomland forested wetland habitats to ensure optimum ecological productivity.

Discussion: The refuge is part of the largest, intact, least disturbed bottomland hardwood system remaining on the Atlantic slope. The river formed the current communities as it carved out guts and creeks and deposited sediments throughout its floodplain. After hundreds of years, such dynamics created a mosaic of ridges, sloughs, and large interior swamps rich in plant diversity. The two major habitat types found within the refuge are bottomland hardwood forests and cypress/tupelo swamps. Marsh habitat and nesting habitat for wood ducks in the form of wood duck boxes are also recognized habitats for discussion in this plan. There are two satellite tracts that the Refuge is responsible for located in Nash and Sampson Counties. They consist of forested-scrub/shrub and pocosin wetlands respectively. The Refuge also administers 98 Farmers Home Administration conservation easements located throughout central and eastern North Carolina. Individual objectives are addressed in detail below.

Habitat surveys and management will be focused on the U.S. Fish and Wildlife Service trust species: migratory birds (songbirds, waterfowl, and colonial nesting birds), interjurisdictional fish (anadromous and catadromous), and threatened and endangered species.

Objective 1: Coastal Plain Bottomland Hardwoods

Protect, study, and manage 7,154 acres of coastal plain bottomland hardwood habitat to maintain it as a natural community.

Discussion: The bottomland hardwood forests associated with the Roanoke River floodplain are present on the natural levees, low ridge, high ridge and alluvial flat features of the river's floodplain. All of these forests have been disturbed in some way either by past species-specific logging, cattle grazing or by the managed flow regime that is present on the river today. Habitat management techniques ranging from minor forest manipulation, to releasing target tree species by removing or killing non-target species, to promoting development of vertical structure, to conversion of high ridge monoculture forest plantations to mixed hardwood stands will be necessary to restore the ecological integrity and biological diversity of this habitat type. This plan will protect this habitat type and where prescribed, forest enhancement management practices will be implemented. This conservation planprovides for more intensive data collection to occur when investigating the impact of a managed flow regime on tree regeneration and overall forest health than is currently being done.

Strategies:

- Protect adjacent areas by suppressing wildfires.

- Establish three permanent forest health inventory plots on a reference site within five years.

- Collect and analyze data on five permanent forest health inventory plots and three plots on a reference site every ten years.

- Establish 60 natural tree regeneration plots on a reference site within five years.

- Collect data on 100 natural tree regeneration plots on the refuge and 60 plots on a reference site annually.

- Collect and analyze data on 100 natural tree regeneration plots on the refuge located on areas prone to inundation from hydroelectric power production annually.

- Inventory overstory, understory, and herbaceous strata of existing forest stands to determine wildlife habitat management prescriptions within 10 years.

- Develop and implement a habitat management plan that will restore plant diversity to previously logged areas within 10 years. The following techniques will be considered: thinning to create favorable understory structure, creating tree fall gaps, and thinning to selectively manage for target species.

- Develop and implement forest pest management plans within 10 years.

- Develop and implement beaver pond management plans within 10 years.

- Provide habitat for resident and wintering waterfowl.

- Recruit agencies, universities, and organizations to perform studies and investigations on the refuge to determine the impacts of a managed flow regime on coastal plain bottomland hardwoods.

- Cooperate with the Corps of Engineers, hydroelectric power company, the North Carolina Department of Environment and Natural Resources, and The Nature Conservancy to examine the impacts of a managed flow regime on the health and sustainability of coastal plain bottomland hardwoods.

- Comply with Service obligations in the Federal Energy Regulatory Commission license that address the impact of hydroelectric power generation on the lower Roanoke River ecosystem.

- Continue to actively participate in the Corps of Engineers' Section 216 study to examine the impacts of flow regimes on the behavior and productivity of colonial nesting birds.

Objective 2: Coastal Plain Bottomland Hardwood (Nash County Satellite)

Protect and manage continuously approximately 45 acres of coastal plain bottomland hardwood habitat on the Nash county tract from trespass and vandalism.

Discussion: The Nash County satellite tract was transferred to the refuge as a Farmers Home Administration inventory property in 1992 through the 1985 Farm Bill. Forty-two of the 45 acres consist of broad-leaved deciduous palustrine forested and scrub-shrub wetland habitat. The forested areas include an abundance of wildlife food producing species. The canopy trees are sufficient to provide high quality nesting cavities and food for a number of trust species including wood duck, mallard, and several species of neotropical migratory songbirds. The wetland's flooding regime and the age and composition of the vegetation combine to provide high quality breeding, feeding, resting, and escape habitat for resident and migratory game and nongame wildlife species. However, the wetland's flooding regime is impacted by beaver activity within, and adjacent to, the tract. This conservation plan provides for the protection of habitat and the developing and implementing of a habitat management plan.

Strategies:

- Patrol the property as time allows.

- Contact the special agent to prosecute violations as violations occur.

- Develop and implement a habitat management plan within seven years.

- Develop and implement a beaver pond management plan by 2009.

Objective 3: Coastal Plain Pocosin (Sampson County)

Protect and manage approximately 129 acres of coastal plain pocosin wetlands habitat on the Sampson County tract from trespass and vandalism.

Discussion: The 129-acre Sampson County satellite tract was transferred to the refuge as a Farmers Home Administration inventory property in 1989 through the 1985 Farm Bill. The tract consisted of pocosin wetlands that had been cleared, ditched, and converted to row-crop agriculture approximately 15 years before the transfer to the refuge occurred. Since the transfer, the Service has planted trees and restored some of the hydrology in the area that had been severely altered. The habitat is also revegetating naturally to a pocosin wetland community. The tract is now considered a valuable wetland that researchers have used for plant studies. This conservation plan provides for the protection of the habitat and for developing and implementing a habitat management plan.

Strategies:

- Patrol the property as time allows.

- Contact the special agent to prosecute violations as violations occur.

- Develop and implement a habitat management plan within seven years.

Objective 4: Cypress/Tupelo Swamp

Protect and manage 13,824 acres of healthy, functional cypress/tupelo swamp habitat to maintain it as a natural community.

Discussion: The cypress/tupelo swamps present on the refuge are found in small sloughs located between alluvial ridges and in the large interior swamps. All of the swamps have been logged for their cypress with only a few monarch cypress remaining. The swamps today are dominated by water tupelo with cypress interspersed amongst the tupelo. The managed flow regime on the river prevents little opportunity for cypress regeneration. Cypress' require at least a 3-year dry down period in order for the seedlings to take hold and survive periods of high water under a natural flow regime. Habitat management strategies in these areas will be geared toward promoting the growth of cypress. This conservation plan provides for the development and implementation of forest and beaver management plans.

Strategies:

- Inventory overstory, understory, and herbaceous strata of existing forest stands to determine wildlife habitat management prescriptions within 10 years.

- Develop and implement a habitat management plan that will restore plant diversity to previously logged areas within 10 years. The following techniques will be considered: thinning to create favorable conditions for regeneration, retaining trees with cavities and hollow bases, and thinning to selectively manage for target species.

- Develop and implement forest pest management plans within 10 years.

- Develop and implement beaver pond management plans within 10 years.

- Provide habitat for resident and wintering waterfowl.

- Recruit agencies, universities, and organizations to perform studies and investigations on the refuge to determine the impacts of a managed flow regime on the cypress/tupelo swamps.

- Cooperate with the Corps of Engineers, the hydroelectric power company, the North Carolina Department of Environment and Natural Resources, and The Nature Conservancy to examine the impacts of managed flow regimes on the health and sustainability of cypress/tupelo swamps.

- Comply with Service obligations in the Federal Energy Regulatory Commission license that address the impact of hydroelectric power generation on the lower Roanoke River ecosystem.

- Continue to actively participate in the Corps of Engineers' Section 216 study to examine the impacts of flow regimes on the behavior and productivity of cypress/tupelo swamps.

Objective 5. Freshwater Marsh

Protect 43 acres of healthy, functional freshwater marsh habitat to maintain it as a natural community.

Discussion: The marsh habitat on the refuge is located on the Great and Goodman Island tracts. It exists as bands of grasses ranging in width from three to 30 meters along the Middle River, Broad and Grennell Creeks of Great Island, and on the northeast end of Goodman Island. It is predicted that this habitat type will increase with the rise of sea level.

No management strategies are planned for this habitat type. As funds from grants become available or partners express an interest in conducting research on the refuge, more intensive surveys will be performed.

Strategies:

- Recruit agencies, universities, and organizations to perform studies and investigations on the refuge to determine the impacts of a managed flow regime on the freshwater marsh.

- Cooperate with the Corps of Engineers, the hydroelectric power company, the North Carolina Department of Environment and Natural Resources, and The Nature Conservancy to examine the impacts of managed flow regimes on the health and sustainability of freshwater marsh.

- Comply with Service obligations in the Federal Energy Regulatory Commission license that address the impact of hydroelectric power generation on the lower Roanoke River ecosystem.

- Continue to actively participate in the Corps of Engineers' Section 216 study to examine the impact of a managed flow regime on the behavior and productivity of freshwater marsh.

Objective 6: Farmer's Home Conservation Easements

Protect 2,870 acres of habitat on 98 easements from trespass and vandalism and develop and implement management plans on select easements.

Discussion: The refuge administers 98 Farmers Home Administration conservation easements involving 19 counties in the Roanoke–Tar–Neuse–Cape Fear Ecosystem. These easements are the result of the 1985 and 1990 Farm Bill in which any lands foreclosed on by Farmers Home Administration were taken into inventory. The Farm Bills allowed the Service to evaluate the habitat on the foreclosed properties. If the property was identified as being valuable to wildlife, it was considered for an easement or fee title transfer to the Service. The easements include approximately 2,870 acres. The average easement size is 29.03 acres with the largest easement totaling 346.2 acres and the smallest tract 1.21 acres. There are currently 75 landowners involved with these easements. The general wetland habitat types defined by the "Department of Environment, Health and Natural Resources 1996, A "Field Guide to North Carolina Wetlands" include bottomland hardwoods, pocosin, swamp forest, headwater forest, and beaver swamp complex. This conservation plan provides for the protection of the habitat in all easements and the development and implementation of management plans on select easements.

Strategies:

- Patrol the easements as time allows.

- Contact the special agent to prosecute violations as violations occur.

- Develop and implement habitat management plans for selected easements within 10 years.

Objective 7: Wood Duck Boxes

Maintain up to 100 wood duck boxes in the appropriate habitat.

Discussion: The forest communities found within the refuge provide excellent nesting and brood habitat for wood ducks and hooded mergansers. Refuge staff have erected and inherited a number of wood duck boxes since the refuge was established. Most of these boxes are located along the river and creeks near the mouth of the river with just a handful located in cypress/tupelo slough habitat. Use of the boxes is very high indicating their effectiveness and the need for more to meet the nesting needs of the local wood duck and hooded merganser population. This conservation plan provides for continued maintenance of the 60 wood duck boxes currently serviced by refuge staff and the erection of 40 new boxes.

Strategies:

- Monitor wood duck boxes three times a year.

- Repair and replace damaged boxes annually.

- Clean out boxes annually.

- Erect 40 new nest boxes within 15 years.

- Relocate annually those boxes subject to continual dump nesting.

Table 10. Projects supporting habitat strategies.

Strategy	Projects
Personnel Projects	
Collect and analyze data, develop and implement management plans, determine the need for beaver dam manipulation, and maintain wood duck boxes.	Utilize existing wildlife biologist and biological technician. Recruit, hire, and train a new resource specialist (forester/ecologist)(RONS 00005), an entomologist (RONS 00011), a hydrologist (RONS 00006), and a forest technician (RONS 99002, two new biological technicians (RONS 91022 and 00004).
Encourage partnerships and recruit partners.	Utilize the existing manager, assistant manager, and wildlife biologist.
Protect habitat.	Utilize existing zone law enforcement officer. Recruit, hire, and train a new law enforcement officer (RONS 05001).
Manage budget, contracts, personnel, and property. Manage refuge Operation Needs System (RONS), Maintenance Management System (MMS), Real Property Inventory (RPI), and Service Asset Maintenance management System (SAMMS).	Utilize existing refuge manager, assistant manager, and office assistant. Recruit, hire, and train new office assistant (RONS 00002) and administrative assistant (RONS 00010).
Apply for flexible funds and other grants.	Utilize existing manager, assistant manager, and wildlife biologist.
Maintain equipment and administrative roads, manipulate beaver dams, and maintain wood duck boxes.	Utilize the existing equipment operator. Recruit, hire, and train a new wage grade supervisor (RONS 00013), three new equipment operators (RONS 97037, 00008 and 00009) and three new maintenance workers (RONS 00012, and 00014, and 00015) to maintain equipment, administrative roads, and wood duck boxes.
Financial Management Projects	
Ensure budget integrity.	Process payroll, travel, purchasing, and contract documents.
Secure adequate funding to operate refuge.	Prepare annual budget requests and maintain the Refuge Operation Needs System (RONS) and Service Asset Maintenance Management Systems (SAMMS). Apply for grants to finance studies and investigations. Apply for grants to construct new wood duck boxes. Request addition to base funding (RONS 00003). Request funding for study on the impact of flooding on habitat (RONS 97035).
Equipment Projects	
Provide vehicles and boats for Refuge staff to protect habitat, collect data, manipulate beaver dams, and maintain wood duck boxes. Provide vehicles and boats for access to the refuge for partners. Provide equipment and tools to perform the inventories. Provide computers and software to maintain records.	Maintain and replace equipment (various MMS projects).
Facility Projects	
Maintain, rehabilitate, and restore facilities to manage habitat.	Maintain roads, rehabilitate roads, and restore wetlands (various MMS projects).

GOAL 3. PUBLIC USE

Provide the public with safe, quality wildlife-dependent recreational and educational opportunities that focus on the wildlife and habitats of the refuge and the National Wildlife Refuge System. Continue to participate in local efforts to sustain economic health through nature-based tourism.

Discussion: As identified in the National Wildlife Refuge System Improvement Act of 1997, there are six priority wildlife-dependent recreation uses. These are hunting, fishing, wildlife observation, wildlife photography, and environmental education and interpretation. Fundamental to the provision of these uses are viable and diverse fish and wildlife populations and the habitats upon which they depend. These priority uses, along with all other uses, must be appropriate and compatible with the refuge, and the purposes and mission of the National Wildlife Refuge System.

Currently, little nonhunting or fishing public use occurs. The refuge does not have the staff to provide on- or off-refuge environmental education, interpretive, or wildlife-dependent recreational programming. The altered flow regime on the river frequently prevents the public from being able to access and partake in permitted hunts. Environmental education programs, wildlife observation, and photography are also impacted by prolonged flooding events.

Objective 1: Hunting

Provide 8,680 hunt days annually to ensure safe, quality hunting opportunities consistent with sound biological principles.

Discussion: Hunting is the largest wildlife-dependent recreational use that occurs on the refuge. Small game, wild turkey, waterfowl, and deer hunts are offered under special permits issued by lottery. The North Carolina Wildlife Resources Commission administers hunt permits for refuge lands in conjunction with the adjacent state-managed Roanoke River Game Lands. To ensure a safe, quality hunt, each permit holder is allowed to hunt on only the tract of land for which he/she applied. Special hunting guidelines for refuge lands are outlined in the North Carolina Special Hunt Opportunities booklet. Camping by hunters is allowed on the refuge during the hunts to facilitate safe access to the refuge. By allowing camping, the need to travel by boat in the dark is eliminated. The refuge currently provides the maximum hunt opportunities while continuing to allow other refuge user groups access during these seasons. This plan expands the hunt program for the refuge by adding 200 waterfowl hunt days annually. The number of hunt opportunities will increase more as the size of the refuge increases within its approved acquisition boundary, and is found compatible with refuge purposes. This conservation plan provides for the development of a refuge hunt brochure and an investigation of the potential of a youth waterfowl hunt.

Strategies:

- Provide 3,750 deer hunt days with modern gun, 1,000 deer hunt days with muzzleloaders, 2,000 deer hunt days with archery, 1,000 small game hunt days, 530 turkey hunt days, and 400 waterfowl hunt days annually.

- Update refuge hunting plan within five years.

- Provide a one-day youth turkey hunt annually.

- Investigate the potential to conduct a one-day youth waterfowl hunt within five years.

- Update refuge hunting regulations in the North Carolina Hunting and Fishing Regulations Digest annually.

- Develop and distribute a special refuge hunt brochure within three years.

- Allow overnight primitive camping to enhance safety.

- Address primitive camping litter and sanitary waste disposal within three years.

Objective 2: Fishing

Provide 5,000 quality fishing opportunities annually consistent with sound biological principles.

Discussion: Providing fishing opportunities has not been a primary objective of the refuge's public use program. A fishery fed by the river during and after periods of floodplain inundation exists on refuge lands. Currently, fishing on the refuge occurs on the banks of the Roanoke River with anglers parking on the shoulder of U.S. Highway 13/17 and accessing the riverbanks by foot. This plan will develop and implement a fishing plan, as well as consider the potential of expanding the fishing program.

Strategies:

- Develop and implement a public fishing plan within three years.

- Assess the potential of expanding public access within three years.

- Develop and distribute a refuge fishing regulations' brochure within three years.

- Address litter situation by erecting signage and enforcing refuge regulations.

Objective 3: Environmental Education

Develop a community-based environmental education program for up to 500 people annually in coordination with area schools and other area educational and community organizations.
Discussion: A quality environmental education program can lead to increased awareness and stewardship of the environment. The impact humans have on the environment will continue to pose threats to the natural resources found on the Roanoke River National Wildlife Refuge and adjoining lands. It is particularly important to reach the local youths to educate them about the value of these resources and instill a sense of ownership of these resources. Currently, the refuge has no staff dedicated to only environmental education. When there are requests from partners or schools for such programs, staff is pulled from other program areas to conduct the program, or the request is declined. This plan provides for an expanded environmental education program for an increased audience.

Strategies:

- Provide up to 12 environmental education programs annually.

- Conduct six tours of the refuge annually.

- Participate in three environmental field days annually.

- Encourage the use of the refuge as an outdoor classroom within one year.

- Develop and implement an environmental education plan within three years.

- Develop and implement environmental education programs for students and teachers within three years.

- Develop and implement programs in cooperation with the Partnership for the Sounds, Cooperative Extension Service, Bertie County Board of Education, North Carolina Wildlife Resources Commission, and North Carolina Museum of Natural History.

- Encourage the refuge friends group to assist with environmental education.

Objective 4: Interpretation

Develop a quality interpretive program for 3,000 people annually that will increase awareness of the habitat features, wildlife values, and management programs on the refuge.

Discussion: Interpretation materials such as brochures, self-guided nature trails, and kiosks are important in creating public understanding and appreciation of the natural environment, including fish and wildlife. Information presented with such tools can supplement environmental education activities that refuge staff or partners are conducting. Often, the material is the only means visitors have to learn about the significance of the natural communities present in the refuge and around its boundaries and the threats to them. This plan provides for a significant expansion of the interpretation program.

Strategies:

- Develop six new kiosks and maintain seven information kiosks.

- Develop a wildlife species list within three years.

- Maintain bird list.

- Extend (add wetland boardwalk loop) for the interpretive Kuralt Trail within 15 years.

- Maintain interpretative Kuralt Trail, update interpretive signage and brochures within five years.

- Develop exhibits for the refuge headquarters within five years.

- Develop an exhibit on forested wetlands for the Cashie River Center within five years.

- Use the refuge video as an interpretive tool within three years.

- Design and implement a remote camera to view the wildlife activity including the Conine Island Rookery from the Roanoke/Cashie River Center within 15 years.

Objective 5: Wildlife Observation

Provide wildlife observation opportunities and facilities for 10,000 people annually.

Discussion: Wildlife observation opportunities are minimal on the refuge at this time. There are two reasons for this. First, much of the refuge is only accessible by boat and many visitors are not equipped to float the river. However, there are old logging roads that exist off U.S. Highway 13/17 that are accessible to visitors on foot. Second, the managed flow regime (hydroelectric and Army Corps of Engineers flood control projects) present on the river results in unpredictably long periods of flooding that are not consistent with a natural flow regime. During periods of high flows, much of the refuge is inaccessible to visitors on foot. This plan provides for a significant expansion of wildlife observation facilities and opportunities.

Strategies:

- Extend (add wetland boardwalk loop) interpretive Kuralt Trail within 15 years.

- Maintain interpretive Kuralt Trail and old logging roads to facilitate observation.

- Provide information to the public to encourage the use of the Kuralt Trail.

- Cooperate with North Carolina Department of Transportation to provide better access and signage for Kuralt Trail.

- Develop a refuge wildlife drive within 15 years.

- Develop a brochure and signage for the refuge drive, and a radio or CD/tape narration describing the trail within 15 years.

- Conduct guided neotropical migratory songbird tours for 12 small groups annually.

- Participate in a canoe and kayak trail partnership with the Roanoke River Partners within 10 years.

Objective 6: Wildlife Photography

Provide wildlife photography opportunities and facilities for 1,000 people annually.

Discussion: Wildlife photography opportunities are minimal on the refuge at this time. Much of the refuge is only accessible by boat and many visitors are not equipped to float the river. However, there are old logging roads that exist off U.S. Highway 13/17 that are accessible to visitors on foot. The managed flow regime (hydroelectric and Army Corps of Engineers flood control projects) present on the river results in unpredictably long periods of flooding that are not consistent with a natural flow regime. During periods of high flows, much of the refuge is inaccessible to visitors on foot. This plan provides for a significant expansion of photography facilities and opportunities.

Strategies:

- Extend (add wetland boardwalk loop) interpretive Kuralt Trail to facilitate photography within 15 years.

- Maintain interpretive Kuralt Trail and old logging roads to facilitate photography.

- Provide information to the public to encourage use of the Kuralt Trail highway tour route.

- Participate in a canoe and kayak trail partnership with the Roanoke River Partners within 10 years.

- Develop a refuge wildlife drive within 15 years.

- Construct two photo blinds within five years; construct a third photo blind within 15 years.

- Promote wildlife photography by sponsoring an annual wildlife photography contest.

Objective 7: Outreach

Provide effective and quality outreach displays for 1,000 people annually at appropriate local, state, and national functions.

Discussion: It is imperative to inform people in the local communities about refuge resources, threats to those resources, and management issues. Being present and available for questions from the public at local and state events is essential for projecting a positive image of the refuge and the Service in general. There are many opportunities for the staff to take part in such activities (e.g., local festivals, county and state fairs, and sporting shows). An effective outreach program is particularly important for the Roanoke River National Wildlife Refuge since the community did not initially support such a program. After 14 years, local residents still have misconceptions about the refuge and its significance. This plan significantly expands the outreach program.

Strategies:

- Develop tools (e.g., exhibits, games, and traveling exhibit) for outreach activities.

- Participate in the relevant local festivals, International Migratory Bird Day, National Wildlife Refuge Week, National Hunting and Fishing Day, and North Carolina State Fair.

- Maintain the refuge web site and the revise the refuge brochure as programs change.

- Write 12 news releases annually.

- Develop and maintain a refuge-specific radio information broadcast within 15 years.

- Develop public service announcements about local natural resources within 10 years.

- Schedule and deliver at least 12 planned presentations annually.

- Develop and implement an outreach plan within five years in cooperation with the Friends of the Roanoke River National Wildlife Refuge (refuge friends group) and the Partnership for the Sounds.

- Recruit membership for the Friends of the Roanoke River National Wildlife Refuge as an advocate for the refuge.

Objective 8. Refuge Support

Develop and maintain ties to past and new organizations that support the refuge.

Discussion: Working closely with partners at the local, county, and state governments and private organizations is essential for the refuge to achieve its goals. One partner that assists the refuge is the Friends of the Roanoke River National Wildlife Refuge. This support group, known as a friends group, raises funds and recruits volunteers to assist the refuge. The Friends of the Roanoke River National Wildlife Refuge is an existing friends group that requires assistance with its organization and evolution. The Partnership for the Sounds is a local nongovernmental organization that promotes sustainable eco-tourism and supports the Service and the refuges on the Albemarle-Pamlico Peninsula as anchors of ecotourism. The Roanoke River Partners is a nonprofit organization that promotes ecotourism in the Lower Roanoke River Valley. The Nature Conservancy and Conservation Fund are national organizations that have been instrumental in acquiring land for conservation and often brokering land for resale to the Service. This plan continues to develop and nurture refuge partnerships.

Strategies:

- Support leadership of and membership recruitment for the Friends of the Roanoke River National Wildlife Refuge.

- Develop fund-raising capability within the Friends of the Roanoke River National Wildlife Refuge.

- Work continuously and formally with the Partnership for the Sounds and the Roanoke River Partners to promote nature-based tourism and compatible public use on the refuge.

- Work with Conservation Fund, The Nature Conservancy, and other nongovernmental organizations to support land acquisition and restoration.

- Work with nongovernmental organizations to support protection of the Roanoke River basin.

- Work with The Nature Conservancy and state and federal agencies to address managed flow issues on the river.

Objective 9. Visitor Welcome and Orientation

Provide visitors with adequate signage and information to locate and navigate the refuge.

Discussion: Visitors require good signage and directions to find the refuge, the various access points on the refuge, and visitor facilities. Access to the refuge is primarily by boat and the locations of public boat ramps and their location relative to the tracts on the refuge is important to visitors. Currently the only access from a public road is at the Kuralt Trail parking lot and interpretive trail.

Strategies:

- Provide adequate directional signage for visitors to access the refuge.

- Provide adequate signage for visitors to find the Kuralt Trail parking lot.

- Provide information to visitors about refuge access by phone and email.

- Develop refuge access map.

- Develop the refuge web site to include access and orientation information.

- Incorporate refuge rules and regulations into general brochure.

Table 11. Projects supporting public use strategies.

Strategy	Projects
Personnel Projects	
Plan, design and conduct programs and outreach.	Utilize existing manager, assistant manager, and other qualified staff. Recruit, hire, and train new park ranger (RONS 93028). Recruit, hire, and train new media specialist (RONS 00007).
Maintain education, interpretation, wildlife observation, and photography facilities.	Utilize existing engineering equipment operator. Recruit, hire, and train a new wage grade supervisor (RONS 00013), three new equipment operators (RONS 97037, 00008 and 00009) and three new maintenance workers (RONS 00012, 00014, and 00015).
Protect visitors.	Utilize existing zone law enforcement officer. Recruit, hire, and train a new law enforcement officer (RONS 05001) and a new assistant manager for facilities (RONS 02001).
Manage budget, contracts, personnel, and property.	Utilize existing refuge manager, assistant manager, and office assistant. Recruit, hire, and train new office assistant (RONS 00002).
Apply for flexible funds and other grants.	Utilize existing refuge manager and assistant manager. Recruit, hire, and train new park ranger (RONS 93028). Recruit, hire, and train new media specialist (RONS 00007).
Financial Management Projects	
Ensure budget integrity.	Process payroll, travel, purchasing, and contract documents.
Secure adequate funding to operate refuge.	Prepare annual budget requests and maintain the Refuge Operation Needs System (RONS) and Service Asset Maintenance Management Systems (SAMMS). Apply for grants to finance materials and facilities to support environmental education, interpretation, wildlife observation, and wildlife photography. Request addition to base funding (RONS 00003). Design and print interpretive brochures (RONS 05005).
Equipment Projects	
Provide vehicles and boats for refuge staff to enforce refuge regulations, to conduct education and interpretative programs. Provide access for partners to the refuge and refuge waters by vehicles and boats. Replace equipment to maintain roads and provide access. Provide computers and software to maintain records.	Maintain and replace equipment (various MMS projects).
Facility Projects	
Maintain, rehabilitate, and restore facilities to manage habitat.	Maintain roads, rehabilitate roads, and restore wetlands (various MMS projects). Design, construct, install interpretative exhibits in the visitor contact station (RONS 00001). Design, construct and install interpretative kiosks on the refuge (RONS 05002). Design, construct, and maintain an office and visitor contact station (MMS 90015).

GOAL 4. RESOURCE PROTECTION

Protect refuge resources by limiting the adverse impacts of human activities and development.

Discussion: Natural and cultural resources found on the refuge are protected by various policies set forth in the National Wildlife Refuge System Administration Act of 1966 and the National Wildlife Refuge System Improvement Act of 1997. The refuge staff has the responsibility to protect resources while addressing requests for special use permits. Consultation with agencies that have an interest in resources found on the refuge and provisions in special use permits are tools the staff can use to ensure that activities are compatible with the purposes and mission of the refuge. Individual objectives for resource protection are addressed below.

Objective 1: Cultural Resources

Avoid all impacts to cultural resources by evaluating all proposed projects and coordinating with the State and Regional Historic Preservation Officers before beginning a project.

Discussion: Native Americans once had villages in the Roanoke River Valley. Some of the lands granted to the Native Americans as a reservation are now refuge lands. There are two known Native American middens on refuge lands. Due to chronic bank sloughing both middens are slowly being eroded. When settlers in the Piedmont Region cleared the land for agriculture, sediment was deposited on the river's coastal plain reach. As a result, the Native American middens that are present on refuge lands, but have not yet been identified, may be buried under several feet of post-colonial sediments. The staff must assume that proposed activities may disturb undiscovered middens and other cultural resources found on the refuge. The State Historic Preservation Office will be notified of refuge projects that have the potential to disturb cultural resources. Proposed projects will also be submitted to the Regional Historic Preservation Officer for review. When it is determined that a site may be of significance, the Regional Historic Preservation Officer will consult with the State Historic Preservation Office to decide how to proceed on on-site investigations. This plan allows for refuge staff to continue patrolling identified sites as part of its routine law enforcement efforts and will inventory all resources so that the Service will be aware of additional resource sites that need protection.

Strategies:

- Evaluate all proposed projects and coordinate with the Regional Historic Preservation Officer before beginning a project.

- Protect identified cultural resource sites.

- Conduct a comprehensive cultural resources inventory within 10 years.

Objective 2: Interagency Coordination

Maintain a reasonable level of coordination with local, state, and federal public agencies and private organizations.

Discussion: The refuge staff coordinates with a wide variety of agencies and organizations to protect the resources on the refuge. The staff conducts much of the coordination through constant communication with local and state law enforcement officials who patrol the area around the refuge. They also conduct meetings to establish rules and regulations and delegate responsibilities during refuge and state game land hunts. To help achieve the goals and objectives put forth in this plan, it is essential that refuge staff continue to coordinate and collaborate with state natural resource agencies and private nongovernmental organizations to the greatest extent possible. Coordination between agencies is important in order for the refuge to be an active participant in addressing flow issues on the river and conducting activities on the refuge. This plan will increase the level of deliberate involvement of refuge staff in cooperative efforts with other government and private organizations.

Strategies:

- Communicate formally and informally in 100 contacts or meetings each year.

- Review and revise formal cooperative agreements annually.

- Coordinate annually with the North Carolina Wildlife Resources Commission on the hunting program and the North Carolina Forest Service and local volunteer fire departments on fire suppression.

- Develop new cooperative agreements with other agencies and organizations as necessary.

- Cooperate with the Corps of Engineers, hydroelectric power company, North Carolina Department of Environment and Natural Resources, and The Nature Conservancy to examine the impacts of managed flow regime on the lower Roanoke River ecosystem.

- Comply with Service obligations in the Federal Energy Regulatory Commission license agreement that address the impact of hydroelectric power generation on the lower Roanoke River ecosystem.

Objective 3: Land Protection

Continue to purchase land from willing sellers within the approved acquisition boundary.

Discussion: The final environmental assessment for the refuge identified a 33,000-acre acquisition boundary. The refuge currently owns in fee title ownership 20,978 acres in five tracts along the Roanoke River. The refuge staff maintains contact with the owners of the tracts within the approved acquisition boundary and with the owners and organizations that may assist in securing the land, either through fee title ownership or conservation easements. Land purchased by the refuge is identified using boundary signs that are maintained on a regular basis. In this plan, the staff will post the boundaries of land acquired, inventory the wildlife and habitat, and manage the habitat. The Nature Conservancy and the State of North Carolina have designated the 190,000-acre, 100-year floodplain of the Roanoke River as priority areas for land protection. The refuge will develop a land protection plan to outline areas that are important habitat and ways to protect the areas (e.g., fee title acquisition, acquisition of easements, management agreements).

Strategies:

- Maintain contact with landowners within the approved acquisition boundary.

- Pursue acquisition of rights-of-way for public access to Town Swamp and Company Swamp from willing sellers.

- Cooperate with willing sellers and the Service's Realty Division to acquire land.

- Develop a land protection plan by 2007 for areas beyond the approved acquisition boundary.

- Inventory wildlife populations and vegetation on additional acreage as it is acquired by the Service.

- Maintain boundary posting and post boundaries on newly purchased lands as they are acquired by the Service.

- Incorporate newly purchased lands into management plans.

Objective 4: Law Enforcement

Maintain highly trained and effective law enforcement personnel to ensure continuous trust resource protection, visitor safety, and enforcement of all refuge related acts and regulations.

Discussion: Protecting the natural resources of the refuge and ensuring the safety of visitors are fundamental responsibilities of the National Wildlife Refuge System. As crime continues to increase in rural America, the refuge continues to be faced with more complicated law enforcement issues beyond violations of wildlife laws. There is currently no law enforcement staff at the refuge to oversee law enforcement activities on 20,978 acres of refuge lands or on the 98 conservation easements. Coordination with the Service's Zone Officer, Division of Law Enforcement, and state conservation officers on law enforcement cases is essential. This plan proposes a major change in the refuge's approach to law enforcement from reactive to proactive. It allows for one full-time officer to carry out law enforcement duties on a regular basis.

Strategies:

- Provide assistance to and coordinate with appropriate local, state, and federal law enforcement agencies to facilitate compliance with local, state, and federal laws.

- Develop written agreements as needed and improve cooperation with law enforcement agencies annually within this 15-year plan.

Objective 5: Permits

Carefully review and evaluate requests for special use permits to ensure compatibility with refuge purpose(s) and mission as applicants submit them.

Discussion: Permits may be issued when individuals or parties request to conduct activities on the refuge that are normally not permissible by the general public. Researchers are examples of the types of requests the staff receives for special use permits. If the proposed activity is found to be compatible with the purposes and mission of the refuge, the staff may issue a special use permit with provisions outlining special conditions that must be followed by the permittee. This plan will allow staff more time to monitor permitted activities to ensure compliance and assess the impact of the use on the environment.

Strategies:

- Protect refuge resources by developing special conditions for those permitted uses that are compatible.

- Develop standardized special conditions where possible.

- Monitor permitted activities to ensure compliance and assess the impact of the use on the environment.

Objective 6: Pest Animals

Record observed incidents of impacts to refuge resources by pest animals as time allows.

Discussion: The introduction of exotic species and the absence of top predators in the bottomland hardwood forest communities has caused pest animals (e.g., beaver and nutria) to become over abundant and in some instances damage refuge resources. For example, beavers can have an adverse impact on tree species, and exotic nutria may be displacing the native muskrat. Feral pigs have been observed on lands adjacent to the refuge. This plan will adapt a proactive approach to developing and implementing a plan to monitor and control pest animals.

Strategies:

- Develop and implement a nuisance animal control plan within 10 years.

- Document adverse effects of pest animals on refuge resources as time allows.

Objective 7: Pest Plants

Improve plant communities and limit impacts to refuge resources by monitoring and controlling pest plants as time allows.

Discussion: Exotic pest plants exist on the refuge and may pose a threat to the integrity of the refuge's bottomland communities. In the wetter areas parrot feather and Japanese stilt grass are the dominant exotics while in the drier areas Chinese privet, kudzu, and Japanese honeysuckle are potential threats. Since there is no immediate threat to refuge resources, limited attention has been given to pest plants. However, the potential for any of the species mentioned above to occur or a new invasion is very likely. This plan will adapt a proactive approach to developing and implementing a plan to monitor and control pest plants.

Strategies:

- Develop and implement a pest plant control plan within five years.

- Record and map pest plant species that occur on the refuge within three years.

Objective 8: Significant Natural Heritage Areas

Limit impacts and retain the natural character of the area.

Discussion: The entire refuge has been designated by the state as a significant natural heritage area. The implementation of a forest management plan will allow the refuge to retain or enhance the natural character of the bottomland hardwood communities in order to fulfill the purpose of the refuge, as well as meeting the goals of the state natural heritage program.

Strategy:

- Protect state designated significant natural heritage areas from vandalism, fire, and timber theft.

Objective 9: Water Quality

Monitor water quality on the refuge as necessary to document the effects of land use on the refuge, land use on adjacent areas, and managed flows on refuge flora and fauna.

Discussion: The staff will alter the orientation of its water quality monitoring program depending on hydrologic events. Monitoring may occur on the river and/or on the floodplain. The Service will collect chemical baseline data at four sites on the refuge. The data will be carefully summarized or shared with other agencies and organizations.

Strategies:

- Monitor water quality in refuge wetland units during selected hydrologic events.

- Cooperate with other agencies and organizations performing water quality sampling on the Roanoke River.

- Monitor chemical baseline water quality data at four selected refuge sites on the refuge and two on adjacent areas as necessary.

- Summarize and share data with other agencies.

- Continue to actively participate in the Corps of Engineers' Section 216 study to examine the impacts of managed flow regimes on the behavior and productivity of colonial nesting birds.

Objective 10: Wilderness Areas

There are no designated or candidate wilderness areas on the refuge.

Discussion: None of the units that the refuge currently own is over 5,000 acres or without roads dissecting the areas. The Fish and Wildlife Service does not own the mineral rights to the islands that could be managed as wilderness areas. As the Service acquires more land within the approved acquisition boundary, the refuge staff will review its suitability as wilderness study areas.

Objective 11: Wildlife Disease Control and Prevention

Coordinate with local, state, and federal agencies as necessary to monitor and control wildlife disease and limit impacts to refuge resources.

Discussion: The Service has strict policies to prevent the introduction or spread of disease to refuge wildlife species. Refuge staff will continue to adhere to Fish and Wildlife Service policy in order to prevent and/or control outbreaks of wildlife diseases. Cooperation with the North Carolina Wildlife Resources Commission on addressing wildlife management issues is also essential to controlling and preventing disease outbreaks. Health checks of the white-tailed deer herds are performed every five years by the University of Georgia, School of Veterinary Medicine, to analyze parasite counts and the potential for disease outbreaks of the deer population found within and in the vicinity of refuge lands. There is no other monitoring of wildlife species for disease.

Strategies:

- Coordinate with local, state, and federal agencies as necessary to monitor and control wildlife disease.

- Cooperate with the University of Georgia to conduct health checks of white-tailed deer.

- Cooperate with the North Carolina Wildlife Resources Commission as necessary to discourage the release of pen-reared waterfowl into the wild.

Table 12. Projects supporting resource protection.

Strategy	Projects
Personnel Projects	
Maintain cooperation with agencies, organizations, and permit holders. Review permits and develop conditions for uses allowed by permits. Maintain contact with owners of property within acquisition boundary.	Utilize existing refuge manager, assistant manager, and wildlife biologist.
Protect cultural resources, enforce refuge regulations and coordinate with other agencies, and enforce permit conditions.	Utilize existing zone law enforcement officer. Recruit, hire, and train a new law enforcement officer (RONS 05001).
Collect and summarize water quality data.	Utilize existing wildlife biologist and biological technician. Recruit, hire, and train a new hydrologist (RONS 00006) and two new biological technicians (RONS 91022 and 00004).
Review permit applications and assess the impacts of permitted activities. Develop and implement a pest plant and animal control program. Limit the impacts of fire and update the fire management plan. Monitor and control wildlife disease. Monitor and control pest animals and plants and wildlife disease.	Utilize existing wildlife biologist and biological technician. Recruit, hire, and train a new hydrologist (RONS 00006) and two new biological technicians (RONS 91022 and 00004).
Coordinate visitor safety and environmental compliance.	Utilize existing refuge manager, assistant manager, and zone officer. Recruit, hire, and train a new assistant manager for facilities (RONS 02001). Recruit, hire, and train a new law enforcement officer (RONS 05001).
Maintain equipment and facilities and implement a fire management program.	Utilize existing engineering equipment operator. Recruit, hire, and train a forester (RONS 00005), new wage grade supervisor (RONS 00013), three new equipment operators (RONS 97037, 00008 and 00009) and three new maintenance workers.
Manage budget, contracts, personnel, and property.	Utilize existing refuge manager, assistant manager, and office assistant. Recruit, hire, and train new office assistant (RONS 00002). Recruit, hire, and train a new administrative assistant (RONS 00010).
Apply for flexible funds and other grants.	Utilize existing refuge manager and assistant manager.
Financial Management Projects	
Insure budget integrity.	Process payroll, travel, purchasing, and contract documents.

Strategy	Projects
Secure adequate funding to operate refuge.	Prepare annual budget requests and maintain the Refuge Operation Needs System (RONS) and Service Asset Maintenance Management System (SAMMS). Apply for grants to finance studies and investigations, a communication system, permit compliance monitoring, pest plant and animal control, water quality monitoring, disease monitoring and control, and the development of the prescribed burning program. Request addition to base funding (RONS 00003). Request funding to support USGS Water Quality Monitoring Cooperative Agreement (RONS 99003), for a communication system (RONS 90008), and a dioxin study (RONS 00017), and a cultural resource survey (RONS 97032).
Equipment Projects	
Provide vehicles and boats for refuge staff to protect cultural resources, gain access to inholdings, monitor compliance with permit conditions, monitor and control pest animals and plants, manage water quality monitoring stations and collect baseline chemical data, monitor impacts of fire to the refuge, monitor and control wildlife disease. Provide vehicles and boats for partners to gain access to the refuge and refuge waters. Calibrate and maintain equipment to monitor water quality. Provide equipment to control pest plants and implement the prescribed burning program.	Maintain and replace equipment (various MMS projects).
Facility Projects	
Provide facilities necessary to meet the refuge purpose.	Maintain, replace and rehabilitate roads, parking lots, kiosks, water control structures, shop, garage, and office (various MMS projects).

GOAL 5. REFUGE ADMINISTRATION

Acquire and manage adequate funding, human resources, facilities, equipment, and infrastructure to accomplish the other refuge goals.

Discussion: The administrative functions associated with a refuge include a wide array of activities that are critical to the mission of the National Wildlife Refuge System and the purpose of each refuge. These functions include staffing, training, budgeting, planning, access, facilities, equipment, and funding in order to accomplish the overall goals and objectives of the refuge.

Objective 1: Facility Management

Provide appropriate office space and maintenance facilities to ensure safe and efficient refuge operations.

Discussion: The refuge currently leases office and maintenance facilities through the General Services Administration. The leased office space is adequate for the current staff with space available for one additional staff member. As staff increases, the refuge will have to either lease additional space or construct a new facility. The leased maintenance facility consists of an old warehouse with wooden floors and a small secure yard. It is inadequate in size and design to carry out the refuge's mission. It is in an area prone to flooding. This plan would provide for an administrative office and a modern maintenance facility to ensure safe and efficient refuge operations.

Strategies:

- Construct a new office and visitor contact station as the staff increases and as funding becomes available.

- Replace existing leased compound when funding becomes available.

- Acquire a new site for the maintenance compound when funding becomes available.

- Design, construct, and occupy a safe modern shop, maintenance, and storage facility when funding becomes available.

Objective 2: Financial Management

Secure an annual budget that will allow the refuge to effectively carry out its mission. Manage budget to ensure the accountability of funds.

Discussion: Financial management affects every aspect of refuge operations. Funding operations is dependent on effective budgeting and requests for funds under the Refuge Operation Needs System (RONS) and Service Asset Maintenance Management Systems (SAMMS). The staff submits RONS requests for increased operations and new equipment. These two systems are the primary source for additional funding above the annual base (e.g., salaries, fuel, office supplies, etc.). The staff submits SAMMS requests for maintenance and equipment replacement. This plan allows the staff to update requests for additional funding to carry out the mission of the refuge.

Strategies:

- Prepare annual budget.

- Maintain RONS and SAMMS annually.

- Administer payroll, travel, purchasing, and contract documents.

Objective 3: Personnel

Provide and continuously manage a full staff complement to accomplish refuge goals, operations, and maintenance. Provide staff with professional, technical, and leadership development training as allowable under current funding levels.

Discussion: The refuge staff would increase to an optimal staff of 24 full-time equivalents (FTEs) and 25 positions. This staffing level would provide for optimal biological, public use, maintenance, and law enforcement programs along with support staff. The manager will evaluate employee performance and reward employees continuously.

Strategies:

- Provide staff with professional, technical, and leadership development training in accordance with Service policy as opportunities occur and funding is available.

- Evaluate performance continuously; manage performance and conduct in accordance with Service policy.

Objective 4: Property Management

Manage property according to Service policy to effectively carry out the mission of the refuge.

Discussion: Property is generally divided into three categories: real property, capitalized property, and non-capitalized property. Real property includes such things as roads, culverts, buildings, etc., and makes up the infrastructure of the refuge. Capitalized property is equipment that cost over $5,000 and certain restricted items such as firearms and laptop computers. Non-capitalized property is equipment under $5,000. The Fish and Wildlife Service Manual has strict requirements for record keeping and how these properties are managed. This plan allows for the staff to continue managing all property in accordance with Fish and Wildlife Service policies.

Strategies:

- Install and manage a refuge wide-communications system when funding for such a system becomes available.

- Acquire all equipment necessary to support refuge programs as the Service provides funds.

- Conduct one capital property inventory, one non-capitalized, and one real property inventory annually.

- Maintain administrative records on capital, non-capitalized, and real property.

- Evaluate the operating condition of capital property annually.

- Maintain and upgrade capital and non-capital property to ensure the safety of the staff and the general public.

- Replace equipment frequently enough to maximize the efficiency of refuge operations.

- Manage all property according to Service policy.

- Acquire or construct buildings and structures to meet refuge program needs.

- Pursue acquisition of rights-of-way for public access to Town Swamp and Company Swamp from willing sellers.

Objective 5: Refuge Access

Provide public access for pedestrians from U.S. Highway 13/17 and the Roanoke River and maintain administrative access agreements.

Discussion: The roads and trails present on the refuge today are remnants of old logging roads. Presently, the only public access to the refuge for pedestrians is from U.S. Highway 13/17; all other areas are accessible by boat from the river. The existing roads are used to carry out refuge operations and are maintained as seasonal roads since they are flooded on a regular basis. Vehicular access in most areas will continue to be restricted to the public in order to protect wildlife resources and to help ensure visitors a quality visit. However, if acquisition of rights-of-way through private holdings can be obtained, there are opportunities that can allow for seasonal public access on the Company Swamp and Town Swamp Units. This plan provides for expanding pedestrian access opportunities to refuge lands and upgrading maintenance on administrative roads as required by the Fish and Wildlife Service Manual.

Strategies:

- Provide public access for pedestrians from U.S. Highway 13/17 and the Roanoke River.

- Acquire a public access right-of-way to Company Swamp and Town Swamp Units to enhance public access.

- Maintain roads for administrative access.

Objective 6: Volunteer Coordination

Use 10,000 annual volunteer hours to assist the refuge in fulfilling its mission.

Discussion: Volunteers play a vital role in helping the Service fulfill its mission. The refuge utilizes volunteers from the community and college interns to assist office and field personnel with some tasks, saving staff valuable time. Volunteers assist in collecting field data, entering data in computers, and accompanying the refuge's equipment operator in the field. The refuge recruits volunteer interns from colleges, and provides housing and a stipend with which to purchase meals. This plan allows for the staff to expand its volunteer program.

Strategies:

- Recruit interns by maintaining contact with college professors.

- Recruit local volunteers through the Friends of Roanoke River National Wildlife Refuge, print media, and the Internet.

- Designate a refuge staff member as a volunteer coordinator.

- Utilize Friends of Roanoke River National Wildlife Refuge to coordinate projects.

Table 13. Projects supporting refuge administration strategies.

Strategy	Projects
Personnel Projects	
Manage budget, contracts, personnel, and property; process payroll and travel vouchers; maintain RONS AND MMS.	Utilize existing refuge manager, assistant manager, and office assistant. Recruit, hire, train new office assistant (RONS 00002).
Recruit, hire, and train a resource specialist (RONS 00005); two biological technicians (RONS 91022 and 00004); a hydrologist (RONS 00006); forest technician (RONS 99002); entomologist (RONS 00011), a law enforcement Officer (RONS 05001), park ranger (RONS 93028), media specialist (RONS 00007), office assistant (RONS 00002), administrative assistant (RONS 00010), a new wage grade supervisor (RONS 00013), three new equipment operators (RONS 97037, 00008 and 00009) and three new maintenance workers (RONS 00012, and 00014, and 00015).	Utilize existing refuge manager, assistant manager, and office assistant. Recruit, hire, train new office assistant (RONS 00002).
Recruit, supervise, and manage volunteers.	Utilize existing refuge manager, assistant manager, wildlife biologist, engineering equipment operator, and office assistant. Recruit, hire, and train a new park ranger (RONS 93028).
Administer contracts for habitat management.	Recruit, hire, train new administrative assistant (RONS 00009).
Maintain equipment and facilities.	Utilize existing engineering equipment operator. Recruit, hire, and train a new wage grade supervisor (RONS 00013), three new equipment operators (RONS 97037, 00008 and 00009) and three new maintenance workers (RONS 00012, and 00014, and 00015).
Manage the Service Asset and Maintenance System (SAMMS) and coordinate safety and environmental compliance	Utilize existing refuge manager, assistant manager. Recruit, hire, and train a new assistant manager for facilities (RONS 02001).
Financial Management Projects	
Ensure budget integrity.	Process payroll, travel, purchasing, and contract documents.

Secure adequate funding to operate refuge.	Prepare annual budget requests and maintain the Refuge Operation Needs System (RONS) and Service Asset Maintenance Management Systems (SAMMS). Apply for grants to finance, a communication system, property acquisition, and support for volunteers. Request addition to base funding (RONS 00003). Request funding for a communication system (RONS 90008)
Equipment Projects	
Provide equipment to administer refuge operations.	Maintain and replace equipment as necessary (various MMS projects).
Facility Projects	
Provide facilities necessary to meet the refuge purpose.	Maintain, rehabilitate, replace, and construct water control structures, kiosks, office, shop, garage, and equipment storage areas as necessary (various MMS projects). Maintain, rehabilitate, and construct roads and parking lots (various MMS projects).

Table 14. Summary of strategies proposed in each wildlife alternative.

Program	Activity	Alternative		
		1	2	3
Colonial Nesting Birds	Survey of Rookeries from the Air	Every 3 Years	Every 3 Years	Every 3 Years
	Observe as Opportunities arise	Yes	Yes	Yes
	Survey the Presence of Yellow-Crowned Night Heron Nests Annually	Yes	Yes	Yes
	Survey Productivity of Yellow-Crowned Night Heron Nests Annually	No	Yes	Yes
	Survey Conine Island Rookery from the Ground Annually	No	Yes	Yes
	Survey of All Refuge Rookeries from the Ground Annually	No	No	Yes As Time Permits
Fish	Manage Refuge to Protect	Yes	Yes	Yes
	Document Utilization of Anadromous Fish on Floodplain as Time Permits	Yes	Yes	Yes
	Inventory Floodplain Fishes Every 5 Years	No	Yes	Yes
Invertebrates	Observe as Opportunities Arise	No	Yes	Yes
	Initiate Floodplain Study on RR with a Reference Site on a River w/ no Managed Flows within 15 Years	No	No	Yes
	Establish Invertebrate Monitoring Protocol	No	Within 10 Years	Within 5 Years
	Monitor Invertebrates	No	No	Yes Within 10 Years
Mammals	Manage White-Tailed Deer by Hunting	Yes	Yes	Yes
	Observe as Opportunities Arise	Yes	Yes	Yes
	Count Parasites of White-Tailed Deer	Every 5 Years	Every 5 Years	Every 5 Years
	Quantify Nutria Effects within 15 Years	No	Yes	Yes
	Survey Small Mammals within 10 Years	No	Yes	Yes
	Survey Road Kills on Highway 13/17 within 15 Years	No	Yes	Yes
	Collect Deer Herd Data Annually on a Random Basis	No	No	Yes
	Participate in Northeastern North Carolina Black Bear Study within 5 Years	No	Yes	Yes

Program	Activity	Alternative		
		1	2	3
Neotropical Migratory Songbirds	Monitor Birds on Levee Plots Annually	40	60	60
	Monitor Birds on Interior Swamp Plots Annually	0	0	40
	Survey Cerulean Warblers along a 20-Mile Transect in Vicinity of Refuge Lands Annually	Yes	Yes	Yes
	Survey Cerulean Warbler along 130-Mile Transect	Every 5 Years	Every 5 Years	Every 3 Years
	Survey Non-Breeding Bird Survey Annually	No	No	100 Plots
Raptors	Observe as Opportunities Arise	Yes	Yes	Yes
	Conduct Osprey Productivity Surveys	As Time Allows	Annually	Annually
	Band Ospreys	As Time Allows	Annually	Annually
	Survey Bald Eagle Nest Productivity as Opportunities Arise	Yes	Yes	Yes
	Survey Road Kills within 10 Years	No	Yes	Yes
	Survey Kite Nests Annually	No	Yes	Yes
	Survey Kite Population Annually	No	No	Yes
Waterfowl	Wood Duck Productivity Surveys Three times a Year	60 Boxes	75 Boxes	100 Boxes
	Band Wood Ducks as Directed	Yes	Yes	Yes
	Establish Winter Waterfowl Survey Protocol within 5 Years	No	Yes	Yes
	Conduct Winter Waterfowl Survey within 5 Years	No	Yes	Yes
	Establish Wood Duck Cavity Monitoring Survey Protocol	No	No	Yes
	Conduct Wood Duck Cavity Monitoring Survey	No	No	Yes
Reptiles and Amphibians	Observe as Opportunities Arise	Yes	Yes	Yes
	Establish Protocol and Survey within 10 Years	No	Yes	Yes
	Monitor Population Trends Every Five Years	No	No	Yes

Table 15. Summary of strategies proposed in each habitat alternative.

Program	Activity	Alternative		
		1	2	3
Coastal Plain Bottomland Hardwoods (On Refuge)	Acreage	7,154	7,154	7,154
	Update Fire Management Plans	Yes	Yes	Yes
	Inventory Five Forest Health Plots on the Refuge Every 10 Years	Yes	Yes	Yes
	Establish Three Forest Health Plots on Reference Site Within 5 Years	No	Yes	Yes
	Inventory Three New Forest Health Plots on Reference Site Every 10 Years	No	Yes	Yes
	Inventory 100 Regeneration Plots on Refuge Annually	Yes	Yes	Yes
	Establish 60 New Regeneration Plots on Reference Site within 5 Years	No	Yes	Yes
	Inventory 60 Regeneration Plots on Reference Site Annually	No	Yes	Yes
	Develop and Implement Habitat Management Plans within 10 Years	No	Yes	Yes
	Develop and Implement Forest Pest Management Plan within 10 Years	No	Yes	Yes
	Develop and Implement Beaver Pond Management Plan within 10 Years	No	Yes	Yes
Coastal Plain Bottomland Hardwood (Nash County)	Acreage Protected	45	45	45
	Develop and Implement Habitat Management Plan within 7 Years	No	No	Yes
Coastal Plain Pine Flatwoods (Sampson County)	Acreage Protected	129	129	129
	Develop and Implement Habitat Management Plan within 7 Years	No	No	Yes
Cypress/ Tupelo Swamp	Acreage	13,824	13,824	13,824
	Develop and Implement Habitat Management Plans within 10 Years	No	Yes	Yes
	Develop and Implement Forest Pest Management Plan within 10 Years	No	Yes	Yes
	Develop and Implement Beaver Pond Management Plan within 10 Years	No	Yes	Yes
Freshwater Marsh	Acreage Protected	43	43	43
Easements	Acreage Protected	2,870	2,870	2,870
	Easements Protected	98	98	98
	Develop and Implement Habitat Management Plan on Selected Easements within 10 Years	No	No	Yes
Wood Duck Boxes	Maintain Annually	60 Boxes	75 Boxes	100 Boxes
	New Boxes Erected within 15 Years	0	15	40
	Relocate Boxes to Reduce Dump Nests	No	Yes	Yes

Table 16. Summary of strategies proposed in each public use alternative.

Topic	Activity	Alternatives		
		1	2	3
Hunting	Update Hunting Regulations Annually	Yes	Yes	Yes
	Update Hunting Plan within 5 Years	Yes	Yes	Yes
	Allow Camping During Hunts	Yes	Yes	Yes
	Address Waste Disposal within 3 Years	Yes	Yes	Yes
	Conduct Youth Turkey Hunt Annually	Yes	Yes	Yes
	Evaluate Youth Waterfowl Hunt within 5 Years	No	Yes	Yes
	Develop and Distribute Refuge Hunt Brochure within 3 Years	No	Yes	Yes
	Annual Hunter Use Days (Total)	8,480	8,480	8,680
	Annual Hunter Use Days (Waterfowl)	200	200	400
	Annual Hunter Use Days (Turkey)	530	530	530
	Annual Hunter Use Days (Small Game)	1,000	1,000	1,000
	Annual Hunter Use Days (Deer with Modern Gun)	3,750	3,750	3,750
	Annual Hunter Use Days (Deer with Muzzleloader)	1,000	1,000	1,000
	Annual Hunter Use Days (Deer with Archery)	2,000	2,000	2,000
Fishing	Annual Angler Use Days	3,000	4,000	5,000
	Develop and Implement Plan within 3 Years	Yes	Yes	Yes
	Evaluate Increased Access within 3 Years	Yes	Yes	Yes
	Develop and Distribute Regulation Brochure within 3 Years	Yes	Yes	Yes
Environmental Education	Host Students Annually	50	500	500
	Conduct Programs Annually	4	4	12
	Conduct Tours Annually	0	6	6
	Participate in Field Days Annually	0	1	3
	Encourage Refuge Use as Classroom within 1 Year	No	Yes	Yes
	Develop and Implement Program with Students and Teachers within 3 Years	No	Yes	Yes
Interpretation	Annual Visitors	1,000	3,000	3,000
	Maintain Kiosks	1	7	7
	Construct New Kiosks	0	6	6
	Maintain Kuralt Trail	Yes	Yes	Yes
	Use Video within 3 Years	Yes	Yes	Yes
	Maintain Bird List	Yes	Yes	Yes
	Develop Wildlife List within 3 Years	No	Yes	Yes
	Extend Kuralt Trail and Erect Signage within 15 Years	No	Yes	Yes
	Develop Exhibits for Headquarters within 5 Years	Yes	Yes	Yes
	Design and Implement Remote Camera in Heron Rookery within 15 Years	No	Yes	Yes

Topic	Activity	Alternatives		
		1	2	3
Wildlife Observation	Annual Visitors	5,000	10,000	10,000
	Conduct Annual Guided Tours	0	6	12
	Maintain Kuralt Trail and Logging Roads	Yes	Yes	Yes
	Provide Kuralt Trail Information	Yes	Yes	Yes
	Extend Kuralt Trail and Erect Signage within 15 Years	No	Yes	Yes
	Participate in Canoe Trail Partnership within 10 Years	No	Yes	Yes
	Develop Wildlife Drive within 15 Years	No	No	Yes
	Develop Brochure, Signage, CD/Tape for Wildlife Drive within 15 Years	No	No	Yes
Wildlife Photography	Annual Visitors	500	1,000	1,000
	Maintain Kuralt Trail and Logging Roads	Yes	Yes	Yes
	Provide Kuralt Trail Information	Yes	Yes	Yes
	Participate in Canoe Trail Partnership within 10 Years	No	Yes	Yes
	Build Photo Blinds within 5 Years	2	2	2
Outreach	Target Outreach Audience	500	1,000	1,000
	Participate in Six Festivals and Fairs	Yes	Yes	Yes
	Maintain Refuge Web Site and Brochure	Yes	Yes	Yes
	Develop News Releases	6	12	12
	Make Presentations to Groups Annually	5 on Request	12 Planned	12 Planned
	Encourage Friends of Roanoke River National Wildlife Refuge to Promote Refuge	Yes	Yes	Yes
	Recruit Membership for Friends of Roanoke River National Wildlife Refuge and Develop It	No	Yes	Yes
	Develop and Maintain Refuge Radio Broadcasts within 15 Years	No	No	Yes
	Develop and Implement Outreach Plan within 5 Years	No	Yes	Yes
	Develop Public Service Announcements About Local Natural Resources within 15 Years	No	No	Yes
Refuge Support	Support Friends of Roanoke River National Wildlife Refuge and Develop Fund-Raising Ability	Yes	Yes	Yes
	Work with Partnership for the Sounds	Yes	Yes	Yes
	Work with nongovernmentalal Organizations to Protect and Support Land Acquisition and Restoration within the Roanoke River Basin	Yes	Yes	Yes

Table 17. Summary of strategies proposed in each protection alternative.

Program	Activity	Alternative		
		1	**2**	**3**
Cultural Resources	Protect Identified Sites	Yes	Yes	Yes
	Evaluate Projects	Yes	Yes	Yes
	Conduct Inventory within 10 Years	No	No	Yes
Interagency Coordination	Participate in Annual Meetings and Contacts	60	80	100
	Revise Agreements	As Needed	Annually	Annually
	Develop New Agreements As Needed	No	No	Yes
	Coordinate with NCWRC on Hunting Annually	Yes	Yes	Yes
	Coordinate with NCFS on Fire Annually	No	Yes	Yes
Land Protection	Additional Acreage	12,022	12,022	12,022
	Total Acreage in Approved Acquisition Boundary (Ownership plus Additional Acreage)	33,000	33,000	33,000
	Post Boundary	Yes	Yes	Yes
	Develop a Land Protection Plan for Future Expansion	No	Yes	Yes
Law Enforcement	Ensure health and Safety by:	Enforce Regulations	Enforce Regulations & Outreach	Enforce Regulations & Outreach
	Coordinate with Others Annually	Yes	Yes	Yes
	Develop Written Agreements As Needed	No	Yes	Yes
Permits	Evaluate Permits Annually	6	15	20
	Develop Special Use Conditions	Yes	Yes	Yes
	Develop Standardized Conditions as Needed	No	Yes	Yes
	Monitor Permitted Activities	No	Yes	Yes
Pest Animals	Record Incidents	Yes	Yes	Yes
	Develop and Implement Monitor and Control Plan within 10 Years	No	Yes	Yes
Pest Plants	Map Species Distribution on Refuge within 3 Years	No	Yes	Yes
	Develop Control Plan within 5 Years	No	Yes	Yes
Significant Natural Heritage Areas	Limit Impacts to Retain Character	Yes	Yes	Yes
Significant Natural Heritage Areas	Implement Fire Strategy	Implement Fire Strategy	Conduct Prescribed Burning	Conduct Prescribed Burning

Program	Activity	Alternative		
		1	2	3
Water Quality	Monitor on Refuge During Selected Hydrologic Events	Yes As Time Permits	Yes As Needed	Yes As Needed
	Cooperate with Agencies	Yes	Yes	Yes
	Monitor Number of Refuge Chemical Baseline Sites	2	4	6
	Share Baseline Site Data	Yes	Yes	Yes
Wilderness Areas	Nominate Areas	0	0	0
Wildlife Disease	Monitor and Control	Yes	Yes	Yes
	Coordinate with Others	Yes	Yes	Yes
	Discourage Pen-Raised Waterfowl Releases	Yes	Yes	Yes

Table 18. Summary of strategies proposed in each administration alternative.

Program	Activity	Alternative		
		1	2	3
Facility Management	Operate and Maintain Office	To Ensure Efficiency, Safety, Aesthetics	To Ensure Efficiency, Safety, Aesthetics	To Ensure Efficiency, Safety, Aesthetics
	Operate and Maintain Shop	To Minimum Standards	To Ensure Efficiency and Safety	To Ensure Efficiency and Safety
	Maintain New Shop and Storage Facility	Yes	Yes	Yes
Financial Management	Prepare and Administer Annual Budget	Yes	Yes	Yes
Personnel	Maintain FTE Levels at:	6	11	24
	Provide Training	As Funding Allows	Per Service Policy	Per Service Policy
	Evaluate Performance Semi-Annually	Yes	Yes	Yes
Property Management	Maintain Administrative Records	Yes	Yes	Yes
	Evaluate Operating Condition	No	Yes	Yes
	Maintain and Replace Capital Property	As Breaks Down	To Ensure Safety	To Ensure Safety, Efficiency
	Install and Maintain Refuge Radio Communication System	No	Yes	Yes
	Maintain Real Property	To Extent Possible	Cleanliness and Safety	Cleanliness and Safety
	Construct Buildings	None	To Adequate Levels	To Meet All Needs
	Conduct Annual Inventories	3	3	3
	Manage Real Property	Per Manual	Per Manual	Per Manual
Refuge Access	Provide Public Access Via Route 13/17 and Roanoke River	Yes	Yes	Yes
	Maintain Roads for Administrative Access	Yes	Yes	Yes
Refuge Access	Acquire Public Access Right-of-Way to Town Swamp and Company Swamp	No	Yes	Yes
Volunteer Coordination	Target Hours	1,500	5,000	10,000
	Intern Recruitment through Professors	Yes	Yes	Yes
	Local Volunteer Recruitment through Media and Internet	No	Yes	Yes

Table 19. Summary of projects proposed in each alternative.

Project Description	Alternatives		
	1	2	3
Staff Projects			
Utilize existing GS-13 manager.	X	X	X
Utilize existing GS-5/7/9 assistant manager.	X	X	X
Utilize existing GS-12 wildlife biologist.	X	X	X
Utilize existing GS- 7 biological technician.	X	X	X
Utilize existing GS-5 office assistant.	X	X	X
Utilize existing WG-8 equipment operator.	X	X	X
Recruit, hire, train a new WG-7 equipment operator (RONS 97037).		X	X
Recruit, hire, train a new GS-7 law enforcement officer (RONS 05001).		X	X
Recruit, hire train a new GS-12 resource specialist (RONS 00005).		X	X
Recruit, hire, train a new GS-9 public use specialist (RONS 93028).		X	X
Recruit, hire, train a new GS-7 biological technician (second total) (RONS 91022).		X	X
Recruit, hire, train a new GS-9 assistant manager (RONS 02001).			X
Recruit, hire, train a new WG-8 equipment operator (RONS 00008).			X
Recruit, hire, train a second new GS-7 biological technician (third total) (RONS 00004).			X
Recruit, hire, train a new WG-4 maintenance mechanic (RONS 00014).			X
Recruit, hire, train a new GS-7 forestry technician (RONS 99002).			X
Recruit, hire, train a new GS-11 media specialist (RONS 00007).			X
Recruit, hire, train a new GS-12 hydrologist (RONS 00006).			X
Recruit, hire, train a new GS-9 administrative assistant (RONS 00010).			X
Recruit, hire, train a new WG-10 wage grade supervisor (RONS 00013).			X
Recruit, hire, train a new GS-12 entomologist (RONS 00011).			X
Recruit, hire, train a new WG-3 maintenance worker (0.4 FTE) (RONS 00015).			X
Recruit, hire, train a new WG-7 equipment operator (RONS 00009).			X
Recruit, hire, train a new WG-4 maintenance mechanic (RONS 00012).			X
Recruit, hire, train a new GS-5 clerk (0.7 FTE) (RONS 00002).			X
Budget Projects			
Process payroll, travel, purchasing, and contract documents.	X	X	X
Prepare annual budget, revise RONS and MMS.	X	X	X
Apply for grants.	X	X	X
Request addition to base funding (RONS 00003).		X	X
Request funding to support USGS Water Quality Monitoring Cooperative Agreement (RONS 99003).		X	X
Request funding for contract for forest insect survey (RONS 90011).			X
Request funding for contract for cultural resource survey (RONS 97032).			X
Request funding for study on the impacts of flooding on habitat (RONS 97035).			X
Request funding for study on the impacts of flooding on wildlife (RONS 97033).			X
Request funding for study on implications of widespread dioxin (RONS 00017).			X
Request funding for study on migratory waterfowl food habits (RONS 05006).			X

Project Description	Alternatives		
	1	2	3
Request funding for study on the impact of flooding on reptiles and amphibians (RONS 05004).			X
Request funding for three interpretive brochures (RONS 05005).			X
Equipment Projects			
Maintain vehicles and boats.	X	X	X
Maintain heavy equipment and hand tools.	X	X	X
Maintain computers and software.	X	X	X
Replace D-6 Crawler Tractor (MMS 01001).	X	X	X
Replace 1999 4X4 Dodge Pickup Truck (MMS 01005).	X	X	X
Replace 1999 4X4 Dodge Pickup (MMS 01007).	X	X	X
Replace 1992 Chevy Fire Truck (MMS 01008).	X	X	X
Replace 1998 400 ATV (MMS 01010).	X	X	X
Replace 2000 4X4 Dodge Pickup Truck (MMS 02001).	X	X	X
Replace 2004 New Holland TS Tractor (MMS 04001).	X	X	X
Replace 2004 New Holland Batwing Mower (MMS 04002).	X	X	X
Replace 2004 Caterpillar Bulldozer (MMS 04003).	X	X	X
Replace 2004 4X4 Ford F-150 Pickup Truck (MMS 04005).	X	X	X
Replace 2004 Chevy ¾ ton Pickup Truck (MMS 04010).	X	X	X
Purchase and install new radio system (RONS 90008).	X	X	X
Purchase and maintain a truck, truck transport, and bulldozer (RONS 90016).	X	X	X
Facility Projects			
Maintain roads.	X	X	X
Maintain parking lots and trails.	X	X	X
Maintain buildings.	X	X	X
Maintain public use facilities.	X	X	X
Design, construct, and maintain a shop and equipment storage area (MMS 90014).	X	X	X
Design, construct, and maintain a 1/2 mile disabled accessible trail (MMS 99001).	X	X	X
Construct 125' X 40' pole shed (MMS 04004)	X	X	X
Rehabilitate public parking lots (MMS 04006)	X	X	X
Design and construct two photo blinds (MMS 05001).	X	X	X
Design, construct, and install forested wetland interpretative exhibits in visitor contact station (RONS 00001).	X	X	X
Install boundary signs (RONS 00016).		X	X
Design, construct, and install seven interpretative kiosks (RONS 05002).			X
Install beaver exclusion devices in beaver ponds (RONS 05003).			X

Table 20. Summary of costs of projects proposed in all alternatives.

Project Description	Costs		
Staff Projects	First Year or One Time Costs	Recurring Costs	Total Costs
Alternative 1			
Cost of Staff Projects	$0	$349,000	$349,000
Cost of Budget Projects	$0	$0	$0
Cost of Equipment Projects	$886,000	$30,000	$916,000
Cost of Facility Projects	$2,182,000	$5,000	$2,187,000
Cost of Land Acquisition (12,000 acres at $700 per acre)	$8,400,000	$0	$8,400,000
Grand Total of Alternative 1	$11,468,000	$384,000	$11,852,000
Alternative 2			
Cost of Staff Projects	$325,000	$667,000	$992,000
Cost of Budget Projects	$0	$130,000	$130,000
Cost of Equipment Projects	$886,000	$30,000	$916,000
Cost of Facility Projects	$2,212,000	$5,000	$2,217,000
Cost of Land Acquisition 12,000 acres at $700 per acre)	$8,400,000	$0	$8,400,000
Grand Total of Alternative 2	$11,823,000	$832,000	$12,655,000
Alternative 3			
Cost of Staff Projects	$1,206,500	$1,521,000	$2,727,500
Cost of Budget Projects	$337,000	$140,000	$477,000
Cost of Equipment Projects	$886,000	$30,000	$916,000
Cost of Facility Projects	$2,292,000	$5,000	$2,297,000
Cost of Land Acquisition (12,000 acres at $700 per acre)	$8,400,000	$0	$8,400,000
Grand Total of Alternative 3	$13,121,500	$1,696,000	$14,817,500

Table 21. Cost of projects proposed in Alternative 1.

Project Description	Costs		
	First Year or One Time Costs	Recurring Costs	Total Costs
Staff Projects			
Existing GS-13 Manager.		Existing Base $349,000	Existing Base $349,000
Existing GS-5/7/9 Assistant Manager.			
Existing GS-12 Wildlife Biologist.			
Existing GS- 7 Biological Technician.			
Existing GS-5 Office Assistant.			
Existing WG-8 Equipment Operator.			
Cost of Staff Projects	$0	$349,000	$349,000
Equipment Projects			
Replace D-6 Crawler Tractor (MMS 01001).	$185,000	$0	$185,000
Replace 1999 4X4 Dodge Pickup Truck (MMS 01005).	$26,000	$0	$26,000
Replace 1999 4X4 Dodge Service Truck (MMS 01007).	$31,000	$0	$31,000
Replace 1992 Chevy Fire Truck (MMS 01008).	$31,000	$0	$31,000
Replace 1998 ATV (MMS 01010).	$6,000	$0	$6,000
Replace 2000 4X4 Dodge Pickup Truck (MMS 02001).	$26,000	$0	$26,000
Replace 2004 New Holland TS Tractor (MMS 04001)	$58,000	$0	$58,000
Replace 2004 New Holland Batwing Mower (MMS 04002)	$19,000	$0	$19,000
Replace 2004 Caterpillar Bulldozer (MMS 04003)	$144,000	$0	$144,000
Replace 2004 Ford F-150 4X4 Pickup Truck (MMS 04005)	$25,000	$0	$25,000
Replace 2004Chevrolet ¾ Ton Pickup Truck (MMS 04010)	$25,000	$0	$25,000
Purchase and Install New Radio System (RONS 90008).	$60,000	$10,000	$70,000
Purchase Truck, Truck Transport, and Bulldozer (RONS 90016).	$250,000	$20,000	$270,000
Cost of Equipment Projects	$886,000	$30,000	$916,000
Facility Projects			
Design, Construct, and Maintain a Shop and Equipment Storage Area (MMS 90014).	$1,271,000	$0	$1,271,000
Design and Construct Kuralt Trail Interpretive Boardwalk (MMS 99001).	$595,000	$0	$595,000
Design and Construct 125' X40' Pole Shed (MMS 04004).	$75,000	$0	$75,000
Rehabilitate Public Use Parking Lots (MMS 04006).	$66,000	$0	$66,000
Design and Construct Two Photo Blinds (MMS 05001).	$10,000	$0	$10,000
Design, Construct, and Install Interpretative Exhibits in Visitor Contact Station (RONS 00001).	$165,000	$5,000	$170,000
Cost of Facility Projects	$2,182,000	$5,000	$2,187,000
Grand Total	$11,468,000	$384,000	$11,852,000

Table 22. Cost of projects proposed in Alternative 2.

Project Description	Costs		
	First Year or One Time Costs	Recurring Costs	Total Costs
Staff Projects			
Existing GS-13 manager.		Existing Base $349,000	Existing Base $349,000
Existing GS-5/7/9 assistant manager.			
Existing GS-12 wildlife biologist.			
Existing GS-7 biological technician.			
Existing GS-5 office assistant.			
Existing WG-8 equipment operator.			
New WG-7 equipment operator (RONS 97037).	$65,000	$51,000	$116,000
New GS-7 law enforcement officer (RONS 05001).	$65,000	$64,000	$129,000
New GS-12 resource specialist (RONS 00005).	$65,000	$87,000	$152,000
New GS-9 public use specialist (RONS 93028).	$65,000	$63,000	$128,000
New GS-7 biological technician (RONS 91022).	$65,000	$53,000	$118,000
Cost of Staff Projects	$325,000	$667,000	$992,000
Budget Projects			
Addition to base funding (RONS 00003).	$0	$65,000	$65,000
Funding to support USGS Water Quality Monitoring Cooperative Agreement (RONS 99003).	$0	$65,000	$65,000
Cost of Budget Projects	$0	$130,000	$130,000
Equipment Projects			
Replace D-6 crawler tractor (MMS 01001).	$185,000	$0	$185,000
Replace 1999 4X4 Dodge Pickup (MMS 01005).	$26,000	$0	$26,000
Replace 1999 4X4 Dodge Service Truck (MMS 01007).	$31,000	$0	$31,000
Replace 1992 Chevy Fire Truck (MMS 01008).	$31,000	$0	$31,000
Replace 1998 ATV (MMS 01010).	$6,000	$0	$6,000
Replace 2000 4X4 Dodge Pickup (MMS 02001).	$26,000	$0	$26,000
Replace 2004 New Holland TS Tractor (MMS 04001)	$58,000	$0	$58,000
Replace 2004 New Holland Batwing Mower (MMS 04002)	$19,000	$0	$19,000
Replace 2004 Caterpillar Bulldozer (MMS 04003)	$144,000	$0	$144,000
Replace 2004 Ford F-150 4X4 Pickup Truck (MMS 04005)	$25,000	$0	$25,000
Replace 2004Chevrolet ¾ Ton Pickup Truck (MMS 04010)	$25,000	$0	$25,000
Purchase and Install New Radio System (RONS 90008).	$60,000	$10,000	$70,000
Purchase Truck, Truck Transport, and Bulldozer (RONS 90016).	$250,000	$20,000	$270,000
Cost of Equipment Projects	$886,000	$30,000	$916,000
Facility Projects			
Design, Construct, and Maintain a Shop and Equipment Storage Area (MMS 90014).	$1,271,000	$0	$1,271,000
Design, Construct, and Maintain a 1/2 Mile Disabled Accessible Trail (MMS 99001).	$595,000	$0	$595,000

Project Description	Costs		
	First Year or One Time Costs	Recurring Costs	Total Costs
Design, Construct, and Maintain a 125' X 40' Pole Shed (MMS 04004).	$75,000	$0	$75,000
Rehabilitate Public Use Parking Lots (MMS 04006).	$66,000	$0	$66,000
Design, Construct, and Maintain Photo Blinds (MMS 05001).	$10,000	$0	$10,000
Design, Construct, and Install Interpretative Exhibits in Visitor Contact Station (RONS 00001).	$165,000	$5,000	$170,000
Install Boundary Signs (RONS 00016).	$30,000	$0	$30,000
Cost of Facility Projects	$2,212,000	$5,000	$2,217,000
Grand Total of Costs	$11,823,000	$832,000	$12,655,000

Table 23. Cost of projects proposed in Alternative 3.

Project Description	Costs		
	First Year or One Time Costs	Recurring Costs	Total Costs
Staff Projects			
Existing GS-13 manager.		Existing Base $349,000	Existing Base $349,000
Existing GS-5/7/9 assistant manager.			
Existing GS-12 wildlife biologist.			
Existing GS-7 biological technician.			
Existing GS-5 office assistant.			
Existing WG-8 equipment operator.			
New WG-7 equipment operator (RONS 97037).	$65,000	$51,000	$116,000
New GS-7 law enforcement officer (RONS 05001).	$65,000	$64,000	$129,000
New GS-12 resource specialist (RONS 00005).	$65,000	$87,000	$152,000
New GS-9 public use specialist (RONS 93028).	$65,000	$63,000	$128,000
New GS-7 biological technician (RONS 91022).	$65,000	$53,000	$118,000
New GS-9 assistant manager (RONS 02001).	$65,500	$69,000	$134,500
New WG-8 equipment operator (RONS 00008).	$195,000	$59,000	$254,000
New GS-7 biological technician (RONS 00004).	$85,000	$59,000	$144,000
New WG-4 maintenance worker (RONS 00014).	$5,000	$46,000	$51,000
New GS-7 forest technician (RONS 99002).	$65,000	$59,000	$124,000
New GS-11 media specialist (RONS 00007).	$65,000	$82,000	$147,000
New GS-12 hydrologist (RONS 00006).	$95,000	$96,000	$191,000
New GS-9 administrative assistant (RONS 00010).	$65,000	$69,000	$134,000
New WG-10 wage grade supervisor (RONS 00013).	$65,000	$66,000	$131,000
New GS-12 entomologist (RONS 00011).	$65,000	$96,000	$161,000
New WG-3 maintenance worker (0.4 FTE) (RONS 00015).	$26,000	$17,000	$43,000
New WG-7 equipment operator (RONS 00009).	$35,000	$56,000	$91,000
New WG-4 maintenance worker (RONS 00012).	$5,000	$46,000	$51,000
New GS-5 clerk (0.7 FTE) (RONS 00002).	$45,500	$34,000	$79,500
Cost of Staff Projects	$1,206,500	$1,521,000	$2,727,500
Budget Projects			
Addition to base funding (RONS 00003).	$0	$65,000	$65,000
Funding to support USGS Water Quality Monitoring Cooperative Agreement (RONS 99003).	$0	$65,000	$65,000
Funding for contract for forest insect survey (RONS 90011).	$30,000	$10,000	$40,000
Funding for contract for cultural resource survey (RONS 97032).	$35,000	$0	$35,000
Funding for study on the impacts of flooding on habitat (RONS 97035).	$30,000	$0	$30,000

Funding for study on the impacts of flooding on wildlife (RONS 97033).	$60,000	$0	$60,000
Funding for water quality study on dioxin (RONS 00017).	$40,000	$0	$40,000
Funding for herpetology impact study (RONS 05004).	$65,000	$0	$65,000
Funding for three interpretive brochures (RONS 05005).	$12,000	$0	$12,000
Funding for migratory waterfowl food study (RONS 05006).	$65,000	$0	$65,000
Cost of Budget Projects	$337,000	$140,000	$477,000
Equipment Projects			
Replace D-6 crawler tractor (MMS 01001).	$185,000	$0	$185,000
Replace 1999 4X4 Dodge Pickup (MMS 01005).	$26,000	$0	$26,000
Replace 1999 4X4 Dodge Service Truck (MMS 01007).	$31,000	$0	$31,000
Replace 1992 Chevy Fire Truck (MMS 01008).	$31,000	$0	$31,000
Replace 1998 ATV (MMS 01010).	$6,000	$0	$6,000
Replace 2000 4X4 Dodge Pickup (MMS 02001).	$26,000	$0	$26,000
Replace 2004 New Holland TS Tractor (MMS 04001)	$58,000	$0	$58,000
Replace 2004 New Holland Batwing Mower (MMS 04002)	$19,000	$0	$19,000
Replace 2004 Caterpillar Bulldozer (MMS 04003)	$144,000	$0	$144,000
Replace 2004 Ford F-150 4X4 Pickup Truck (MMS 04005)	$25,000	$0	$25,000
Replace 2004 Chevrolet ¾ Ton Pickup Truck (MMS 04010)	$25,000	$0	$25,000
Purchase and Install New Radio System (RONS 90008).	$60,000	$10,000	$70,000
Purchase Truck, Truck Transport, and Bulldozer (RONS 90016).	$250,000	$20,000	$270,000
Cost of Equipment Projects	$886,000	$30,000	$916,000
Facility Projects			
Design, Construct, and Maintain a Shop and Equipment Storage Area (MMS 90014).	$1,271,000	$0	$1,271,000
Design, Construct, and Maintain a 1/2 Mile Disabled Accessible Trail (MMS 99001).	$595,000	$0	$595,000
Design, Construct, and Maintain a 125' X 40' Pole Shed (MMS 04004).	$75,000	$0	$75,000
Rehabilitate Public Use Parking Lots (MMS 04006).	$66,000	$0	$66,000
Design, Construct, and Maintain Photo Blinds (MMS 05001).	$10,000	$0	$10,000
Design, Construct, and Install Interpretative Exhibits in Visitor Contact Station (RONS 00001).	$165,000	$5,000	$170,000
Install Boundary Signs (RONS 00016).	$30,000	$0	$30,000
Design, Construct, and Install Seven Interpretive Kiosks (RONS 05002).	$30,000	$0	$30,000
Install Beaver Exclusion Devices (RONS 05003).	$50,000	$0	$50,000
Cost of Facility Projects	$2,292,000	$5,000	$2,297,000

STAFFING AND FUNDING

Currently a staff of six permanent positions has been approved for the refuge. To complete the extensive wildlife habitat management and restoration projects and to conduct the necessary inventorying, monitoring, and mapping activities, more staff is required. The proposed staffing plan (Figure 9) would enable the refuge to achieve its plan objectives and strategies within a reasonable time. The annual recurring cost (including salaries and benefits) would be $1.433 million. The rate at which this refuge realizes its full potential to contribute locally, regionally, and nationally to wildlife conservation and appropriate wildlife-dependent recreation and environmental education is totally dependent upon receiving adequate staffing and funding.

PARTNERSHIP OPPORTUNITIES

A major objective of this comprehensive conservation plan is to establish partnerships with local volunteers, landowners, private organizations, and state and federal natural resource agencies. In the immediate vicinity of the refuge, opportunities exist to establish partnerships with sporting clubs, elementary and secondary schools, and community organizations. At regional and state levels, partnerships might be established with organizations such as the North Carolina Wildlife Resources Commission, The Nature Conservancy, Ducks Unlimited, National Audubon Society, and National Wild Turkey Federation.

The refuge volunteer program and other partnerships generated will depend upon the number of staff positions the Service provides the refuge. As staff and resources are committed, opportunities to expand the volunteer program and develop partnerships will be enhanced.

MONITORING AND EVALUATION

Adaptive management is a flexible approach to long-term management of resources that is directed over time by the results of ongoing monitoring activities and other information. More specifically, adaptive management is a process by which projects are implemented within a framework of scientifically driven experiments to test the predictions and assumptions outlined within a plan.

Adaptive management applies to all refuge programs. The staff can use it to alter its approach to managing wildlife populations, habitat, public use opportunities, staff, buildings, property, or land. To apply adaptive management, specific survey, inventory, and monitoring protocols will be adopted for the refuge. For example, the habitat management strategies will be systematically evaluated to determine management effects on wildlife populations. This information will be used to refine approaches and determine how effectively the objectives are being accomplished. Evaluations will include ecosystem team and other appropriate partner participation. If monitoring and evaluation indicate undesirable effects for target and non-target species and/or communities, then alterations to the management projects will be made. Subsequently, this plan will be revised.

Specific monitoring and evaluation activities will be described in the step-down management plans.

Under the Technical Settlement Agreement issued by the Federal Energy Regulatory Commission to Dominion Power in 2004, Dominion Power has agreed to an adaptive management approach to address the impacts of hydropower generation on downstream terrestrial and aquatic ecosystems. The first 5 years of the agreement term is a period of baseline data collection. After the initial 5-year period, those impacts will be assessed and flow releases will be adapted to minimize impacts. The staff adaptation of the comprehensive conservation plan will consider those adaptations.

Figure 9. Proposed staffing plan for the Roanoke River National Wildlife Refuge

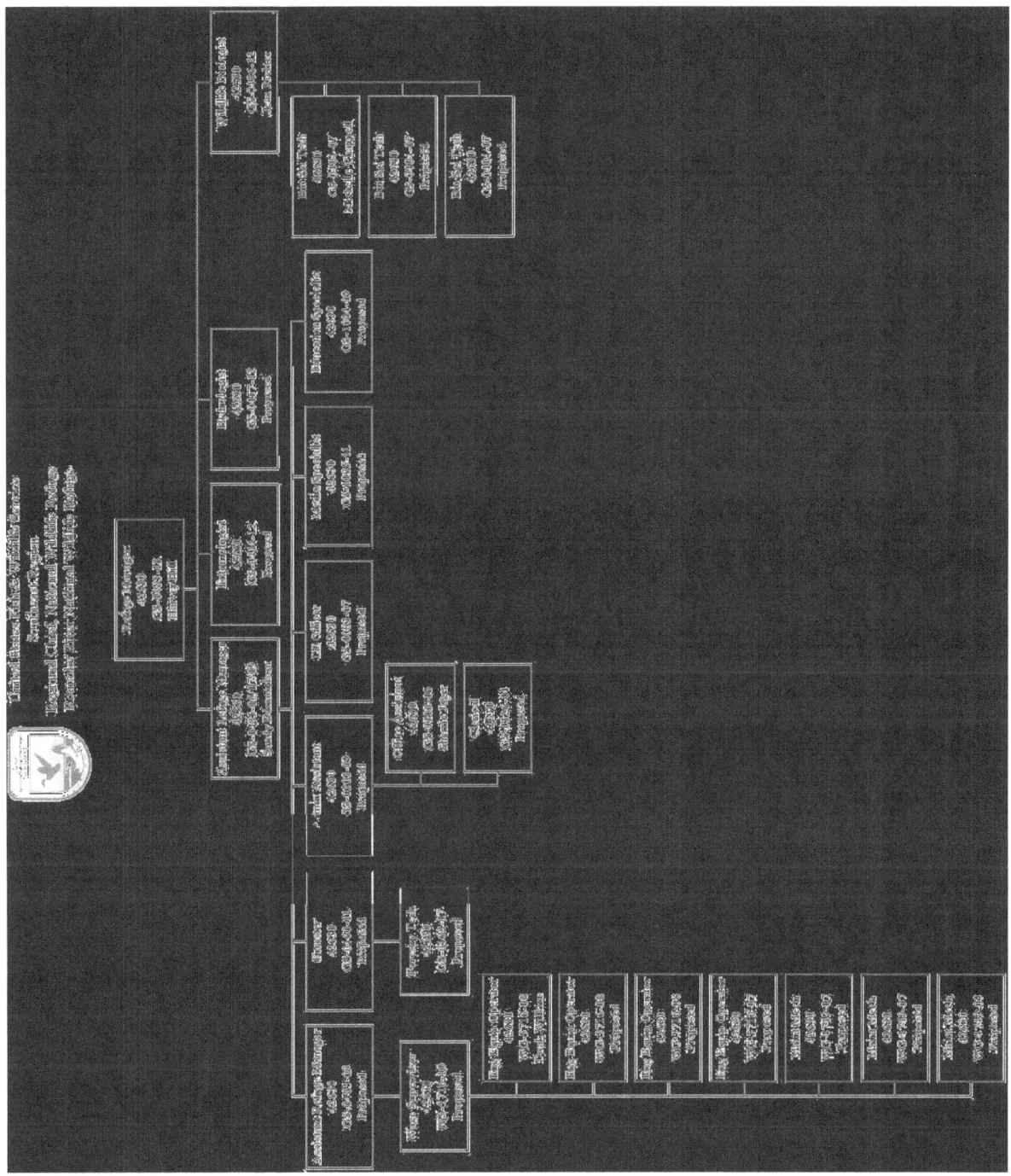

Concurrently, the Army Corps of Engineers has been authorized to review its flood control operations on the Roanoke River under Section 216 of the Flood Control Act of 1970. That review may also result in a change of its release of flood waters on the downstream ecosystem. The staff adaptation of the comprehensive conservation plan will consider those adaptations.

MANAGEMENT COMMON TO ALL ALTERNATIVES

COMPATIBLE USES

The National Wildlife Refuge System Administration Act of 1966, as amended by the National Wildlife Refuge System Improvement Act of 1997, states that national wildlife refuges must be protected from incompatible or harmful human activities to ensure that Americans can enjoy refuge system lands and waters. Before activities or uses are allowed on a national wildlife refuge, the uses must be found to be compatible. A compatible use "...will not materially interfere with or detract from the fulfillment of the mission of the refuge system or the purposes of the refuge." In addition, "wildlife-dependent recreational uses may be authorized on a refuge when they are compatible and not inconsistent with public safety."

An interim compatibility determination is a document that assesses the compatibility of an activity during the period of time the Service first acquires a parcel of land to the time a formal, long-term management plan for that parcel is prepared and adopted. The Service has completed an interim compatibility determination for the six priority general public uses of the system, as listed in the National Wildlife Refuge System Improvement Act of 1997. These uses are hunting, fishing, wildlife observation, wildlife photography, environmental education and interpretation.

OTHER MANAGEMENT

The Service would manage all activities that could affect natural resources, including subsurface mineral reservations, utility lines and easements, soil, water, air, and historical and archaeological resources to comply with all laws and regulations. The Service has a legal responsibility to consider the effects of its actions on cultural resources. Under all alternatives, the Service would manage these resources in accordance with public law and agency policy. Individual projects would require additional consultation with the Advisory Council on Historic Preservation and the State of North Carolina's Historic Preservation Office. The Service would require additional consultation, surveys, and clearance where it develops projects on the refuge or when activities would affect properties that are listed or eligible for listing in the National Register of Historic Places.

LAND ACQUISITION

The acquisition of land within the approved refuge acquisition boundary will continue. All land acquisitions are subject to contaminant surveys.

Funding for land acquisition would come from the Land and Water Conservation Fund, Migratory Bird Conservation Fund, or donations from conservation organizations. Conservation easements and leases can sometimes be used to obtain minimum interests necessary to satisfy refuge objectives if the refuge staff can adequately manage uses of the areas for the benefit of wildlife. The Service can negotiate management agreements with local, state, and federal agencies, and accept conservation easements. Some tracts within the proposed refuge acquisition boundary may be owned by other public or private conservation organizations. The Service would work with interested organizations to identify additional areas needing protection and provide technical assistance if needed. The acquisition of private lands is entirely contingent on the landowners and their willingness to participate.

REFUGE REVENUE SHARING

Annual refuge revenue-sharing payments to Bertie County would continue at similar rates under each alternative. If lands are acquired and added to the refuge, the payments would increase accordingly and be paid to the counties in which the land lies.

EDUCATION AND VISITOR SERVICES

As the refuge's visitor service program is developed, the staff would continue to assess the program and its potential impact on refuge resources. Changes in the program would be implemented as needed to address any impacts identified and to respond to anticipated wildlife population increases. To ensure a quality wildlife-dependent recreation experience while achieving the "wildlife first" mandate, the number of users and conflicts among users may be limited by the following: (1) permitting uses; (2) designating roads, trails, and sites for specific kinds of wildlife-dependent recreational use; and (3) permitting uses at certain times of the year.

There are a number of situations where future refuge closures or restrictions on access may be warranted. Examples of these situations include, but are not limited to, the following: protection of endangered species; protection of nesting birds and bear den sites; restriction of recreation activities to achieve specific wildlife population objectives; safety concerns due to high water; minimization of conflicts with other refuge management programs; and limitations from inadequate funds and/or staff to administer use.

REFUGE ADMINISTRATION

The maintenance and operation of the refuge's administrative facilities would continue, regardless of the alternative selected. Periodic updating of facilities is necessary for safety and accessibility and to support staff and management needs. Funding needs have been identified for several projects, including providing additional facilities and equipment to support refuge operation and maintenance.

IV. Environmental Consequences

This section analyzes and discusses the potential environmental effects or consequences that can be reasonably expected by the implementation of each of the three management alternatives described in Section III of this environmental impact statement. The planning team selected the following impact topics for analysis:

- Effects on biological environment;
- Effects on physical environment;
- Effects on social environment; and
- Effects on economic environment.

These topics were chosen based on the important issues and concerns raised at the public scoping meeting and the planning team meetings. Each alternative portrays the expected outcomes for fish and wildlife species through 2019, varying as to the intensity of management. TableIV-1 outlines a comparison of the effects of Alternatives 2 and 3 to the existing condition (Alternative 1).

COMPARISON OF EFFECTS AMONG MANAGEMENT ALTERNATIVES

OVERVIEW

The refuge's current management actions described in Alternative 1 would have minimal to no effects on the biological or socioeconomic environment. The proposed management actions described in Alternative 2 would have moderately positive effects on the biological environment and society. The proposed management actions described in Alternative 3 would have significantly positive effects on the biological environment and society. Land acquisition proposed in Alternatives 2 and 3 would have a negative economic effect on the local property tax receipts and industries, such as pulp and paper production, that rely on the current land use. However, that implementation would produce new economic opportunities from the salaries of the new staff, refuge expenditures in the local economy, and refuge visitors participating in outdoor recreation and environmental education opportunities.

BIOLOGICAL ENVIRONMENT

Effects of Biological (Wildlife and Habitat) Alternatives

Each alternative would protect existing habitat important to migratory birds, mammals, reptiles, amphibians, fish, and invertebrates. Alternative 1 limits the biological program to providing limited data on neotropical migratory songbirds in bottomland hardwoods on the refuge, but does not provide for any habitat management except wood duck box maintenance. Alternative 2 would provide data on some species and a balanced effort to moderately increase habitat management for neotropical migratory songbirds and forest-dependent waterfowl on the refuge. Alternative 3 would provide data on all species on the refuge and a balanced effort to significantly increase habitat management for neotropical migratory songbirds and forest-dependent waterfowl on and off the refuge on Farmers Home Administration easements.

The condition of nesting and foraging habitat for waterfowl and songbirds would improve moderately under Alternative 2 and significantly under Alternative 3 because of improved forest management.

Wood duck and songbird populations would increase moderately under Alternative 2 and significantly under Alternative 3.

Roanoke River National Wildlife Refuge is part of the range of the cerulean warbler, a management indicator species. This species, now rarely seen, was once common in the area that is now the refuge. Cerulean warblers feed and nest in large (greater than 50,000 acres) forest patches of mature, dense canopy tree stands (over 40 years in age) and typically choose stands with the largest trees for nesting (over 100 years in age) (Hunter 1999). Mississippi kites, another management indicator species, nest in similar habitats. The remaining mature forests on Roanoke River National Wildlife Refuge have been degraded due to years of timber harvest. High levels of crown closure interspersed with large, emergent trees are positively correlated with nest site location and success for these birds. The forest management activities outlined in Alternatives 2 and 3 would cause long-term benefits in improving the nesting habitat for these species to moderate levels in Alternative 2 and to significant levels in Alternative 3.

The Swainson's warbler, another management indicator species, is a passerine migrant that inhabits canebrakes, spending most of its time near the ground searching for insects. It breeds in large swamps and bottomlands and prefers nesting in dense cane near or over water. The existing habitat on the refuge has largely been degraded due to past land management practices and clearing of swamps and bottomlands. The forest habitat restoration programs described under Alternatives 2 and 3 would positively benefit nesting and feeding habitat for this species, as well as other priority bird species such as the Cerulean warbler, Swainson's warbler, prothonotary warbler, American woodcock, wood thrush, and hooded warbler.

The exact extent of active management required to improve habitat to support specific populations is not currently known, but will be determined by the surveys outlined in the plan. The precise habitat requirements for most individual species are not known in quantitative terms, and less is known about optimum habitat for suites of species. References such as "The Land Manager's Guide to the Birds of the Southeast" (Hamel 1992) are the best compendia of recommendations against which to compare survey data and plan management.

Effects of Resource Protection Alternatives

Each alternative proposes to protect sites important to forest interior breeding birds and the black bear by acquiring inholdings within the approved acquisition boundary. Alternatives 2 and 3 have the potential to provide greater management capabilities and larger areas of habitat protection.

All alternatives would provide additional protection to wetlands beyond the protection afforded by existing wetland regulations. They would also protect landscape characteristics such as habitat connectivity and would provide sufficient proprietary interest in properties to restore habitats for forest interior breeding birds.

A zone law enforcement officer administers the law enforcement program under Alternative 1. This situation does not provide a permanent law enforcement visibility on the refuge. Wildlife species are subject to poaching and habitat subject to damage and timber theft. Increases in law enforcement ability proposed in Alternatives 2 and 3 will provide a permanent presence and allow a more proactive approach to regulation, ensuring that moderate to significant gains in wildlife populations and habitat condition would be secured.

As the refuge program develops and attracts more visitors, requests for special use permits will increase. The increases in permit review and administration in Alternatives 2 and 3 will allow proper handling of those permits and monitoring of the permitted activities. In the long run, this will also secure the moderate and significant improvements made by habitat management in Alternatives 2 and 3.

The staff would develop an integrated pest management plan under all alternatives. Alternative 1 would provide the least active management, while Alternatives 2 and 3 would provide the most management and would have significant impacts on the biological environment by managing undesirable plants and animals. Whenever possible, all alternatives would use techniques other than pesticides to control these species. However, some quantity of pesticides would be used on an as-needed basis.

Effects of Public Use Alternatives

Under all public use alternatives, the level of recreation use and ground-based disturbance from pedestrians would be largely concentrated to boardwalks, trails, and the office and maintenance areas. Public use could still have a negative effect on nesting bird populations. The increased public use provided in Alternatives 2 and 3 may have a slightly negative effect on the refuge's wildlife populations due to disturbance and habitat trampling. The staff would monitor the impact and mitigate the effects by limiting the amount, time, or areas of access.

It is unlikely that species such as bald eagles would establish nests near developed facilities. Although no bald eagle nesting areas are known on the refuge, bald eagles have been sighted. Bald eagles are vulnerable to human activity around nesting areas and do not tolerate human disturbances during the breeding season. Recreational activities including hiking, hunting, and small fishing craft can be a major disturbance to bald eagles. The level of recreational use is least disturbing to wildlife under Alternative 1, and most disturbing under Alternatives 2 and 3. The moderate increase in the level of recreational use expected under Alternatives 2 and 3 would increase disturbances related to hiking, hunting, and fishing and could preclude the possibility of eagles establishing a nest where most of the proposed recreational activities would occur. The expansion of forest management activities described in Alternatives 2 and 3 may also negatively affect bald eagles locating on the refuge over the short term. Hunting is primarily a winter season activity. Over the long term, Alternatives 2 and 3 would produce a number of suitable nesting and roosting trees for bald eagles.

The refuge's deer population is currently at a healthy carrying capacity. Under the other alternatives, forest management actions could increase the deer population slightly under Alternative 2 and moderately under Alternative 3. The refuge's forests and adjacent croplands provide rich sources of forage for deer. Under all alternatives, the staff would monitor deer populations and use hunting to manage populations in order to provide a compatible recreational activity and prevent habitat damage. Hunting would also ensure the health of the deer herd and minimize the effects to other wildlife species and habitat.

Effects of Administrative Alternatives

Under all alternatives, the Service would design, construct, and occupy a new shop. The new shop will allow the staff to maintain the refuge more efficiently and safely, resulting in less time spent on maintenance and more time on habitat management. Under Alternative 1, the staff can only maintain office space and access roads to provide safe facilities for the employees and the public. Under Alternatives 2 and 3, the maintenance goal for office space and roads would be safety and efficiency. The increased efficiency would provide for more habitat management and an improved biological environment.

Under Alternative 1, the staff administers a program to meet the minimum requirements for the management of real property, capital property, and personnel. Under Alternative 2, the staff would improve that management to ensure safe operation of the refuge. This alternative provides better conditions under which the staff can work and the public can visit. Under Alternative 3, the staff would moderately improve that management to ensure safe operation of the refuge and meet all the needs of the refuge. This alternative significantly improves management by providing the resources to meet all the wildlife monitoring and habitat management needs of the refuge

The refuge administers a volunteer program with a goal of 1,500 hours. These volunteers allow the staff to perform much more wildlife and habitat monitoring than would be performed without them. Alternative 2 provides for the recruitment, training, and management of 5,000 hours of volunteer assistance. The additional assistance will allow the staff to pursue the moderate improvement in biological monitoring and habitat management outlined in this plan. Alternative 3 provides for the recruitment, training, and management of 10,000 hours of volunteer assistance. The additional assistance will allow the staff to pursue the significantly higher level of biological monitoring and habitat management outlined in this plan.

Under Alternative 1, there is substandard access for resource management and visitors caused by the inferior quality of roads and trails. Under Alternatives 2 and 3, the Service would improve access to the edge of the refuge by securing rights-of-way to Company and Broadneck Swamps. This improved access would facilitate moderate increases in resource management.

Alternative 1 does not address the current shortage of critical staff, and the staffing level would remain as it is now. Critical refuge and resource management and protection, visitor services and protection, and facilities and equipment maintenance goals and objectives would remain unfulfilled. Alternative 2 provides staffing to facilitate moderate improvements in essential refuge operations that will have a corresponding effect on the biological environment. Alternative 3 provides the staffing to achieve significant improvements in all refuge operations that will have a corresponding effect on the biological environment.

PHYSICAL ENVIRONMENT

The most critical issue on the refuge is the management of water in the Roanoke River by the Corps of Engineers for flood control and by Dominion Generation for hydroelectric power generation. All alternatives propose continued communication and coordination with the Corps of Engineers, Dominion Generation, and the Federal Energy Regulatory Commission to influence the management of flows to minimize the impact on the Roanoke River floodplain. The effect of that coordination is very unpredictable. Management of the flows is dependent on the policies that govern the Corps of Engineers, the economics of hydroelectric power generation, and weather patterns. Conscientious coordination would not ensure a positive effect.

All alternatives have a significantly positive long-term effect on soil formation processes on lands the refuge acquires as the lands recover from intensive forest management and timber harvest. Some short-term disturbances to surface soils and topography would occur at those locations selected for administrative and public use facilities, maintenance operations, and forest management. Since the proposed increase in public use is essentially equal under Alternatives 2 and 3, both alternatives would have the same moderately negative effect in the vicinity of developed facilities.

All alternatives would have a negligible effect on the water quality in individual streams and wetlands due to a relatively low level of soil disturbance and fertilizer and pesticide application. All alternatives would also have the same positive effects from the protection of groundwater recharge areas, sediment retention, and the minimization of runoff and non-point source pollution.

Each alternative would protect the aesthetic characteristics associated with bottomland hardwood forests. Forest management activities designed to improve forest composition and structure would be carried out in such a way to minimize any short-term aesthetic effects.

SOCIAL ENVIRONMENT

Alternative 1 of the public use program concentrates on providing opportunities for hunting. The North Carolina Wildlife Resources Commission administers the permit program. The zone law enforcement officer provides law enforcement. The refuge allows the other priority public uses (fishing, wildlife observation, wildlife photography, environmental education, and interpretation) but does not provide programs to support them. Poor roads would limit access to the refuge to only those traveling by foot or boat. Lack of programming, staff, and facilities limit opportunities for environmental education, interpretation, wildlife observation, and photography. The staff conducts environmental education as requested and participates in major local outreach events. The program outlined in Alternative 1 provides social benefits that the refuge lands did not provide when in private ownership, but leaves much room for improvement.

Under Alternatives 2 and 3, fishing, wildlife observation, wildlife photography, and environmental education and interpretation opportunities would increase equally, and each would provide moderate increases in social benefits. Under each alternative, most of the newly acquired lands would be opened for public hunting, resulting in a net gain of public hunting opportunities in the area so there would be no difference in social benefits from hunting.

Poor roads would still limit access to the refuge to only those traveling by foot or boat. Visitor access would increase in Alternatives 2 and 3, where foot trails, boardwalks, wildlife viewing platforms, and photo blinds would be developed. Alternative 3 provides slightly more facilities than Alternative 2. Under both alternatives, the refuge would acquire rights-of-way for public access to Company and Town Swamps.

Visitor use management on refuges concentrates on the experience, not the number of people coming into a refuge. The types and intensity of visitor activities would vary from tract-to-tract depending on its size, habitat type(s), and wildlife uses. Because much of the land in Bertie County is currently in private ownership, the general public realizes only minimal access privileges on that private land.

The more proactive outreach effort in Alternative 3 would increase planned presentations and an active refuge support group, resulting in a moderate increase in the awareness of the public about the natural resources of the area.

The improved public use program in Alternatives 2 and 3 would provide a moderate increase in opportunities for all local citizens to learn about and enjoy the natural environment. In addition to the human use patterns that would undoubtedly shift with such normal ecological changes as forest maturation and publicity by outside groups, the improved refuge management will further increase usage. The retention of the existing hunting and fishing programs would continue to provide a recreation outlet and economic opportunities for citizens and local businesses. The refuge would remain a reliable site for nature-based tourism publicized and conducted by others.

The refuge's current base budget is $349,000, most of which pays salaries for employees who live in the local communities, or provides for maintenance of refuge equipment and facilities. Improving management of the refuge would produce additional economic impact due to an increase in visitation. In addition to the increased salaries ($667,000 in Alternative 2 and $1,521,000 in Alternative 3) from increased staffing levels, the improved program would result in the refuge purchasing more supplies and equipment from the local economy and attracting more visitors to the area.

An estimated 17,000 refuge visits were reported in 2000. The wildlife-dependent recreational activities described under Alternatives 2 and 3 (i.e., expanded opportunities to 8,000 visits in fishing, wildlife observation, wildlife photography, environmental education, and interpretation) would increase visitation to the refuge and generate greater purchases of local goods and services in the surrounding communities.

Refuge visitation to support priority public uses would generally increase slowly over time as the refuge hires a public use specialist, develops visitor service programs and facilities, secures operational funds, and acquires refuge lands. Initially, much of the public use on the refuge should come from local, county, and state residents, although an increase in the number of spring and fall tourists is predicted for fishing, hiking, and wildlife observation. The number of visitors would depend on the season and would grow as the refuge land base increases and more public use programs are provided.

Many of the wildlife-dependent recreational activities offered have yet to be discovered by local citizens. As a generator of economic benefits, each alternative identifies hunting and wildlife observation as important tourist attractions. Under Alternatives 2 and 3, development of wildlife-dependent recreation programs and facilities and improved publicity would lead to the moderate increase in the economic benefit from increased tourism.

Service estimates of economic impacts of hunters and anglers are $74 per day for hunters and $69 for anglers (U.S. Fish and Wildlife Service 2001). A local estimate of the economic impact of participants in non-consumptive wildlife dependent recreation activities is $100 per day (Vogelsang 2001). The current 7,000 hunters, 3,000 anglers, and 7,000 other visitors represent $1,425,000 spent locally on food, lodging, fuel, supplies, and equipment. The 8,000 additional visitors to the refuge in Alternatives 2 and 3 would spend an additional $800,000 locally on food, lodging, fuel, supplies, and equipment.

Land acquisition within the approved acquisition boundary would decrease the gross property tax revenues of Bertie, Martin, Halifax, and Washington counties. However, there would be an increase in refuge revenue-sharing payments. Because the Service is a federal agency, it is not subject to state and local taxes. Under the Refuge Revenue Sharing Act, the Service would make annual payments to the counties to offset the loss of property tax revenues. These annual refuge revenue-sharing payments for owned and acquired lands are computed on whichever of the following formulas is greatest: (1) three-fourths of 1 percent of the fair market value of the lands acquired in fee title; (2) 25 percent of the net refuge receipts collected; or (3) 75 cents per acre of the lands acquired in fee title within the counties. The Refuge Revenue Sharing Act also requires that Service lands be appraised every five years to ensure that payments to local governments remain equitable. In 2001, Bertie County received a revenue-sharing payment of $36,427 for 17,977 acres at Roanoke River National Wildlife Refuge, which was appraised at $9,358,625 for the value of the land and timber. That amount represented only 52 percent of its entitlement due to a lack of congressional funding of the act.

North Carolina taxes land on the area of the state in which the land is located (Major Land Resource Area), the soil type on the land, and the present use of the land (North Carolina Use-Value Advisory Board 2003). Roanoke River National Wildlife Refuge is in the Upper Coastal Plain Major Land Resource Area and the land use is forestry. The soils on the 17,977 acres on which taxes were paid in 2002 are: Wehadkee loam, 6,100 acres; Dorovan muck, 5,900 acres; Chewacla loam, 5,710 acres; Wickham sandy loam, 130 acres; Tarboro loamy sand 35 acres; Conetoe loamy sand, 50 acres; Chastain silt loam, 25 acres; Seabrook sand, 20 acres; Bibb loam, 10 acres; Winton fine sandy loam, 10 acres; Udorthents, 5 acres; Roanoke fine sandy loam, 5 acres; and Wahee fine sandy loam, 2 acres. The present use value of the refuge land is $2,143,690. If the property had been in private ownership, the taxes would have been $19,076.84 on that acreage based on a tax rate of $.89 per $100 of assessed value.

The revenue-sharing payment of $36,427 was almost twice the $19,076.84 that private landowners would have paid in taxes. The Service will apply revenue-sharing to all acquired and newly acquired fee simple lands that are removed from the tax bases of the counties.

EFFECTS COMMON TO ALL MANAGEMENT ALTERNATIVES

HEALTH AND SAFETY EFFECTS

All of the 3 alternatives have potentially negative effects on public health and safety. They all pose potential safety problems involving the possibility of boat accidents of visitors gaining access to the refuge by water, hiking accidents occurring on the refuge's roads and trails, and accidents occurring during the hunting season and while engaged in management activities. As indicated below in the Mitigation Measures section, time and space zoning has been used successfully on national wildlife refuges to minimize the possibility of potential accidents and conflicts between hunters and other refuge user groups.

REGULATORY EFFECTS

As indicated in the Background section of this plan, the Service must comply with a number of federal laws, administrative orders, and policies in the development and implementation of its management actions and programs. Among these mandates are the Endangered Species Act of 1973; the Clean Water Act of 1977; and compliance with Executive Orders 11990 (Protection of Wetlands) and 11988 (Floodplain Management). The implementation of any of the three alternatives described in this environmental impact statement would not lead to a violation of these or other mandates.

CULTURAL AND HISTORIC RESOURCES EFFECTS

All alternatives afford additional land protection and low levels of development, thereby producing little negative effect on the refuge's cultural and historic resources. Potentially negative effects could include logging and construction of new trails. In most cases, these management actions would require review by the Service's Regional Cultural Resource Officer in consultation with the State of North Carolina's Historic Preservation Office, as mandated by Section 106 of the National Historic Preservation Act. Therefore, the determination of whether a particular action within an alternative has the potential to affect cultural resources is an ongoing process that would occur during the planning stages of every project. Alternative 3 provides for a comprehensive cultural resources survey that would identify those resources well before planning a project and would best allow the staff to avoid an impact.

Service acquisition of land with known or potential archaeological or historical sites provides two major types of protection for these resources: protection from damage by federal activity and protection from vandalism or theft. The National Historic Preservation Act requires that any actions by a federal agency which may affect archaeological or historical resources be reviewed by the State Historic Preservation Office, and that the identified effects must be avoided or mitigated. The Service's policy is to preserve these cultural, historic, and archaeological resources in the public trust, and avoid any adverse effects wherever possible.

Land acquisition by the Service would provide some degree of protection to significant cultural and historic resources. If acquisition of private lands does not occur and these lands remain under private ownership, the landowner would be responsible for protecting and preserving cultural resources. Development of off-refuge lands has the potential to destroy archaeological artifacts and other historical resources, thereby decreasing opportunities for cultural resource interpretation and research.

UNCERTAINTY OF FUTURE ACTION EFFECTS

In general, one of the components of each alternative is the inventory and monitoring of fish and wildlife populations on the refuge. Once this information is known, the Service will develop detailed step-down management plans to manage the fish and wildlife populations on the refuge, based on the application of sound fish and wildlife management principles and concepts. The specific content of the step-down management plans will provide the basis for further analysis of environmental effects.

The alternatives in this plan do present sufficient information to assess the full potential environmental effects of plans to be developed in the future.

CUMULATIVE EFFECTS

Cumulative effects on the environment result from incremental effects of a proposed action when these are added to other past, present, and reasonably foreseeable future actions. While cumulative effects may result from individually minor actions, they may, viewed as a whole, become significant over time.

The implementation of any of the three alternatives described in this document includes actions relating to site development, fish and wildlife habitat and population management, land acquisition, and recreational use programs. These actions would have both direct and indirect affects. For example, recreation site development would result in increased public use and increases in social and economic benefits, but could also increase littering, noise, and vehicular traffic. Habitat management would improve wildlife populations in the long term, but could increase erosion and runoff in the short term. However, the cumulative effects of a single action over the 15-year planning period are not expected to be significant.

The Service can only assess the real potential for cumulative effects in detail after the refuge staff prepares the step down plans that will lay out the specifics of road improvement, habitat management, and public use programs and facilities. If the plans propose intensive development and management all in the same area at the same time, the potential for cumulative effects could be significant. Since the general level of development increases from Alternative 1 to Alternative 2 to Alternative 3, the potential for cumulative impacts will increase through the same progression.

.

Table 24. Comparison of the effects of Alternatives 2 and 3 to Alternative 1.

Area of Concern	Alternative 2	Alternative 3
Effects on Wildlife		
Colonial Nesting Bird Population	Slight Increase	Slight Increase
Fish Population	Slight Increase	Slight Increase
Invertebrate Population	Slight Increase	Slight Increase
Mammal Population	Slight Increase	Moderate Increase
Neotropical Migratory Bird Population	Moderate Increase	Significant Increase
Raptor Population	Slight Increase	Slight Increase
Reptile and Amphibian Population	Slight Increase	Slight Increase
Waterfowl Population	Moderate Increase	Significant Increase
Effects on Habitat		
Coastal Plain Bottomland Hardwood Habitat Conditions	Significant Increase	Significant Increase
Coastal Plain Bottomland Hardwood (Nash County) Habitat Conditions	No Difference	Significant Increase
Coastal Plain Pocosin (Sampson County) Habitat Conditions	No Difference	Significant Increase
Cypress/Tupelo Swamp Habitat Conditions	Significant Increase	Significant Increase
Freshwater Marsh Habitat Conditions	No Difference	No Difference
Easement Habitat Condition	No Difference	Slight Increase
Wood Duck Box Condition	Moderate Increase	Significant Increase
Effects on Physical Environment		
Flooding from Managed Flows	No Difference	No Difference
Soil Condition of Newly Acquired Land	No Difference	No Difference
Soil Condition of Developed Facilities	Moderate Decrease	Moderate Decrease
Soil Condition Away from Developed Facilities	No Difference	No Difference
Water Runoff and Infiltration	No Difference	No Difference
Effects on Social Environment		
Hunting	No Difference	No Difference
Fishing	Slight Increase	Moderate Increase
Environmental Education	Moderate Increase	Moderate Increase
Interpretation	Moderate Increase	Moderate Increase
Wildlife Observation	Moderate Increase	Moderate Increase
Wildlife Photography	Moderate Increase	Moderate Increase
Outreach	Moderate Increase	Moderate Increase
Refuge Support	No Difference	No Difference
Cultural Resource Protection	No Difference	Slight Increase
Effects on Economic Environment		
Local Expenditures	Moderate Increase	Significant Increase
Local Property Taxes	No Difference	No Difference

The data and staff needed to develop step down plans do not currently exist. It will probably take the 15-year duration of this plan to gather that data and hire the staff required to develop those plans

MITIGATION MEASURES

Described below are the measures used to mitigate and minimize the potential adverse effects.

Wildlife Disturbances

Disturbance to wildlife at some level is an unavoidable consequence of any public use program, regardless of the activity involved. Obviously, some activities innately have the potential to be more disturbing than others. All of the proposed alternative public use activities contained in this document have been carefully planned to avoid unacceptable levels of impact.

As currently proposed, the known and anticipated level of disturbance of the proposed alternative (Alternative 3) is not considered significant and is well within the tolerance level of known wildlife species and populations present in the area. Implementation of the proposed public use program will take place through carefully controlled time and space zoning, including the management of waterfowl sanctuary areas, establishment of protection zones around key sites such as rookeries and eagle nests (if necessary), and the routing of roads and trails to avoid contact with sensitive areas such as rookery habitats, etc. In addition, the refuge will conduct all public hunting activities (e.g., season lengths, bag limits, number of hunters) within the constraints of sound biological principles and refuge-specific regulations established to restrict illegal or nonconforming activities. Providing fishing opportunities will allow the use of a renewable natural resource without adversely impacting other resources. The North Carolina Wildlife Resources commission sets the hunting and fishing seasons and bag and creel limits enforced on the refuge.

General wildlife observation/photography activities may result in minimal disturbances to wildlife. To mitigate these potential disturbances, the Service will design and construct all visitor trails and observation points with a buffer around key wildlife forage and resting areas. The visitors will be educated through signs and brochures to avoid disturbing wildlife. Also, any area on the refuge may be closed to the public if disturbance becomes excessive.

Temporary initial disturbances to wildlife and habitat will occur during the construction of new facilities such as trails, wildlife observation platforms, photo blinds, and interpretive sites. However, once the construction of such facilities is completed, the experience gained by the public will offset these disturbances. Allowing these non-consumptive recreational opportunities on the refuge will help to maintain and build public support for the refuge and the Roanoke-Tar-Neuse-Cape Fear ecosystem.

The Service will monitor the impacts of activities through wildlife inventories and assessments of public use levels and activities. Public use programs will be adjusted as needed to limit disturbance to acceptable levels.

User Group Conflicts

As public use levels expand across time, unanticipated conflicts between user groups may occur. The staff will adjust the refuge's public use programs as needed to eliminate or minimize each problem and provide quality wildlife-dependent recreational opportunities. Experience has proven that time and space zoning (e.g., establishment of separate use areas, use periods, and restrictions on the number of users) is an effective tool in eliminating conflicts between user groups. The current practice of discouraging all public uses except hunting during hunting season will continue.

Effects on Adjacent Landowners

Acquiring right-of-way access to the Company Swamp and Town Swamp Units will result in increased disturbance to adjacent landowners as visitors cross the adjacent property. The refuge will maintain the road, pick up litter, and encourage visitors to respect the rights of the adjacent landowners. Implementation of other provisions of the proposed action will not impact adjacent or in-holding landowners. The plan allows essential access to private property through the issuance of special use permits. Future land acquisitions will occur on a willing seller basis only and at fair market values. In addition, under the preferred alternative of the proposed comprehensive conservation plan, the staff will conduct water quality sampling and monitoring activities to document current conditions and seek to improve the water quality, if necessary. Existing state water quality criteria and use classifications are adequate to achieve desired on-refuge conditions. Thus, implementation of the proposed alternative will not impact adjacent landowners or users beyond the constraints already implemented under existing state standards and laws.

Land Ownership and Site Development

Land acquisition within the approved acquisition boundary would result in changes in land and recreational use patterns, since all uses on national wildlife refuges must meet compatibility standards. Land ownership by the Service also precludes any future economic development by the private sector on these lands. The land within the approved acquisition boundary is subject to regulation under the Clean Water Act that would limit development of the land for residential, commercial, industrial, or agricultural use.

Potential development of access roads, buildings, trails, water control structures, visitor parking areas, and other improvements could lead to minor short-term negative impacts on plants, soils, and some wildlife species. When the refuge proposes site development activities, each activity will receive the appropriate National Environmental Policy Act consideration during pre-construction planning. At that time, any required mitigation activities, if necessary, will be incorporated into the specific project to reduce the level of impacts to the human environment and to protect fish and wildlife and their habitats.

As indicated earlier, one of the direct effects of site development is increased public use. This increased use may lead to more littering, noise, and vehicle traffic. While Service funding and personnel will be allocated to minimize these indirect effects, such allocations would make the resources unavailable for other programs.

V. Consultation and Coordination

A core planning team composed of representatives from various Service divisions (Table 25) was formed to prepare the Comprehensive Conservation Plan and Environmental Impact Statement for Roanoke River National Wildlife Refuge. Initially, the team focused on identifying the issues and concerns pertinent to refuge management. The team met on several occasions from December 2000 to June 2002.

A biological review team (Table 26) with representatives from different programs in the Service, state agencies, nongovernmental organizations, and a consulting forester met on the refuges in the ecosystem four times between December 1999 and December 2000. They assessed the habitats on the refuges and the needs of wildlife species in the ecosystem, and made recommendations on land management and acquisition needs.

The core planning team also sought the contributions of experts (Table 27) from various fields.

Table 25. Roanoke River National Wildlife Refuge comprehensive conservation planning team members.

NAME	TITLE	LOCATION
Jerry Holloman, USFWS	Former Manager, Roanoke River National Wildlife Refuge	Windsor, North Carolina
Harvey Hill, USFWS	Manager, Roanoke River National Wildlife Refuge	Windsor, North Carolina
Mike Canada, USFWS	Former Assistant Manager, Roanoke River National Wildlife Refuge	Windsor, North Carolina
Sandy Edmondson, USFWS	Assistant Manager, Roanoke River National Wildlife Refuge	Windsor, North Carolina
Jean Richter, USFWS	Wildlife Biologist, Roanoke River National Wildlife Refuge	Windsor, North Carolina
Robert Glennon, USFWS	Natural Resource Planner, Ecosystem Planning Office	Edenton, North Carolina
David Brown, USFWS	Habitat Protection Biologist, Ecosystem Planning Office	Edenton, North Carolina

Table 26. Biological Review Team members.

NAME	TITLE	LOCATION
Bob Noffsinger, USFWS	Former Supervisory Wildlife Management Biologist, Wildlife and Habitat Management Office	Manteo, North Carolina
Frank Bowers, USFWS	Former Migratory Bird Coordinator, Southeast Regional Office	Atlanta, Georgia
Chuck Hunter, USFWS	Former Nongame Migratory Bird Coordinator, Southeast Regional Office	Atlanta, Georgia
Ronnie Smith, USFWS	Fisheries Biologist, Edenton Fisheries Assistance Office	Edenton, North Carolina
John Stanton, USFWS	Former Wildlife Biologist, Mattamuskeet National Wildlife Refuge	Swanquarter, North Carolina
Wendy Stanton, USFWS	Wildlife Biologist, Pocosin Lakes National Wildlife Refuge	Columbia, North Carolina
Dennis Stewart, USFWS	Wildlife Biologist, Alligator River National Wildlife Refuge	Manteo, North Carolina
Ralph Keel, USFWS	Former Wildlife Biologist, Great Dismal Swamp National Wildlife Refuge	Suffolk, Virginia
John Gallegos, USFWS	Wildlife Biologist, Back Bay National Wildlife Refuge	Virginia Beach, Virginia
David Allen	Nongame Biologist, North Carolina Wildlife Resources Commission	Trenton, North Carolina
Jeff Horton	Site Manager, The Nature Conservancy	Windsor, North Carolina
Fred Liverman	Forester (Retired), Champion Paper Company	Roanoke Rapids, North Carolina

Table 27. Expert contributors to the Roanoke River National Wildlife Refuge Comprehensive Conservation Plan and their area(s) of expertise.

Name	Field of Expertise
Bill Grabill, Former Refuge Supervisor U.S. Fish and Wildlife Service Southeast Regional Office Atlanta, Georgia	Refuge Management
Bruce Bell, Former NEPA Specialist U.S. Fish and Wildlife Service Southeast Regional Office Atlanta, Georgia	National Environmental Policy Act (NEPA) Requirements
Richard Kanaski, Regional Archaeologist U.S. Fish and Wildlife Service Southeast Regional Office Atlanta, Georgia	Cultural Resources
John Ann Shearer, Private Lands Biologist U.S. Fish and Wildlife Service Ecological Services Field Office Raleigh, North Carolina	Habitat Opportunities on Private Lands Waterfowl Management, Refuge Management
John Gagnon, Soil Scientist Natural Resources Conservation Service United States Department of Agriculture Edenton, North Carolina	Soils

On May 22 and 24, 2001, the planning team held public meetings to gain the insights of local citizens and their perceptions of the issues and concerns facing the refuge.

The issues and alternatives generated from these meetings, coupled with the input of the planning team, are contained in Chapters 1 and 3 of this environmental impact statement. The refuge staff presented the alternatives to the North Carolina Wildlife Resources Commission staff on March 20, 2002, and to the public on April 9 and 11, 2002, to get their input before selecting a preferred alternative.

I. Glossary

Adaptive Management	A process in which projects are implemented within a framework of scientifically driven experiments to test predictions and assumptions outlined within the comprehensive conservation plan. The analysis of the outcome of project implementation helps managers determine whether current management should continue as is or whether it should be modified to achieve desired conditions.
Alternative	A different means of accomplishing refuge purposes, goals, and objectives and contributing to the National Wildlife Refuge System. An alternative is a reasonable way to fix the identified problem or satisfy the stated need.
Approved Acquisition Boundary	A project boundary that the Director of the Fish and Wildlife Service approves upon completion of the detailed planning and environmental compliance process.
Biological Diversity	The variety of life and its processes, including the variety of living organisms, the genetic differences among them, and the communities and ecosystems in which they occur. The National Wildlife Refuge System focus is on indigenous species, biotic communities, and ecological processes.
Biological Integrity	The biotic composition, structure, and functioning at genetic, organism, and community levels comparable with historic conditions, including the natural biological processes that shape genomes, organisms, and communities.
Canopy	A layer of foliage, generally the uppermost layer, in a forest stand. It can be used to refer to mid- or understory vegetation in multilayered stands. Canopy closure is an estimate of the amount of overhead tree cover (also canopy cover).
Categorical Exclusion	A category of actions that do not individually or cumulatively have a significant effect on the human environment and have been found to have no such effect in procedures adopted by a federal agency, pursuant to the National Environmental Policy Act of 1969.
CFR	Code of Federal Regulations.

Compatible Use	A wildlife-dependent recreational use or any other use of a refuge that, in the sound professional judgment of the Refuge Manager, will not materially interfere with, or detract from, the fulfillment of the mission or the purposes of the refuge. A compatibility determination supports the selection of compatible uses and identifies stipulations or limits necessary to ensure compatibility.
Comprehensive Conservation Plan	A document that describes the desired future conditions of the refuge; provides long-range guidance and management direction for the Refuge Manager to accomplish the purposes, goals, and objectives of the refuge; and contributes to the mission of the National Wildlife Refuge System and meets relevant mandates.
Conservation Easement	A legal document that provides specific land-use rights to a secondary party. A perpetual conservation easement usually grants conservation and management rights to a party in perpetuity.
Cooperative Agreement	A simple habitat protection action in which no property rights are acquired. An agreement is usually long-term and can be modified by either party. Lands under a cooperative agreement do not necessarily become part of the National Wildlife Refuge System.
Corridor	A route that allows movement of individuals from one region or place to another.
Cover Type	The present vegetation of an area.
Cultural Resources	The remains of sites, structures, or objects used by people of the past.
Cypress and Tupelo Swamp	Found in low-lying areas–swales and open ponds–that hold water several months, if not all of the year. Large hollow trees are used as bear den sites.
Deciduous	Pertaining to perennial plants that are leafless for sometime during the year.
Ecological Succession	The orderly progression of an area through time in the absence of disturbance from one vegetative community to another.
Ecosystem	A dynamic and interrelated complex of plant and animal communities and their associated non-living environment.
Ecosystem Management	Management of natural resources using systemwide concepts to ensure that all plants and animals in ecosystems are maintained at viable levels in native habitats and basic ecosystem processes are perpetuated indefinitely.
Environmental Health	The composition, structure, and functioning of soil, water, air, and other abiotic features comparable with historic conditions, including the natural abiotic processes that shape the environment.

Even-Aged Forests	Forests that are composed of trees with a time span of less than 20 years between oldest and youngest individuals.
Endangered Species	A plant or animal species listed under the Endangered Species Act that is in danger of extinction throughout all or a significant portion of its range.
Endemic Species	Plants or animals that occur naturally in a certain region and whose distribution is relatively limited to a particular locality.
Environmental Assessment	A concise document, prepared in compliance with the National Environmental Policy Act of 1969, that briefly discusses the purpose and need for an action, alternatives to such action, and provides sufficient evidence and analysis of impacts to determine whether to prepare an environmental impact statement or finding of no significant impact.
Fauna	All the vertebrate or invertebrate animals of an area.
Federal Trust Species	All species where the Federal Government has primary jurisdiction including federally threatened or endangered species, migratory birds, anadromous fish, and certain marine mammals.
Fee-title	The acquisition of most or all of the rights to a tract of land. There is a total transfer of property rights with the formal conveyance of a title. While a fee title acquisition involves most rights to a property, certain rights may be reserved or not purchased, including water rights, mineral rights, or use reservation (the ability to continue using the land for a specified time period, or the reminder of the owner's life).
Finding of No Significant Impact	A document prepared in compliance with the National Environmental Policy Act of 1969, supported by an environmental assessment, that briefly presents why a federal action will have no significant effect on the human environment and for which an environmental impact statement, therefore, will not be prepared.
Floodplain Woods	Bottomland hardwood forests consist of hardwoods (old growth and mid-succession age timber) cypress tupelo stands found on low ridges that drain slowly and are subject to flooding. Species include overcup, willow, and water oaks; sweetgum; and green ash. Old growth stands typically exceed 120 years of age.
Fragmentation	The process of reducing the size and connectivity of habitat patches. The disruption of extensive habitats into isolated and small patches.
Goal	Descriptive, open-ended, and often broad statements of desired future conditions that convey a purpose but does not define measurable units.

Geographic Information System	A computer system capable of storing and manipulating spatial data.
Ground Story (flora)	Vascular plants less than one meter in height, excluding tree seedlings.
Herbaceous Wetland	Annually or seasonally inundated with vegetation consisting primarily of grasses, sedges, rushes, and cattail.
Historic Conditions	These are the composition, structure, and functioning of ecosystems resulting from natural processes that we believe, based on sound professional judgment, were present prior to substantial human related changes to the landscape.
Habitat	The place where an organism lives. The existing environmental conditions required by an organism for survival and reproduction.
Indicator Species	A species of plant or animal that is assumed to be sensitive to habitat changes and represents the needs of a larger group of species.
In-holding	Privately owned land inside the boundary of a national wildlife refuge.
Issue	Any unsettled matter that requires a management decision.
Managed Flows	River flows that result in significant deviations from the natural hydrograph due to hydro electric power and flood control projects located upstream of refuge lands.
Migratory	The seasonal movement from one area to another and back.
Monitoring	The process of collecting information to track changes of selected parameters over time.
National Environmental Policy Act	Requires all agencies, including the Service, to examine the environmental impacts of their actions, incorporate environmental information, and use public participation in the planning and implementation of all actions. Federal agencies must integrate this Act with other planning requirements, and prepare appropriate policy documents to facilitate better environmental decision making.
National Wildlife Refuge	A designated area of land, water, or an interest in land or water within the National Wildlife Refuge System.
National Wildlife Refuge System	Various categories of areas administered by the Secretary of the Interior for the conservation of fish and wildlife, including species threatened with extinction, all lands, waters, and interests therein administered by the Secretary as wildlife refuges, wildlife ranges, game ranges, wildlife management areas, or waterfowl production areas.
Native Species	Species that normally live and thrive in a particular ecosystem.

Neotropical Migratory Bird	A bird species that breeds north of the United States/Mexican border and winters primarily south of that border.
Objective	An objective is a concise quantitative (where possible) target statement of what will be achieved. Objectives are derived from goals and provide the basis for determining management strategies. Objectives should be attainable and time-specific.
Planning Area	A planning area may include lands outside existing planning unit boundaries that are being studied for inclusion in the unit and/or partnership planning efforts. It may also include watersheds or ecosystems that affect the planning area.
Planning Team	A planning team prepares the Comprehensive Conservation Plan. Planning teams are interdisciplinary in membership and function. A team generally consists of the a planning team leader; refuge manager and staff biologists; staff specialists or other representatives of Service programs, ecosystems or regional offices; and state partnering wildlife agencies as appropriate.
Preferred Alternative	This is the alternative determined by the decision maker to best achieve the refuge purpose, vision, and goals; contributes to the refuge system mission, addresses the significant issues; and is consistent with principles of sound fish and wildlife management.
Purpose of the Refuge	The purpose of the refuge is specified in or derived from the law, proclamation, Executive Order, agreement, public land order, donation document, or administrative memorandum establishing, authorizing, or expanding a refuge and refuge unit.
Refuge Operating Needs System	This is a national database that contains the unfunded operational needs of each refuge. Projects included are those required to implement approved plans and meet goals, objectives, and legal mandates.
Refuge Purposes	The purposes specified in or derived from the law, proclamation, executive order, agreement, public land order, donation document, or administrative memorandum establishing, authorizing, or expanding a refuge, refuge unit, or refuge subunit.
Seral Forest	A forest in the mature stage of development, usually dominated by large, old trees.
Sink	A habitat in which local mortality exceeds local reproductive success for a given species.
Sink Population	A population in a low-quality habitat in which birth rate is generally less than the death rate and population density is maintained by immigrants from source populations.

Source	A habitat in which local reproductive success exceeds local mortality for a given species.
Source Population	A population in a high quality habitat in which its birth rate greatly exceeds death rate and the excess individuals leave as migrants.
Step-down Management Plans	Step-down management plans provide the details necessary to implement management strategies and projects identified in the Comprehensive Conservation Plan.
Strategy	A specific action, tool, or technique or combination of actions, tools, and techniques used to meet unit objectives.
Stream Classification	WSIII – waters protecting a drinking water supply which are generally in a low to moderately developed watershed. C – freshwaters protected for secondary recreation, fishing, and aquatic life, including propagation, survival, and wildlife. CSw – freshwaters with low velocities protected for secondary recreation, fishing, and aquatic life, including propagation, survival, and wildlife.
Threatened Species	Species listed under the Endangered Species Act that are likely to become endangered within the foreseeable future throughout all or a significant portion of their range.
Trust Species	Species for which the U.S. Fish and Wildlife Service has primary responsibility, including most federally listed threatened and endangered species, anadromous fish once they enter the inland coastal waterways, migratory birds, and certain marine mammals.
Understory	Any vegetation with canopy below or closer to the ground than canopies of other plants.
Wildlife Corridor	A landscape feature that facilitates the biologically effective transport of animals between larger patches of habitat dedicated to conservation functions. Such corridors may facilitate several kinds of traffic, including frequent foraging movement, seasonal migration, or the once in a lifetime dispersal of juvenile animals. These are transition habitats and need not contain all habitat elements required by migrants for long-term survival or reproduction.
Wildlife-dependent Recreation	A use of a refuge involving hunting, fishing, wildlife observation, wildlife photography, environmental education, and interpretation. The National Wildlife Refuge System Improvement Act of 1997 specifies that these are the six priority general public uses of the system.

II. References and Literature Cited

Albemarle Region Chamber of Commerce. 2002. Historic Jackson.

Barick, F. B., and T. S. Critcher. 1975. *Wildlife and land use planning with particular reference to coastal counties.* North Carolina Wildlife Resources Commission, Raleigh, NC. 168 pp.

Beasley, C. A., and J. E. Hightower. 2000. Effects of a low-head dam on the distribution and characteristics of spawning habitat used by striped bass and American shad. *Transactions of the American Fisheries Society* 129:1372-1386.

Bellrose, F. C. 1976. *Ducks, geese, and swans of North America.* Stackpole Books, Harrisburg, PA. 544 pp.

Boon, P., J., P. Calow and G. E. Petts. 1992. *River conservation and management.* John Wiley and Sons, New York. 470 pp.

Bryan, C. F., and J. V. Connor. 1981. Use of bottomland hardwood zones by fishes. Pages 249-253 *in* J. R. Clark and J. Benforado, eds., *Wetlands of bottomland hardwood forests.* Elsevier Scientific Publishing Company, New York, NY. 401 pp.

Carnes, W. C. 1965. *Survey and classification of the Roanoke River watershed, North Carolina.* N.C. Wildlife Resources Commission, Raleigh. Final Report, Federal Aid in Fish Restoration, Project F-14-R, Job I-Q. 23 pp. + Appendices.

Collier, M., R. H. Web and J. C. Schmidt. 1996. *Dams and rivers: primer on the downstream effects of dams.* United States Geological Survey, Denver, Colorado.

Cowardin, L., et al. 1979. *Classification of wetlands and deepwater habitats of the United States.* U.S. Fish and Wildlife Service, Office of Biological Services FWS/OBS-79/31. 131 pp.

Drobney, R. D. 1982. Body weight and composition changes and adaptations for breeding in wood ducks. *Condor* 84:300-305.

Drobney, R. D. 1984. Effect of diet on visceral morphology of breeding wood ducks. *The Auk* 101:93-98.

Eubanks, Ted, Paul Kerlinger and R. H. Payne. 1993. High Island, Texas: a case study in avitourism. *Birding* 25(6):415-420).

Eubanks, Ted, and John Stoll. 1999. *Avitourism in Texas: two studies of birders in Texas and their potential support for the proposed World Birding Center.* Texas Parks and Wildlife, Contract No. 44467.

Fish, F. 1968. *A catalog of the inland fishing water in North Carolina.* N.C. Wildlife Resources Commission, Raleigh. Final Report, Federal Aid in Fish Restoration Project, F-14-R. 312 pp.

Fontaine, T. D. and S. M. Bartell. 1983. *Dynamics of lotic ecosystems.* Ann Arbor Science Publishers, Ann Arbor, Michigan.

Frayer, W. E., T. J. Monahan, D. C. Bowen and F. A. Graybill. 1983. *Status and trends of wetlands and deepwater habitats in the conterminous United States: 1950s to 1970s.* U.S. Fish and Wildlife Service, Washington, DC. 32 pp.

Fredrickson, L. H. 1980. Management of lowland hardwood wetlands for wildlife: problems and potential. *Transactions of the 45th North American Wildlife and Natural Resources Conference*, pages 376-386.

Fredrickson, L. H. and M. E. Heitmeyer. 1988. Waterfowl Use of Forested Wetlands of the Southern United States: An Overview. Pages 307-323 *in* M.W. Weller, ed., *Waterfowl in winter.* University of Minnesota Press, Minneapolis, Minnesota.

Hall, S. 1999. *Inventory of the macro-lepidoptera of the Devil's Gut Preserve.* N.C. Natural Heritage Program, Division of Parks and Recreation. 1615 MSC. Raleigh, NC.110 pg.

Hamel, P. B. 1992. *The land manager's guide to the birds of the south.* The Nature Conservancy and the United States Department of Agriculture Forest Service. Atlanta, Georgia.

Hassler, W. H., N. L. Hill and J. T. Brown. 1981. *The status and abundance of striped bass, Morone saxatilis, in the Roanoke River and Albemarle Sound, North Carolina, 1966-1980.* N.C. Division of Marine Fisheries, Morehead City. Special Scientific Report No. 38, Project AFS-14. 156 pp.

Hefner, J. H. and J. D. Brown. 1984. Wetland trends in the southeastern United States. *Wetlands* 4:1-11.

Hunt, C. E. 1988. *Down by the river: the impact of federal water projects and policies on biological diversity.* Island Press, Washington, D.C. 266 pp.

Hunter, W. C., D. N. Pashley and R. E .F. Escano. 1992. Neotropical migratory landbird species and their habitats of special concern within the Southeast region. Pages 159-169 *in* D.M. Finch and P. W. Stangel, eds., *Status and management of neotropical migratory birds.* U.S. Forest Service, General Technical Report RM-229, Fort Collins, Colorado.

Hunter, W. C., L. H. Peoples and J. A. Collazo. 2001. South Atlantic Coastal Plain Partners in Flight Bird Conservation Plan. Partners in Flight, www.partnersinflight.org.

Jackson, Donald C., and G. Marmulla 1999. *The influence of dams on river fisheries.* Special Consultant's Report to the United Nations Food and Agriculture Organization, Mississippi State University.

Johnson, H. B., S. E. Winslow, D. W. Crocker, B. J. Hollard, Jr., J. W. Gillikin and D. L. Taylor. 1981. *Biology and management of mid-Atlantic anadromous fishes under extended jurisdiction - Part I: North Carolina.* N.C. Division of Marine Fisheries, Morehead City. Special Scientific Report No. 36, Project AFCS-9. 191 pp.

Jordan, W. P. 1954. *James and Henry Bertie: namesakes of the county.* The Chronicle of the Bertie County Historical Association, vol. 2, no. 2, illus.

Kerlinger, P. 1994. *The economic impact of birding ecotourism on communities surrounding eight national wildlife refuges.* Washington, DC: National Fish and Wildlife Association.

Kerlinger, P. 1999. Birding Tourism and Dauphin Island.

Lee, E. Lawrence. 1963. *Indian wars in North Carolina, 1663-1763.* Carolina Tercentenary Commission, pp. 3-13 and 46-50.

Lee, R. 1993. Personal Communication. North Carolina Bottomland Hardwood Cooperative.

LeGrand, H. 1994. Personal Communication. North Carolina National Heritage Program, Raleigh, NC.

Ligon, F. K., W. E. Dietrich, and W. J. Trush. 1995. Downstream ecological effects of dams. *BioScience* 45:183-192.

Loesch, C. R., D. J. Twedt, K. Tripp, W. C. Hunter, and M. S. Woodrey. 1999. Development of management objectives for waterfowl and shorebirds in the Mississippi Alluvial Valley. *In* R. Bonney, D. N. Pashley, R. J. Cooper, and L. Niles, eds., *Strategies for Bird Conservation: The Partners in Flight Planning Process.* Cornell University, Cornell Lab of Ornithology.

Lynch, J. M., and J. Crawford. 1980. *Reconnaissance survey on the lower Roanoke River floodplain, N.C., with additional notes on the Chowan River floodplain.* Report submitted to The Nature Conservancy and the North Carolina Natural Heritage Program, Raleigh, NC. 55 pp.

Lynch, J. M. 1981. *Roanoke River preserve design project.* Report to North Carolina Natural Heritage Program and North Carolina Nature Conservancy, Raleigh, NC. 246 pp.

Maki, T. E., A. J. Weber, D. W. Hazel, S. C. Hunter, B. T. Hyberg, D. M. Flinchum, J. P. Lollois, J. B Rongstad and J. D. Gregory. 1980. *Effects of stream channelization on bottomland and swamp forest ecosystems.* Report No.147. Water Resources Research Institute of the University of North Carolina, Raleigh, NC. 135 pp.

McClanahan, R. D. 1979. *Investigation into potentially detrimental impacts of high water upon wild turkey populations along the Roanoke River, Bertie and Martin Counties.* Field Report, N.C. Wildlife Resources Commission. Raleigh, NC. 3 pp.

Mérona, B. D., G. Mendes dos Santos, and G. Almeida. 2001. Short-term effects of Tucurui Dam (Amasonia, Brazil) on the trophic organization of fish communities. *Environmental Biology of Fishes* 60:375-392.

Mitsch, W. J., and J. G. Gosselink. 1993. *Wetlands.* Second Edition. Van Nostrand Reinhold, New York, New York. 722 pp.

Moore, L. 1993. *Population dynamics and habitat requirements of wild turkeys in the Ouachita Mountain range.* Annual Progress Report, University of Arkansas Cooperative Wildlife and Fish Unit, Fayetteville, Arkansas. 4 pp.

Mueller, A. J., D. J. Twedt, and C. R. Loesch. 1999. Development of Management Objectives for breeding birds in the Mississippi Alluvial Valley. *In* R. Bonney, D. N. Pashley, R. J. Cooper, and L. Niles, eds., *Strategies for Bird Conservation: The Partners in Flight Planning Process.* Cornell University, Cornell Lab of Ornithology.

National Audubon Society. 1998. Campaign on HR 3267.

New Jersey Department of Environmental Protection. 2000. Wildlife-associated Recreation on the New Jersey Delaware Bayshore.

North Carolina Department of Economic Security. 1999. Largest Employers by County.

North Carolina Department of Economic Security. 2002. Unemployment Rates by County.

North Carolina Division of Parks and Recreation. 2001. North Carolina Coastal Plain Paddle Trails Guide.

North Carolina Natural Heritage Program. 1988. Letter of comment on draft environmental assessment for Roanoke River National Wildlife Refuge. Division of Parks and Recreation, North Carolina Department of Natural Resources and Community Development, Raleigh, NC. 2 pp.

North Carolina Office of Archives and History. 2002. Historic Halifax.

North Carolina Use-Value Advisory Board. 2003. 2004 Use-value Manual for Agricultural, Horticultural and Forestland. Raleigh, NC. 72 pp.

North Carolina Wildlife Resources Commission. Unpublished data.

Northampton County Chamber of Commerce. 2002a. County profile.

Northampton County Chamber of Commerce. 2002b. Historical Overview.

Occaneechi Band of the Saponi Nation. 2002. A Brief History of the Occaneechi Band of the Saponi Nation.

Osborne, J. S. 1981. *Population dynamics of white-tailed deer in northeastern North Carolina.* Report No. W-57-II-B4, N.C. Wildlife Resources Commission, Raleigh, NC. 27+ pp.

Pascal, Herbert R., Jr. 1958. *The Tuscarora in Bertie.* The Chronicle of the Bertie City Historical Association, vol.6, no.1.

Peters, D., et al. 1998. Utilization of Flooded Swamp Habitat on the Lower Roanoke River by Anadromous Clupeids. Unpublished. National Marine Fisheries Service, Beaufort, NC.

Petts, G. E. 1984. *Impounded rivers: perspectives for ecological management.* John Wiley and Sons, New York, NY. 326 pp.

Poff, N. L., and D. D. Hart. 2002. How dams vary and why it matters for the emerging science of dam removal. *BioScience* 52:659-668.

Powell, William S. 1975. *Human settlement and profile history, North Carolina atlas: portrait of a changing southern state.* University of North Carolina, p. 14, illus.

Pringle, C. M., M. C. Freeman, and B. J. Freeman. 2000. Regional effects of hydrologic alterations on riverine macrobiota in the new world: tropical-temperate comparisons. *BioScience* 50:807-823.

Reincke, K. J., and C. K. Baxter. 1996. Waterfowl habitat management in the Mississippi alluvial valley. Pages 159-167 *in* J. T. Ratti, ed., *Seventh International Waterfowl Symposium.*

Riggs, S. R., and D. K. Belknap. 1988. Upper Cenozoic processes and environments of continental margin sedimentation: eastern United States. Pages 131-176 *in* R. E. Sheridan and J. A. Graw, eds., *The Geology of North America, Volumes 1-2, the Atlantic Continental Margin.* U.S. Geological Society of America.

Riggs, S. R., L. L. York, J. F. Wehmiller and S. W. Snyder. 1992. *Depositional patterns resulting from high frequency quaternary sea-level fluctuations in northeastern North Carolina.* Quaternary Coasts of the United States: Marine and Lacustrine Systems. SEPM Special Publication No. 40, p. 141-153.

Roanoke Valley Chamber of Commerce. 2002. Location.

Ruane, R. J., C. E. Bohac, W. M. Seawell and R.M. Shane. 1986. Improving the downstream environment by reservoir release modifications. Pages 270-277 *in* G. E. Hall and M. J. Van Den Avyle, eds., *Reservoir fisheries management strategies for the 80's.* Reservoir Committee, Southern Division American Fisheries Society, Bethesda, MD.

Rulifson, R. A. 1992. Personal Communication. East Carolina University. Greenville, NC.

Rulifson, R. A., J. E. Cooper, D. W. Stanley, M. E. Shepherd, S. F. Wood and D. A. Daniel. 1992a. *Food and feeding of young striped bass in Roanoke River and western Albemarle Sound, North Carolina, 1990-1991.* N.C. Wildlife Resources Commission, Raleigh, Completion Report for Project F-27.

Rulifson, R. A., J. E. Cooper, D. W. Stanley, M. E. Shepherd, S. F. Wood and D. A. Daniel. 1992b. *Food and feeding of young striped bass in Roanoke River and western Albemarle Sound, North Carolina, 1990-1991.* N.C. Wildlife Resources Commission, Raleigh, and North Carolina Striped Bass Study Management Board, Completion Report for Projects 90-2 and 91-2. 62 pp.

Rundle, W. D. and M. W. Sayre. 1983. Feeding ecology of migrant soras in southeastern Missouri. *Journal of Wildlife Management* 47:1153-1159.

Schafale, M. P., and A. S. Weakely. 1990. *Classification of the natural communities of North Carolina.* Third Approximation. N.C. Natural Heritage Program, Raleigh, NC. 325 pp.

Shea, D., C. S. Hofeltet, D. R. Luellen, A. Huysman, P. R. Lazaro, R. Zarzecki, and J. R. Kelly. 2001. *Chemical contamination at national wildlife refuges in the lower Mississippi River ecosystem.* Report by North Carolina State University to the U.S. Fish and Wildlife Service, Atlanta, GA. 40 pp.

Teskey, R. O., and T.M. Hinckley. 1977. *Impact of water level changes on woody riparian and wetland communities.* Volume II: Southern Forest Region. USFWS, Biological Services Program. FWS/OBS-77/59. 46 pp.

Tetterton B., and G. Tetterton. 1998. North Carolina County Fact Book, Vols. I and II. Broadfoot's of Wendell, Wendell, NC, 1998.

Tinkle, D. W. 1959. Observations of reptiles and amphibians in a Louisiana swamp. *American Midland Naturalist* 62(1): 189-205.

Trush, W. J., S. M. McBain and L. B. Leopold. 2000. Attributes of an alluvial river and their relation to water policy and management. Proceedings of the National Academy of Sciences 97(22):11858-11863.

U. S. Department of Agriculture. 1997. Census of Agriculture, North Carolina, 1997. Washington, D.C.: U.S. Department of Agriculture.

U. S. Department of Agriculture, Forest Service. 1991. Forest Statistics for North Carolina Counties, 1991. Washington, D.C.: U.S. Government Printing Office.

U. S. Department of Agriculture, Forest Service. 2003. Forest Statistics for the Northern Coastal Plain of North Carolina, 2000. Washington, D.C.: U.S. Government Printing Office.

U. S. Department of Agriculture, Soil Conservation Service. 1925. Soil Survey of Northampton County, North Carolina.

U. S. Department of Agriculture, Soil Conservation Service. 1990. Soil Survey of Bertie County, North Carolina.

U. S. Department of Agriculture, Soil Conservation Service. 1994. Soil Survey of Northampton County, North Carolina.

U. S. Department of Agriculture, Soil Conservation Service. 1981. Soil Survey of Washington County, North Carolina.

U. S. Department of Agriculture, Soil Conservation Service. 1985. Hydric soils of the State of North Carolina, 1985. U.S. Department of Agriculture, Soil Conservation Service in cooperation with the National Technical Committee for Hydric Soils. Washington, DC.

U. S. Department of Agriculture, Soil Conservation Service. 1989. Soil Survey of Martin County, North Carolina.

U. S. Department of Commerce, Bureau of the Census. 2000. U.S.A. Counties 2000, General Profile, Bertie County, North Carolina. Washington, D.C. U.S. Government Printing Office.

U. S. Department of Commerce, Bureau of the Census. 2000. U.S.A. Counties 2000, General Profile, Halifax County, North Carolina. Washington, D.C. U.S. Government Printing Office.

U. S. Department of Commerce, Bureau of the Census. 2000. U.S.A. Counties 2000, General Profile, Martin County, North Carolina. Washington, D.C. U.S. Government Printing Office.

U. S. Department of Commerce, Bureau of the Census. 2000. U.S.A. Counties 1996, General Profile, Northampton County, North Carolina. Washington, D.C. U.S. Government Printing Office.

U. S. Department of Commerce, Bureau of the Census. 2000. U.S.A. Counties 1996, General Profile, Washington County, North Carolina. Washington, D.C. U.S. Government Printing Office.

U. S. Department of Commerce, Bureau of the Census. 2000. County Business Patterns, Bertie County, North Carolina. Washington, D.C.: U.S. Government Printing Office.

U. S. Department of Commerce, Bureau of the Census. 2000. County Business Patterns, Halifax County, North Carolina. Washington, D.C.: U.S. Government Printing Office.

U. S. Department of Commerce, Bureau of the Census. 2000. County Business Patterns, Martin County, North Carolina. Washington, D.C.: U.S. Government Printing Office.

U. S. Department of Commerce, Bureau of the Census. 2000. County Business Patterns, Northampton County, North Carolina. Washington, D.C.: U.S. Government Printing Office.

U. S. Department of Commerce, Bureau of the Census. 2000. County Business Patterns, Washington County, North Carolina. Washington, D.C.: U.S. Government Printing Office.

U. S. Department of Commerce, Bureau of the Census, Small Area Income and Poverty Estimates Program. 2000. Model-based Income and Poverty Estimates for Bertie County, North Carolina. Washington, D.C.: U.S. Government Printing Office.

U. S. Department of Commerce, Bureau of the Census, Small Area Income and Poverty Estimates Program. 2000. Model-based Income and Poverty Estimates for Halifax County, North Carolina. Washington, D.C.: U.S. Government Printing Office.

U. S. Department of Commerce, Bureau of the Census, Small Area Income and Poverty Estimates Program. 2000. Model-based Income and Poverty Estimates for Martin County, North Carolina. Washington, D.C.: U.S. Government Printing Office.

U. S. Department of Commerce, Bureau of the Census, Small Area Income and Poverty Estimates Program. 2000. Model-based Income and Poverty Estimates for Northampton County, North Carolina. Washington, D.C.: U.S. Government Printing Office.

U. S. Department of Commerce, Bureau of the Census, Small Area Income and Poverty Estimates Program. 2000. Model-based Income and Poverty Estimates for Washington County, North Carolina. Washington, D.C.: U.S. Government Printing Office.

U. S. Department of Commerce, Bureau of the Census, Small Area Income and Poverty Estimates Program. 2000. Model-based Income and Poverty Estimates for Bertie County, North Carolina. Washington, D.C.: U.S. Government Printing Office.

U.S. Environmental Protection Agency. 1997. Nature-based Tourism.

U.S. Fish and Wildlife Service. 1981. *Significant wildlife resource areas of North Carolina.* U.S. Fish and Wildlife Service, Asheville Office, Asheville, NC. 139 pp.

U.S. Fish and Wildlife Service. 1983. *Distribution of waterfowl species harvested in states and counties during 1971-1980 hunting seasons.* U.S. Fish and Wildlife Service, Special Scientific Report No. 254. Washington, DC. 114 pp.

U.S. Fish and Wildlife Service. 1985. *A biological proposal for acquisition: Roanoke River bottomlands, North Carolina.* U.S. Fish and Wildlife Service, Atlanta, GA. 10 pp.

U.S. Fish and Wildlife Service. 1988. *Category plan for preservation of wintering black duck habitat, Atlantic Coast, Priority Category 20.* U.S. Fish and Wildlife Service, Newton Corner, MA. 25 pp.

U. S. Fish and Wildlife Service. 1996. National Survey of Fishing, Hunting and Wildlife-associated Recreation. Washington, DC.

U.S. Fish and Wildlife Service. 2001. National Survey of Fishing, Hunting, and Wildlife-associated Recreation - North Carolina. Washington, DC.

Vaughn, C. C. and C. M. Taylor. 1999. Impoundments and the decline of freshwater mussels: a case study of an extinction gradient. *Conservation Biology* 13: 912–920.

Vogelsang, Hans. 2001. Assessing the Economic Impact of Ecotourism Developments on the Albemarle/Pamlico Region.

Ward, L. W., R. H. Bailey and J. G. Carter. 1991. Chapter 16, Pliocene and Early Pleistocene stratigraphy, depositional history, and molluscan paleobiography of the Coastal Plain. Pages 79-92 *in* J. W. Horton, Jr. and V. Zullo, eds., *The geology of the Carolinas.* Carolina Geological Society, 50th Anniversary Volume. Knoxville, Tennessee: The University of Tennessee Press.

Wharton, C. H., V. W. Lambou, J. Newsom, P. V. Winger, L. L. Gaddy, and R. Mancke. 1981. The fauna of bottomland hardwoods in southeastern states. Pages 87-160 *in* J. R. Clark and J. Benforado, eds., *Wetlands of bottomland hardwood forests.* Elsevier Scientific Publishing Company, New York, NY. 401 pp.

Wharton, C. H., W. M. Kitchens, E. C. Pendleton and T. W. Sipe. 1982. *The ecology of bottomland hardwood swamps of the southeast: a community profile.* U.S. Fish and Wildlife Service, Biological Services Program, Washington, DC. FWS/OBS-81/37. 133 pp.

III. Relevant Legal Mandates

NATIONAL WILDLIFE REFUGE SYSTEM AUTHORITIES

The mission of the Fish and Wildlife Service is to conserve, protect, and enhance the Nation's fish and wildlife and their habitats for the continuing benefit of the American people. The Service is the primary federal agency responsible for migratory birds, endangered plants and animals, certain marine mammals, and anadromous fish. This responsibility to conserve our Nation's fish and wildlife resources is shared with other federal agencies and state and tribal governments.

As part of this responsibility, the Service manages the National Wildlife Refuge System. This system is the only nationwide system of federal land managed and protected for wildlife and their habitats. The mission of the National Wildlife Refuge System is to administer a national network of lands and waters for the conservation, management, and where appropriate, restoration of the fish, wildlife, and plant resources and their habitats within the United States for the benefit of present and future generations of Americans.

Roanoke River National Wildlife Refuge is managed as part of this system in accordance with the National Wildlife Refuge System Administration Act of 1966, as amended by the National Wildlife Refuge System Improvement Act of 1997, the Refuge Recreation Act of 1962, Executive Order 12996 (Management and General Public Use of the National Wildlife Refuge System), and other relevant legislation, Executive Orders, regulations, and policies.

KEY LEGISLATION/POLICIES FOR PLAN IMPLEMENTATION

The Roanoke River National Wildlife Refuge Draft Comprehensive Conservation Plan describes and illustrates management area projects with standards and guidelines for future decision-making and may be adjusted through monitoring and evaluation, as well as amendment and revision. The plan approval establishes conservation and land protection goals, objectives, and specific strategies for the refuge and its expansion. Compatible recreation uses specific to the refuge have been identified and approved by the Refuge Manager. This plan provides for systematic stepping down from the overall direction as outlined when making project or activity level decisions. This level involves site-specific analysis (e.g., Forest Habitat Management Plan) to meet National Environmental Policy Act requirements for decision-making.

Antiquities Act (1906): Authorizes the scientific investigation of antiquities on federal land and provides penalties for unauthorized removal of objects taken or collected without a permit.

Migratory Bird Treaty Act (1918): Designates the protection of migratory birds as a federal responsibility. This Act enables the setting of seasons, and other regulations including the closing of areas, federal or non-federal, to the hunting of migratory birds.

Migratory Bird Conservation Act (1929): Establishes procedures for acquisition by purchase, rental, or gift of areas approved by the Migratory Bird Conservation Commission.

Migratory Bird Hunting and Conservation Stamp Act (1934): Authorized the opening of part of a refuge to waterfowl hunting.

Fish and Wildlife Act (1956): Established a comprehensive national fish and wildlife policy and broadened the authority for acquisition and development of refuges.

Fish and Wildlife Coordination Act (1958): Allows the Fish and Wildlife Service to enter into agreements with private landowners for wildlife management purposes.

Refuge Recreation Act (1962): Allows the use of refuges for recreation when such uses are compatible with the refuge's primary purposes and when sufficient funds are available to manage the uses.

Land and Water Conservation Fund Act (1965): Uses the receipts from the sale of surplus federal land, outer continental shelf oil and gas sales, and other sources for land acquisition under several authorities.

National Wildlife Refuge System Administration Act of 1966 as amended by the National Wildlife Refuge System Improvement Act of 1997, 16 U.S.C. 668dd-668ee (Refuge Administration Act): Defines the National Wildlife Refuge System and authorizes the Secretary of the Interior to permit any use of a refuge provided such use is compatible with the major purposes for which the refuge was established. The Refuge Improvement Act clearly defines a unifying mission for the refuge system; establishes the legitimacy and appropriateness of the six priority public uses (hunting, fishing, wildlife observation, wildlife photography and environmental education and interpretation); establishes a formal process for determining compatibility; established the responsibilities of the Secretary of the Interior for managing and protecting the System; and requires a comprehensive conservation plan for each refuge by the year 2012. The Refuge Improvement Act amended portions of the Refuge Recreation Act and National Wildlife Refuge System Administration Act of 1966.

Architectural Barriers Act (1968): Requires federally owned, leased, or funded buildings and facilities to be accessible to persons with disabilities.

National Environmental Policy Act (1969): Requires the disclosure of the environmental impacts of any major federal action significantly affecting the quality of the human environment.

Rehabilitation Act (1973): Requires that programmatic and physical accessibility be made available in any facility funded by the Federal Government, ensuring that anyone can participate in any program.

Clean Water Act (1977): Requires consultation with the U.S. Army Corps of Engineers for major wetland modifications.

Executive Order 11988 (1977): Each federal agency shall provide leadership and take action to reduce the risk of flood loss and minimize the impact of floods on human safety, and preserve the natural and beneficial values served by the floodplain.

Emergency Wetlands Resources Act (1986): The purpose of the Act is "To promote the conservation of migratory waterfowl and to offset or prevent the serious loss of wetlands by the acquisition of wetlands and other essential habitat, and for other purposes."

Federal Noxious Weed Act (1990): Requires the use of integrated management systems to control or contain undesirable plant species; and an interdisciplinary approach with the cooperation of other federal and state agencies.

Americans with Disabilities Act (1992): Prohibits discrimination in public accommodations and services.

Executive Order 12996 Management and General Public Use of the National Wildlife Refuge System (1996): Defines the mission, purpose, and priority public uses of the National Wildlife Refuge System. It also presents four principles to guide management of the system.

Executive Order 13007 Indian Sacred Sites (1996): Directs federal land management agencies to accommodate access to and ceremonial use of Indian sacred sites by Indian religious practitioners, avoid adversely affecting the physical integrity of such sacred sites, and where appropriate, maintain the confidentiality of sacred sites.

Emergency Wetland Resources Act of 1986: This Act authorized the purchase of wetlands from Land and Water Conservation Fund moneys, removing a prior prohibition on such acquisitions. The Act also requires the Secretary of the Interior to establish a National Wetlands Priority Conservation Plan, requires the states to include wetlands in their comprehensive outdoor recreation plans, and transfers to the Migratory Bird Conservation Fund an amount equal to import duties on arms and ammunition.

Endangered Species Act of 1973 (16 U.S.C. 1531-1544, 87 Stat. 884), as amended: Public Law 93-205, approved December 28, 1973, repealed the Endangered Species Conservation Act of December 5, 1969 (P.L. 91-135, 83 Stat. 275). The 1969 Act amended the Endangered Species Preservation Act of October 15, 1966 (P.L. 89-669, 80 Stat. 926). The 1973 Endangered Species Act provided for the conservation of ecosystems upon which threatened and endangered species of fish, wildlife, and plants depend, both through federal action and by encouraging the establishment of state programs. The Act authorizes the determination and listing of species as threatened and endangered; prohibits unauthorized taking, possession, sale, and transport of endangered species; provides authority to acquire land for the conservation of listed species, using land and water conservation funds; authorizes establishment of cooperative agreements and grants-in-aid to states that establish and maintain active and adequate programs for threatened and endangered wildlife and plants; authorizes the assessment of civil and criminal penalties for violating the Act or regulations; and authorizes the payment of rewards to anyone furnishing information leading to arrest and conviction of anyone violating the Act and any regulation issued thereunder.

Environmental Education Act of 1990(20 USC 5501-5510; 104 Stat. 3325): Public Law 101-619, signed November 16, 1990, established the Office of Environmental Education within the Environmental Protection Agency to develop and administer a federal environmental education program. Responsibilities of the Office include developing and supporting programs to improve understanding of the natural and developed environment, and the relationships between humans and their environment; supporting the dissemination of educational materials; developing and supporting training programs and environmental education seminars; managing a federal grant program; and administering an environmental internship and fellowship program. The Office is required to develop and support environmental programs in consultation with other federal natural resource management agencies, including the Fish and Wildlife Service.

Executive Order 11988, Flood Plain Management: The purpose of this Executive Order, signed May 24, 1977, is to prevent federal agencies from contributing to the "adverse impacts associated with occupancy and modification of floodplains" and the "direct or indirect support of flood plain development." In the course of fulfilling their respective authorities, federal agencies "shall take action to reduce the risk of flood loss, to minimize the impact of floods on human safety, health and welfare, and to restore and preserve the natural and beneficial values served by floodplains."

Fish and Wildlife Improvement Act of 1978: This Act was passed to improve the administration of fish and wildlife programs and amends several earlier laws, including the Refuge Recreation Act, the National Wildlife Refuge System Administration Act, and the Fish and Wildlife Act of 1956. It authorizes the Secretary of the Interior to accept gifts and bequests of real and personal property on behalf of the United States. It also authorizes the use of volunteers on Service projects and appropriations to carry out volunteer programs.

Antiquities Act (16 USC 431 - 433)--The Act of June 8, 1906, (34 Stat. 225): This Act authorizes the President of the United States to designate as National Monuments objects or areas of historic or scientific interests on lands owned or controlled by the United States. The Act required that a permit be obtained for examination of ruins, excavation of archaeological sites and the gathering of objects of antiquity on lands under the jurisdiction of the Secretaries of Interior, Agriculture, and Army, and provided penalties for violations.

Archaeological Resources Protection Act (16 U.S.C. 470aa - 47011): Public Law 96-95, approved October 31, 1979, (93 Stat. 721): This Act largely supplanted the resource protection provisions of the Antiquities Act for archaeological items. It established detailed requirements for issuance of permits for any excavation for, or removal of, archaeological resources from federal and Indian lands. It also established civil and criminal penalties for the unauthorized excavation, removal, or damage of any such resources; for any trafficking in such resources removed from federal and Indian lands in violation of any provision of federal law; and for interstate and foreign commerce in such resources acquired, transported, or received in violation of any state or local law.

Public Law 100-588, approved November 3, 1988, (102 Stat. 2983) lowered the threshold value of artifacts triggering the felony provisions of the Act from $5,000 to $500, made attempting to commit an action prohibited by the Act a violation, and required the land managing agencies to establish public awareness programs regarding the value of archaeological resources to the nation.

Archaeological and Historic Preservation Act (16 U.S.C. 469-469c): Public Law 86-523, approved June 27, 1960, (74 Stat. 220), and amended by Public Law 93-291, approved May 24, 1974, (88 Stat. 174): This Act directed federal agencies to notify the Secretary of the Interior whenever a federal, federally assisted, or licensed or permitted project may cause loss or destruction of significant scientific, prehistoric or archaeological data. The Act authorized use of appropriated, donated, and/or transferred funds for the recovery, protection, and preservation of such data.

Historic Sites, Buildings and Antiquities Act (16 U.S.C. 461-462, 464-467): The Act of August 21,1935, (49 Stat. 666) popularly known as the Historic Sites Act, as amended by Public Law 89-249, approved October 9,1965, (79 Stat. 971): This Act declared it a national policy to preserve historic sites and objects of national significance, including those located on refuges. It provided procedures for designation, acquisition, administration, and protection of such sites. Among other things, National Historic and Natural Landmarks are designated under authority of this Act. As of January 1989, 31 national wildlife refuges contained such sites.

National Historic Preservation Act of 1966 (16 U.S.C. 470-470b, 470c-470n): Public Law 89-665, approved October 15, 1966, (80 Stat. 915) and repeatedly amended: This Act provided for preservation of significant historical features (e.g., buildings, objects, and sites) through a grant-in-aid program to the states. It established a National Register of Historic Places and a program of matching grants under the existing National Trust for Historic Preservation (16 U.S.C. 468-468d). The Act established an Advisory Council on Historic Preservation, which was made a permanent independent agency in Public Law 94-422, approved September 28, 1976 (90 Stat. 1319). That Act also created the Historic Preservation Fund. Federal agencies are directed to take into account the effects of their actions on items or sites listed in, or eligible for listing in, the National Register of Historic Places. As of January 1989, 91 such sites on national wildlife refuges are listed in this Register.

Land and Water Conservation Fund Act of 1948: This Act provides funding through receipts from the sale of surplus federal land, appropriations from oil and gas receipts from the outer continental shelf, and other sources of land acquisition under several authorities. Appropriations from the fund may be used for matching grants to states for outdoor recreation projects and for land acquisition by various federal agencies, including the Fish and Wildlife Service.

Migratory Bird Hunting and Conservation Stamp Act (16 U.S.C. 718-718j, 48 Stat. 452), as amended: The "Duck Stamp Act" of March 16, 1934, requires each waterfowl hunter, 16 years of age or older, to possess a valid federal hunting stamp. Receipts from the sale of the stamp are deposited in a special Treasury account known as the Migratory Bird Conservation Fund and are not subject to appropriations.

National and Community Service Act of 1960 (42 U.S.C. 12401:104 Stat. 3127), Public Law 101-610, signed November 16,1990: This Act authorizes several programs to engage citizens of the United States in full- and/or part-time projects designed to combat illiteracy and poverty, provide job skills, enhance educational skills, and fulfill environmental needs. Several provisions are of particular interest to the Fish and Wildlife Service.

American Conservation and Youth Service Corps: A federal grant program established under Subtitle C of the law, the Corps offers an opportunity for young adults between the ages of 16-25, or in the case of summer programs, 15-21, to engage in approved human and natural resources projects which benefit the public or are carried out on federal or Indian lands. To be eligible for assistance, natural resource programs must focus on improvement of wildlife habitat and recreational areas, fish culture, fishery assistance, erosion, wetlands protection, pollution control and similar projects. A stipend of not more than 100 percent of the poverty level will be paid to participants. A Commission established to administer the Youth Service Corps will make grants to States, the Secretaries of Agriculture and Interior, and the Director of ACTION to carry out these responsibilities.

National Environmental Policy Act of 1959 (P.L. 91-190,42 U.S.C. 4321-4347, January 1, 1970, 83 Stat. 852) as amended by Public Law 94-52, July 3, 1975, 89 Stat. 258, and Public Law 94-83, August 9, 1975, 89 Stat. 424): Title I of the 1969 National Environmental Policy Act requires that all federal agencies prepare detailed environmental impact statements for "every recommendation or report on proposals for legislation and other major federal actions significantly affecting the quality of the human environment." The 1969 statute stipulated the factors to be considered in environmental impact statements, and required that federal agencies employ an interdisciplinary approach in related decision-making and develop means to ensure that unquantified environmental values are given appropriate consideration, along with economic and technical considerations. Title II of this statute requires annual reports on environmental quality from the President to the Congress, and established a Council on Environmental Quality in the Executive Office of the President with specific duties and functions.

National Wildlife Refuge System Improvement Act of 1997: Public Law 105-57, amended the National Wildlife Refuge System Act of 1966 (16 U.S.C. 668dd-ee), and provided guidance for management and public use of the refuge system. The Act mandates that the refuge system be consistently directed and managed as a national system of lands and waters devoted to wildlife conservation and management. The Act establishes priorities for recreational uses of the refuge system. Six wildlife-dependent uses are specifically named in the Act: hunting, fishing, wildlife observation, wildlife photography, and environmental education and interpretation. These activities are to be promoted within the Refuge System and subject to compatibility determinations. A compatible use is one that, in the sound professional judgment of the refuge manager, will not materially interfere with, or detract from, fulfillment of the National Wildlife Refuge System Mission or refuge purpose(s). As stated in the Act, "The mission of the system is to administer a national network of lands and waters for the conservation, management, and where appropriate, restoration of the fish, wildlife, and plant resources and their habitats within the United States for the benefit of present and future generations of Americans." The Act also requires the development of a comprehensive conservation plan for each refuge and that management be consistent with the plan. When writing a plan for expanded or new refuges, and when making management decisions, the Act requires effective coordination with other federal agencies, state fish and wildlife or conservation agencies, and refuge neighbors. A refuge must also provide opportunities for public involvement when making a compatibility determination.

North American Wetlands Conservation Act (103 Stat. 1968; 16 U.S.C. 4401~4412) Public Law 101-233, enacted December 13, 1989: This act provides funding and administrative direction for implementation of the North American Waterfowl Management Plan and the Tripartite Agreement on Wetlands between Canada, the United States, and Mexico. The Act converts the Pittman-Robertson account into a trust fund, with the interest available without appropriation through the year 2006, to carry out the programs authorized by the Act, along with an authorization for annual appropriation of $15 million plus an amount equal to the fines and forfeitures collected under the Migratory Bird Treaty Act. Available funds may be expended, upon approval of the Migratory Bird Conservation Commission, for payment of not to exceed 50 percent of the United States' share of the cost of wetlands conservation projects in Canada, Mexico, or the United States (or 100 percent of the cost of projects on federal lands). At least 50 percent and no more than 70 percent of the funds received are to go to Canada and Mexico each year.

Refuge Recreation Act of 1952: This Act authorizes the Secretary of the Interior to administer refuges, hatcheries, and other conservation areas for recreational use, when such uses do not interfere with the area's primary purposes. It authorizes construction and maintenance of recreational facilities and the acquisition of land for incidental fish and wildlife oriented recreational development or protection of natural resources. It also authorizes the charging of fees for public uses.

Refuge Revenue Sharing Act (16 U.S.C. 715s): Section 401 of the Act of June 15, 1935, (49 Stat. 383) provided for payments to counties in lieu of taxes, using revenues derived from the sale of products from refuges. Public Law 88-523, approved August 30, 1964, (78 Stat. 701) made major revisions by requiring that all revenues received from refuge products, such as animals, timber and minerals, or from leases or other privileges, be deposited in a special Treasury account and net receipts distributed to counties for public schools and roads. Public Law 93-509, approved December 3, 1974, (88 Stat. 1603) required that moneys remaining in the fund after payments be transferred to the Migratory Bird Conservation Fund for land acquisition under provisions of the Migratory Bird Conservation Act. Public Law 95-469, approved October 17, 1978, (92 Stat. 1319) expanded the revenue sharing system to include National Fish Hatcheries and Service research stations. It also included in the Refuge Revenue Sharing Fund receipts from the sale of salmonid carcasses. Payments to counties were established as follows: on acquired land, the greatest amount calculated on the basis of 75 cents per acre, three-fourths of one percent of the appraised value, or 25 percent of the net receipts produced from the land; and on land withdrawn from the public domain, 25 percent of net receipts and basic payments under Public Law 94-565 (31 U.S.C. 1601-1607, 90 Stat. 2662). This amendment also authorized appropriations to make up any difference between the amount in the fund and the amount scheduled for payment in any year. The stipulation that payments be used for schools and roads was removed, but counties were required to pass payments along to other units of local government within the county that suffer losses in revenues due to the establishment of Service areas.

Wilderness Act of 1954: Public Law 88-577, approved September 3,1964, directed the Secretary of the Interior, within 10 years, to review every roadless area of 5,000 or more acres and every roadless island (regardless of size) within National Wildlife Refuge and National Park Systems for inclusion in the National Wilderness Preservation System.

IV. Refuge Acquisition

Fee Title Acquisitions in Bertie County

YEAR	TRACT	ACRES	COST	COST ACRE	TOTAL ACREAGE	TOTAL COST
1990	Rainbow Without Timber	2,782	$991,054	$340	2,782	$991,054
1991	Rainbow Timber		$1,638,946	$562		$2,630,000
1991	Askew	1,276	$691,633	$542	4,058	$3,321,633
1992	Broadneck	2,000	$985,000	$493	6,058	$4,196,633
1993	Conine Island	3,748	$2,425,000	$647	9,806	$6,621,633
1993	Company Swamp	1,502	$1,310,000	$873	11,308	$7,931,633
1995	Hampton Swamp	1,122	$245,000	$218	12,430	$8,186,633
1997	Great Island, Goodman Island, Sunken Marsh	4,993	$438,625	$88	16,423	$8,615,258
1997	Rhodes	554	$400,000	$740	17,977	$9,015,258
2003	Town Swamp, Rainbow	3,001	$2,000,000	$667	20,978	$11,015,258
Total		20,978				$11,015,258

Fee Simple Acquisitions Outside of Bertie County
(Transferred from Farmers Home Administration)

DATE	COUNTY	ACREAGE
1992	Nash County	45
1995	Sampson County	129

Conservation Easement Acquisitions
(Transferred from Farmers Home Administration)

COUNTY	REFUGE TRACTS	NUMBER OF LANDOWNERS	ACREAGE
Alamance	2	4	11.40
Bertie	2	1	50.32
Bladen	1	1	37.96
Caswell	3	3	101.23
Cumberland	3	4	140.98
Edgecombe	2	2	60.67
Franklin	3	3	119.80
Gates	1	1	82.20
Halifax	6	4	83.80
Harnett	2	2	42.05
Hertford	1	1	130.72
Martin	1	1	26.93
Nash	17	8	260.79
Northampton	11	10	243.75
Orange	5	6	47.60
Rockingham	1	1	74.73
Sampson	34	20	1318.26
Wake	2	2	25.44
Wilson	1	1	11.94
Total	98	75	2870.87

V. Refuge Biota

Fauna

Total Species - 191, Breeding Species - 88
A = Abundant, C = Common, U = Uncommon, O = Occasional, R = Rare
*species with confirmed breeding records

FAUNA				
BIRDS				
SPECIES	SPRING	SUMMER	FALL	WINTER
Anhinga*	U	U		
Bittern, Least*	O	O		
Blackbird, Red-winged*	C	R	A	A
Blackbird, Rusty	O		O	O
Bluebird, Eastern*	C	C	C	C
Bobolink	U		U	
Bobwhite, Northern	U	U	U	U
Bufflehead			U	U
Bunting, Indigo*	A	A	A	
Catbird, Gray*	U	O	U	O
Cardinal, Northern*	A	A	A	A
Chat, Yellow-breasted*	U	U	U	R
Chickadee, Carolina*	C	C	C	C
Chuck-will's Widow*	U	U	O	
Comorant, Double-crested*	C	U	U	U
Coot, American			U	U
Cowbird, Brown-headed*	C	C	U	U
Creeper, Brown	U		U	U
Crow, American*	C	C	C	C
Crow, Fish*	C	C	U	U
Cuckoo, Black-billed	R		R	
Cuckoo, Yellow-billed	C	C	C	
Dickcissel	R	R	R	
Dove, Mourning*	A	A	A	A
Dove, Rock*	C	C	C	C
Duck, American Black	U		U	C
Duck, Ring-necked			C	C
Duck, Ruddy			O	O
Duck, Wood*	C	C	C	C
Eagle, Bald* (Threatened)	U	U	U	U
Egret, Cattle	O	O		
Egret, Great*	C	C	U	R
Egret, Snowy	O	O		
Falcon, Peregrine			R	
Finch, House	O	O	O	O
Finch, Purple	U		U	U

SPECIES	SPRING	SUMMER	FALL	WINTER
Flycatcher, Acadian*	A	A	A	
Flycatcher, Great Crested*	C	C	U	
Gadwall			U	U
Gnatcatcher, Blue-gray*	C	C	C	
Goldfinch, American*	C	U	C	C
Goose, Canada*	C	C	O	U
Goose, Snow			R	R
Grackle, Common*	A	A	A	A
Grebe, Pied-billed	U		O	U
Grosbeak, Blue*	C	C	C	
Grosbeak, Evening	O		O	O
Grosbeak, Rose-breasted	U		U	
Gull, Herring	O		O	O
Gull, Ring-billed	A		C	C
Harrier, Northern	U		U	U
Hawk, Broad-winged	R		R	
Hawk, Cooper's*	U	R	U	U
Hawk, Red-shouldered*	C	C	C	C
Hawk, Red-tailed*	C	C	C	C
Hawk, Sharp-shinned	U		C	U
Heron, Black-crowned Night*	R			R
Heron, Great Blue*	C	C	C	U
Heron, Green*	U	U	U	
Heron, Little Blue	O	O		
Heron, Yellow-crowned Night*	U	U	U	
Hummingbird, Ruby-throated*	C	C	C	
Jay, Blue*	C	C	C	C
Junco, Dark-eyed	C		C	C
Kestrel, American	U		U	U
Killdeer	U	U	U	U
Kingbird, Eastern*	U	U	U	
Kingfisher, Belted*	C	C	C	C
Kinglet, Golden-crowned	C		C	C
Kinglet, Ruby-crowned	C		C	C
Kite, Mississippi*	U	U		
Lark, Horned	U	U	U	U
Loon, Common	R		R	R
Mallard*	U	O	C	C
Martin, Purple	U	U	U	
Meadowlark, Eastern*	C	U	U	C
Merganser, Hooded*	C	R	U	C

FAUNA (CONTINUED)				
BIRDS (CONTINUED)				
SPECIES	SPRING	SUMMER	FALL	WINTER
Merlin	R		O	R
Mockingbird, Northern *	C	C	C	C
Moorhen, Common	R	R	R	
Nighthawk, Common	U	O	U	
Nuthatch, Brown-headed*	O	O	O	O
Nuthatch, Red-breasted	O		O	O
Nuthatch, White-breasted*	C	C	C	C
Oriole, Northern	O		O	
Oriole, Orchard*	U	U	O	
Osprey*	C	C	U	
Ovenbird*	U	U	U	
Owl, Barred*	C	C	C	C
Owl, Eastern Screech*	U	U	U	U
Owl, Great Horned*	U	U	U	U
Phoebe, Eastern*	U	O	U	U
Pintail, Northern			U	U
Pipit, American Water	O		O	U
Robin, American*	U	U	C	C
Sandpiper, Least	O		O	
Sandpiper, Solitary	O		O	
Sandpiper, Spotted	C		U	
Sapsucker, Yellow-bellied	U		U	U
Scaup, Greater			R	R
Scaup, Lesser			U	U
Shoveler, Northern			O	O
Shrike, Loggerhead	R	R	R	R
Siskin, Pine	O		O	O
Snipe, Common			O	O
Sora	O		O	
Sparrow, Chipping*	U	U	U	U
Sparrow, Field*	U	U	U	U
Sparrow, Fox			O	U
Sparrow, Savannah	C		C	C
Sparrow, Song	C		C	C
Sparrow, Swamp	C		C	C
Sparrow, White-crowned			R	R
Sparrow, White-throated	A		A	A
Starling, European	U	U	C	C
Stork, Wood	R			
Swift, Chimney*	C	C	C	
Swallow, Bank	R		R	
Swallow, Barn*	C	C	C	

SPECIES	SPRING	SUMMER	FALL	WINTER
Swallow, Cliff*	R		R	
Swallow, Northern Rough-winged*	U	U	R	
Swallow, Tree*	C	R	C	R
Tanager, Scarlet*	U	U	U	
Tanager, Summer*	C	C	U	
Teal, American Green-winged			C	C
Teal, Blue-winged	O		O	R
Tern, Black	R		R	
Tern, Caspian	O		O	
Tern, Common	O			
Tern, Forster's	R		R	
Thrasher, Brown*	U	U	U	U
Thrush, Hermit	U		U	U
Thrush, Swainson's	O		O	
Thrush, Wood*	C	C	U	
Titmouse, Tufted*	A	A	A	A
Towhee, Rufous-sided*	U	U	U	U
Turkey, Wild*	C	C	C	C
Veery	O		O	
Vireo, Blue-headed (Solitary)		U	U	R
Vireo, Philadelphia			O	
Vireo, Red-eyed*	A	A	C	
Vireo, Warbling	R	R		
Vireo, White-eyed*	C	C	C	R
Vireo, Yellow-throated*	U	U	U	
Vulture, Black*	U	U	U	U
Vulture, Turkey*	C	C	C	C
Warbler, Bay-breasted	R		O	
Warbler, Black-and-white*	U	O	C	
Warbler, Black-throated Blue	U		U	
Warbler, Black-throated Green	R	R	R	
Warbler, Blackburnian	R		O	
Warbler, Blackpoll	U		U	
Warbler, Blue-winged	U		U	
Warbler, Canada	R		O	
Warbler, Cape May	R		U	
Warbler, Cerulean*	U	U	U	
Warbler, Chestnut-sided	R		O	
Warbler, Hooded*	U	U	U	
Warbler, Kentucky*	U	U	U	
Warbler, Magnolia			U	

FAUNA (CONTINUED)				
BIRDS (CONTINUED)				
SPECIES	**SPRING**	**SUMMER**	**FALL**	**WINTER**
Warbler, Northern Parula*	A	A	C	
Warbler, Orange-crowned			O	O
Warbler, Palm	U		U	O
Warbler, Pine*	U	U	U	U
Warbler, Prairie*	U	U	U	
Warbler, Prothonatary*	A	A	C	
Warbler, Swainson's*	U	U	O	
Warbler, Tennessee	R		U	
Warbler, Wilson's	R		R	
Warbler, Worm-eating*	R	R	R	
Warbler, Yellow	O		U	
Warbler, Yellow-rumped	C		A	A
Warbler, Yellow-throated*	C	C	U	
Waterthrush, Louisiana*	U	U	U	
Waterthrush, Northern	U		U	
Waxwing, Cedar*	C	R	C	C
Wigeon, American			C	C
Woodcock, American*	U	O	U	U
Woodpecker, Downy*	C	C	C	C
Woodpecker, Hairy*	U	U	U	U
Woodpecker, Pileated*	C	C	C	C
Woodpecker, Red-bellied*	C	C	C	C
Woodpecker, Red-headed*	U	O	U	U
Sapsucker, Yellow-bellied	C	C	C	C
Wood-pewee, Eastern*	U	U	U	
Wren, Carolina*	A	A	A	A
Wren, House	O		O	O
Wren, Winter	U		U	U
Yellow-throat, Common*	C	C	C	O
Yellowlegs, Greater	O		O	R
Whip-poor-will*	U	U	O	

FAUNA (CONTINUED)	
FISH	
COMMON NAME	**SCIENTIFIC NAME**
Alewife	*Alosa pseudoharengus*
Bass, Largemouth	*Micropterus salmoides*
Bass, Striped	*Morone saxatilis*
Bluegill	*Lepomis macrochirus*
Bowfin	*Amia calva*
Carp	*Cyprinus carpio*
Catfish, Brown Bullhead	*Ictalurus nebulosus*
Catfish, Channel	*Ictalurus punctatus*
Catfish, White	*Ictalurus catus*
Catfish, Yellow	*Ictalurus natalis*
Chub, Bluehead	*Nocomis leptocephalus*
Chub, Creek	*Semotilus atromaculatus*
Chubsucker, Creek	*Erimyzon oblongus*
Crappie, Black	*Pomoxis nigromaculatus*
Crappie, White	*Pomoxis annularis*
Darter, Glassy	*Etheostoma vitreum*
Darter, Johnny	*Etheostoma nigrum*
Darter, Sawcheek	*Etheostoma serriferum*
Darter, Swamp	*Etheostoma fusiforme*
Darter, Tessellated	*Etheostoma olmstedi*
Eel, American	*Anguilla rostrata*
Flier	*Centrarchus macropterus*
Gar, Longnose	*lepiosteus osseus*
Herring, Blueback	*Alosa aestivalis*
Madtom, Margined	*Noturus insignis*
Madtom, Tadpole	*Noturus gyrinus*
Menhaden, Atlantic	*Brevortia tyrannus*
Minnow, Silvery	*Hybognathus regius*
Mosquitofish	*Gambusia affinis*
Mudminnow, Eastern	*Umbra pygmaea*
Perch, Pirate	*Aphredoderus sayanus*
Perch, White	*Morone americana*
Perch, Yellow	*Perca flavescens*
Pickerel, Chain	*Esox niger*
Pickerel, Redfin	*Esox americanus*
Pumpkinseed	*Lepomis gibbosus*
Redhorse, Shorthead	*Moxostoma macrolepidotum*
Redhorse, Silver	*Moxostoma anisurum*
Redhorse, Suckermouth	*Moxostoma papallosum*
Shad, American	*Alosa sapidissima*
Shad, Gizzard	*Dorosoma cepedianum*

FAUNA (CONTINUED)	
FISH (CONTINUED)	
COMMON NAME	**SCIENTIFIC NAME**
Shad, Hickory	*Alosa mediocris*
Shiner, Golden	*Notemigonus crysoleucas*
Shiner, Ironcolor	*Notropis chalybaeus*
Shiner, Satinfin	*Notropis analostanus*
Shiner, Spottail	*Notropis hudsonius*
Shiner, Swallowtail	*Notropis procne*
Sturgeon, Atlantic	*Acipenser oxyrhynchus*
Sturgeon, Shortnose	*Acipenser brevirostrum*
Sunfish, Banded	*Enneacanthus obesus*
Sunfish, Banded Pygmy	*Elassoma zonatum*
Sunfish, Blackbanded	*Enneacanthus chaetodon*
Sunfish, Bluespotted	*Enneacanthus gloriosus*
Sunfish, Green	*Lepomis cynellus*
Sunfish, Mud	*Acantharchus pomotis*
Sunfish, Redbreast	*Lepomis auritus*
Swampfish	*Chologaster cornuta*
Topminnow, Lined	*Fundulus lineolatus*
Warmouth	*Lepomis gulosus*
AMPHIBIANS	
COMMON NAME	**SCIENTIFIC NAME**
Amphiuma, Two-toed	*Amphiuma means*
Bullfrog	*Rana catesbeiana*
Frog, Brimley's Chorus	*Pseudacris brimleyi*
Frog, Carpenter	*Rana virgatipes*
Frog, Green	*Rana clamitans*
Frog, Little Grass	*Limnaoedus ocularis*
Frog, Northern Cricket	*Acris crepitans*
Frog, Pickerel	*Rana palustris*
Frog, Southern Cricket	*Acris gryllus*
Frog, Southern Leopard	*Rana sphenocephala*
Frog, Upland Chorus	*Pseudacris triseriata*
Mudpuppy, Dwarf	*Necturus punctatus*
Newt, Eastern	*Notophthalmus viridescens*
Peeper, Spring	*Hyla crucifer*
Salamander, Drawf	*Eurycea quadridigitata*
Salamander, Mabee's	*Ambystoma mabeei*
Salamander, Marbled	*Ambystoma opacum*
Salamander, Mud	*Pseudotriton montanus*
Salamander, Southern Dusky	*Desmognathus auriculatus*
Salamander, Spotted	*Ambystoma opacum*
Salamander, Redback	*Plethodon cinereus*
Salamander, Slimy	*Plethodon glutinosus*
Salamander, Three-toed	*Eurycea guttolineata*

FAUNA (CONTINUED)	
AMPHIBIANS (CONTINUED)	
COMMON NAME	**SCIENTIFIC NAME**
Salamander, Tiger	*Ambystoma tigrinum*
Salamander, Two-lined	*Eurycea bislineata*
Siren, Greater	*Siren lacertina*
Siren, Lesser	*Siren intermedia*
Toad, American	*Bufo americanus*
Toad, Eastern Spadefoot	*Scaphoplis holbrooki*
Toad, Eastern Narrowmouth	*Gastrophryne carolinensis*
Toad, Fowler's	*Bufo woodhousii*
Toad, Oak	*Bufo quercicus*
Toad, Southerm	*Bufo terrestris*
Treefrog, Barking	*Hyla gratiosa*
Treefrog, Gray	*Hyla chrysoscelis*
Treefrog, Gray	*Hyla versicolor*
Treefrog, Green	*Hyla cineres*
Treefrog, Pine Woods	*Hyla femoralis*
Treefrog, Squirrel	*Hyla squirella*
REPTILES	
COMMON NAME	**SCIENTIFIC NAME**
Anole, Carolina	*Anolis carolinensis*
Cooter, Florida	*Chrysemys floridana*
Cooter, River	*Chrysemys concinna*
Copperhead	*Agkistrodon contortrix*
Cottonmouth	*Agkistrodon piscivorus*
Lizard, Eastern Fence	*Sceloporus undulatus*
Lizard, Eastern Glass	*Ophisaurus ventralis*
Lizard, Slender Glass	*Ophisaurus atlenuatus*
Racer, Black	*Coluber constrictor*
Rattlescake, Timber	*Crotalus horridus*
Skink, Broadhead	*Eumeces laticeps*
Skink, Five-lined	*Eumeces fasciatus*
Skink, Ground	*Scincella lateralis*
Skink, Southeastern Five-lined	*Eumeces inexpectatus*
Slider, Yellowbelly	*Chrysemys scripta*
Snake, Banded Water	*Nerodia fasciata*
Snake, Brown	*Storeria dekayi*
Snake, Brown Water	*Nerodia taxispilota*
Snake, Eastern Garter	*Thamnophis sirtalis*
Snake, Eastern Hognose	*Heterodon platyrhinos*
Snake, Eastern King	*Lampropeltis getulus*
Snake, Eastern Ribbon	*Thamnophis sauritus*
Snake, Mud	*Farancia abacura*
Snake, Northern Water	*Nerodia sipeodon*
Snake, Rat	*Elaphe obsoleta*
Snake, Redbelly	*Storeria occipitomaculata*
Snake, Redbelly Water	*Nerodia erythrogaster*

FAUNA (CONTINUED)	
REPTILES (CONTINUED)	
COMMON NAME	**SCIENTIFIC NAME**
Snake, Ringneck	*Diadophis punctatus*
Snake, Rough Garter	*Virginia striatula*
Snake, Rough Green	*Opheodrys aestivus*
Snake, Worm	*Carphophis amoenus*
Turtle, Eastern Box	*Terrapene carolina*
Turtle, Eastern Mud	*Kinosternum subrubrum*
Turtle, Eastern Musk	*Sternotherus oboratus*
Turtle, Painted	*Chrysemys picta*
Turtle, Snapping	*Chelydra serpentina*
Turtle, Spotted	*Clemmys guttana*
MAMMALS	
COMMON NAME	**SCIENTIFIC NAME**
Bat, Evening	*Nycticelus numeralis*
Bat, Hoary	*Lasiurus cinereus*
Bat, Red	*Lasiurus borealis*
Bat, Silver-haired	*Lasionycteris noctivagans*
Bear, Black	*Ursus americana*
Beaver	*Castor canadensis*
Bobcat	*Lynx rufus*
Deer, White-tailed	*Odocoileus virginianus*
Fox, Gray	*Urocyon cinereoargenteus*
Mink	*Mustela vison*
Mole, Eastern	*Scalopus aquaticus*
Mouse, Cotton	*Peromyscus gossypinus*
Mouse, Golden	*Ochrotomys nuttalli*
Mouse, House	*Mus musculus*
Mouse, White-footed	*Peromyscus leucopus*
Muskrat	*Ondatra zibethica*
Opossum	*Didelphis virginiana*
Otter, River	*lutra canadensis*
Pipistrelle, Eastern	*Pipistrellus subflavus*
Rabbit, Eastern Cottontail	*Sylvilagus floridanus*
Rabbit, Marsh	*Sylvilagus palustris*
Raccoon	*Procyon lotor*
Rat, Hispid Cotton	*Sigmodon hispidus*
Rat, Norway	*Rattus norvegicus*
Rat, Rice	*Oryzomys palustris*
Shrew, Carolina Short-tailed	*Blarina carolinensis*
Shrew, Short-tailed	*Blarina brevicauda*
Shrew, Southeastern	*Sorex longirostris*
Squirrel, Gray	*Sciurus carolinensis*
Squirrel, Southern Flying	*Glaucomys volans*
Vole, Meadow	*Microtus pennsylvanicus*
Weasel, Long-tailed	*Mustela frenata*
Woodchuck	*Marmota monax*

VEGETATION

CLASS=Wetland Indicator Status:
OBL=Obligate Wetland (occurs in wetlands more than 99% of the time),
FACW=Facultative Wetland (occurs in wetlands 67-99% of the time),
FAC=Facultative (occurs in wetlands 34-66% of the time),
FACU=Facultative Upland, (occurs in wetlands 1-33% of the time)
UPL=Upland (occurs in wetlands less than 1% of the time)
NI=No Indicator Status Established
+ means the species occurs more in wetter situations than indicated
- means the species occurs more in drier situations than indicated
HABITAT PRESENCE:
BH=Bottomland Hardwoods;
BHL=Logged Bottomland Hardwoods;
GC=Gum/Cypress;
GCL=Logged Gum/Cypress
TC=Transmission Corridor

TREES

COMMON NAME	SCIENTIFIC NAME	CLASS	HABITAT PRESENCE				
			BH	BHL	GC	GCL	TC
Ash	Fraxinus sp.		X	X	X	X	
Ash, Green	Fraxinus pennsylvanica	FACW	X				
Baldcypress	Taxodium distichum	OBL	X	X	X	X	
Basswood	Tilia americana	FACU	X				
Birch, River	Betula nigra	OBL		X			
Boxelder	Acer negundo	FACW	X	X		X	
Cottonwood, Swamp	Populus heterophylla	OBL		X	X	X	X
Elm, American	Ulmus americana	FACW	X	X	X	X	
Elm, Winged	Ulmus alata	FACU+	X	X			
Gum, Tupelo	Nyssa aquatica	OBL	X	X	X	X	
Hickory, Water	Carya aquatica	OBL	X	X		X	X
Holly, American	Ilex opaca	FAC-	X	X			
Holly, Deciduous	Ilex decidua	FACW-	X	X			
Hornbeam, American	Carpinus caroliniana	FAC	X	X	X	X	
Maple, Red	Acer rubrum	FAC	X	X	X	X	X
Maple, Silver	Acer saccharinum	FACW	X	X		X	
Mulberry, Red	Morus rubra	FAC	X				
Oak, Cherrybark	Quercus pagoda	FAC+	X				
Oak, Laurel	Quercus laurifolia	FACW	X				
Oak, Overcup	Quercus lyrata	OBL	X	X	X	X	
Oak, Southern Red	Quercus falcata	FACU-	X				
Oak, Water	Quercus nigra	FAC	X	X			
Oak, Willow	Quercus phellos	FACW-	X	X			
Paw-paw	Asimina sp.	FACU	X		X		
Persimmon	Diospyros virginiana	FAC	X	X			

TREES

COMMON NAME	SCIENTIFIC NAME	CLASS	HABITAT PRESENCE				
			BH	BHL	GC	GCL	TC
Pine, Loblolly	*Pinus taeda*	FAC	X	X			
Sugarberry	*Celtis laevigata*	FACW	X	X			
Sweetgum	*Liquidambar styraciflua*	FAC+	X	X			
Sycamore	*Platanus occidentalis*	FACW-	X	X	X	X	

SHRUBS

COMMON NAME	SCIENTIFIC NAME	CLASS	HABITAT PRESENCE				
			BH	BHL	GC	GCL	TC
Beautyberry	*Callicapa americana*	FACU	X	X			
Blackberry	*Rubus sp.*	FAC	X				
Buckeye	*Aesculus sylvatica*	FAC	X	X			
Hawthorne, Green	*Crataegus viridis*	FACW	X	X			
Holly, Winterberry	*Ilex verticillata*	FACW	X	X			
Spicebush	*Lindera benzoin*	FACW	X	X			

WOODY VINES

COMMON NAME	SCIENTIFIC NAME	CLASS	HABITAT PRESENCE				
			BH	BHL	GC	GCL	TC
Crossvine	*Anisostichus capreolata*	FAC	X	X			
Grape	*Vitis sp.*	FAC	X	X	X		
Greenbrier, Catbrier	*Smilax bona-nox*	FAC	X	X			
Greenbrier, Common	*Smilax rotundifolia*	FAC	X	X	X	X	X
Peppervine	*Ampelopsis arborea*	FAC+	X	X	X	X	X
Poison Ivy	*Toxicodendron radicans*	FAC	X	X	X		
Rattan-vine	*Berchemia scandens*	FACW	X	X	X		
Trumpetcreeper, Common	*Campsis radicans*	FAC	X	X		X	X

GRASS-LIKE PLANTS

COMMON NAME	SCIENTIFIC NAME	CLASS	HABITAT PRESENCE				
			BH	BHL	GC	GCL	TC
Nutgrass	*Cyperus rotundus*	FAC-	X				
Rush, Soft	*Juncus effusus*	FACW					X
Sedge, Bladder	*Carex intumescens*	FACW	X	X		X	
Sedge, Bristlebract	*Carex tribuloides*	FACW+		X			
Sedge, Cattail	*Carex typhina*	OBL	X	X		X	X
Sedge, Gray's	*Carex grayi*	FACW		X			
Sedge	*Carex sp.*	Varies	X	X	X	X	X
Woolgrass	*Scirpus cyperinus*	OBL				X	X

VEGETATION (CONTINUED)

GRASSES

COMMON NAME	SCIENTIFIC NAME	CLASS	HABITAT PRESENCE				
			BH	BHL	GC	GCL	TC
Barnyardgrass	*Echinochloa crus-galli*	FACW-			X	X	
Giant Cane	*Arundinaria gigantea*	FACW	X	X			
Grass, Gaping	*Steinchisma hians*	OBL			X	X	
Junglerice	*Echinochloa colona*	FACW					X
Mannagrass, Fowl	*Glyceria striata*	OBL				X	
Woodoats, Indian	*Chasmanthium latifolium*	FAC-	X				
Wildrye, Virginia	*Elymus virginicus*	FAC	X				

FORBS (BROADLEAVED HERBACEOUS PLANTS)

COMMON NAME	SCIENTIFIC NAME	CLASS	HABITAT PRESENCE				
			BH	BHL	GC	GCL	TC
Angle-pod	*Matalea suberosa*	FACW	X				
Arrow Arum	*Peltandra virginica*	OBL				X	
Arrowhead, Broadleaf	*Sagittaria latifolia*	OBL			X	X	
Aster	*Aster sp.*	Varies	X	X			X
Bedstraw, Bluntleaf	*Galium obtusum*	FACW-					X
Beggarticks	*Bidens discoidea*	FACW	X	X	X	X	X
Bugleweed, Virginia	*Lycopos virginicus*	OBL		X	X		
Burhead, Creeping	*Echinodorus cordifolius*	OBL		X	X		
Buttonweed, Virginia	*Diodia virginiana*	FACW		X		X	X
Cocklebur	*Xanthium strumarium*	FAC					X
Cucumber, Creeping	*Melothria pendula*	FACW-	X				
Dayflower, Marsh	*Murdannia keisak*	OBL			X	X	
Dayflower, Virginia	*Commelina virginiana*	FACW	X	X		X	X
Dicliptera	*Dicliptera brachiata*	FACW	X				
Dogbane, Climbing	*Trachelospermum difforme*	FACW	X	X		X	X
Duckweeds	*Lemna sp.*	OBL			X		
Duckweed, Swollen	*Lemna gibba*	OBL			X		
Duckweed, Yellow	*Lemna perpusilla*	OBL			X		
Falsedandelion, Carolina	*Pyrrhopappus carolinianus*	NI	X	X		X	X
Frog's-bit	*Limnobium spongia*	OBL			X	X	
Groundcherry	*Physalis sp.*	Varies	X				
Heliotrope, Indian	*Heliotropium indicum*	FAC+					X
Hempweed, Climbing	*Mikiana scandens*	FACW+	X	X			
Joepyeweed	*Eupatorium capillifolium*	NI			X		X
Jump seed	*Polygonum virginianum*	FAC		X			

VEGETATION (CONTINUED)							
FORBS (BROADLEAVED HERBACEOUS PLANTS)							
COMMON NAME	SCIENTIFIC NAME	CLASS	HABITAT PRESENCE				
			BH	BHL	GC	GCL	TC
Lambsquarters	Chenopodium album	FAC-					X
Lizard's Tails	Saururus cernuus	OBL	X	X	X	X	X
Marsh Mermaid Weed	Proserpinaca palustris	OBL			X	X	
Mecardonia, Purple	Mecardonia acuminata	FACW			X	X	
Mercury, Three-Seeded	Acalypha rhomboidea	NI	X	X	X	X	X
Mistletoe	Phoradendron flavescens	NI				X	
Monkey-Flower, Sharp-winged	Mimulus alatus	OBL	X				
Morning-glory, Small White	Ipomea lacunosa	NA					X
Moss		NI			X		
Mustard	Brassica sp.	Varies					X
Nettle, False	Boehmeria cylindrica	FACU+	X	X	X	X	
Nettle, Horse	Solanum carolinense	NI		X	X		X
Pennywort, Whorled	Hydrocotyle verticillata	OBL			X		
Pokeberry, Common	Phytolacca americana	FACU+	X	X	X		
Primrose Willow	Ludwigia sp.	OBL	X				
Purslane, Marsh	Ludwigia palustris	OBL			X	X	
Ragweed, Common	Ambrosia artemisiifolia	FACU		X		X	X
Rosemallow, Swamp	Hibiscus moscheutos	OBL					X
Saint Johnswort	Hypericum sp.	Varies			X		
Sida, Broomjute	Sida rhombifolia	FACU					X
Smartweed	Polygonum pennsylvanicum	FACW					X
Smartweed	Polygonum sp.	Varies	X	X	X	X	X
Stinkweed	Pluchea camphorata	FACW			X	X	
Thoroughwort, Small-Flowered	Eupatorium semiserratum	FACW-	X	X			
Touch-me-not, Spotted	Impatiens capensis	FACW			X	X	
Violet	Viola sp.	Varies	X	X	X		
Watermeal	Wolffia papulifera	OBL			X		
Watermilfoil, Parrot Feather	Myriophyllum brasiliense	OBL			X	X	
Waterplantain, Subcordate	Alisma subcordatum	OBL				X	

VEGETATION (CONTINUED)							
FORBS (BROADLEAVED HERBACEOUS PLANTS)							
COMMON NAME	SCIENTIFIC NAME	CLASS	HABITAT PRESENCE				
			BH	BHL	GC	GCL	TC
Yellow-cress, Marsh	*Rorippa palustris*	OBL				X	
Yerba de Tajo	*Ecilpta alba*	FACW-			X	X	

VI. History of the Counties in the Lower Roanoke River Valley

Bertie County

Bertie County received its name from James and Henry Bertie. The state established the county in 1722 from part of Chowan County (Jordan 1954). Settlers established Windsor in 1766 and it became the county seat in 1774. It was an important trading post before the Civil War. The state established the current boundaries in 1759 after adding parts of Tyrrell, Edgecombe, Northampton, and Hertford Counties.

The Tuscarora Tribe of Native Americans lived in Bertie County when the European settlers arrived. In 1701, John Lawson, Surveyor General, identified 15 major Tuscarora towns along the waterways in North Carolina. The Tuscarora were friendly and the northern tribes of Tuscarora avoided early conflicts with settlers that the southern tribes of Tuscarora experienced in the area south of the Pamlico River. Eventually, there was a full scale Tuscarora War in 1711, but the northern tribes did not participate. In 1717, the government established a reservation between Roquist Creek and Roanoke River on 56,000 acres of land centered on Quitsna. The reservation included most of the refuge's approved acquisition boundary. Between 1717 and 1803, most of the Tuscarora joined the Iroquois, with whom they shared a common language in New York. Originally, there were 800 Tuscarora on the reservation; by 1731 there were 600; by 1760 there were 255. In 1760, 155 moved to New York and only 100 older Tuscarora remained. By 1803, all of the Tuscarora had left the reservation. In 1831, the Tuscarora gave up their rights to the land. The Tuscarora now have their own reservation in Lewiston, New York, north of Buffalo. Descendants of the Tuscarora still reside in the area.

The first European settlers in Bertie County were English. Settlement began as early as 1657. Nathaniel Batts is considered the first homesteader in the area. His land along the Albemarle Sound near the mouth of the Roanoke River was one of the first permanent homesteads in North Carolina. His home has become known as Batt's House. From 1667 to 1700, the English population had grown from about 100 to more than 1,000 (Powell 1975).

The early settlers were primarily self-sufficient. Game and fish were plentiful. Cattle and pigs were allowed to roam the woods freely, and along with poultry, could be raised at little expense.

Logging and farming have been the primary sources of livelihood in Bertie County since early settlement. Around 1750, Nathaniel Hill and James Castello built a gristmill on what is now Hoggard's Mill Pond. They built a sawmill several years later. The county gained another sawmill and gristmill on Hayden's Mill Pond during the same period.

Most of the lumber produced the last half of the 18th century and most of the 19th century was used locally. Beginning in the late 1800s, most of the lumber was exported to the Northern States.

Within the refuge's approved acquisition boundary, the major industry is forestry. Farmers have cleared many terraces in the Roanoke's old floodplain, Mush Island, the northern section of the Broadneck Swamp, and lands adjacent to the north boundary of the Company Swamp and Askew Tracts for agriculture. Timber companies have converted some of the old Broadneck Plantation to sycamore and sweetgum. The surrounding area consists of old plantations, some derived from the original royal grants, while newer ones are still over 100 years old.

The forest industry has a major role in management of the Roanoke River bottomland hardwoods and thus will have a major influence on the future value of the area for fish and wildlife. The floodplain forests upstream from Williamston have been altered the most by logging operations, presumably due to relatively easier access. The least disturbed areas occur near the river mouth downstream from Jamesville (Lynch and Crawford 1980). Presently, some old-growth tracts occur along the entire floodplain. Landscape modification by construction of access roads, canals, and ditches is limited mainly to the middle and upper refuge units. The pressure for timber resources continues to increase. The southern United States is expected to remain a major wood producer for national and foreign markets for at least a quarter century (Zoebel 1979). With increased demand and a smaller timber and fiber base, less old-growth tracts will remain or reach maturity resulting in a decreased diversity of habitats. Areas where non-permanent landscape alteration has occurred have the ability to recover rapidly. Low intensity timber management can probably continue without undue stress on the ecological/hydrological systems (Lynch and Crawford 1980).

True Temper Corporation, a tool handle manufacturing company, practiced timber removal the most advantageous to wildlife along the Roanoke River. The company selectively cut primarily hickory and ash. It left the remaining forest to mature and provide wildlife food, cover, and den sites. In addition, timber was floated out by barge, minimizing damage from road building. Over the last several years, True Temper Corporation has sold all of its holdings along the Roanoke River. The Corporation sold some to The Nature Conservancy, which transferred them to the North Carolina Wildlife Resources Commission, and other tracts to other timber corporations.

Forestry practices vary among the remaining companies. Some clear-cut mature stands of most species present and usually rely on natural regeneration. Others have clear-cut large tracts at slightly higher elevations along the river, provided rudimentary drainage by cutting through the natural ridges and levees, and replanted uniform stands of sycamore, sweetgum, and pine for short-term pulp production. In some areas loggers are clear cutting hardwood bottoms, constructing drainage systems, and converting the areas to sycamore plantations (Broadneck Swamp). In recent years, loggers removed cypress by helicopter in the normally flooded timberlands, while most project area logging has consisted of more conventional methods during relatively dry periods. The remaining high-quality habitat in the Roanoke River bottoms may be due more to the current negative economy of logging and the depressed hardwood market than decision(s) by corporate interests to manage for old growth timber.

There is limited residential construction in the floodplain, probably due to the history of rampaging floods along the Roanoke River prior to construction of the reservoirs. Several hunt club cabins are on the Broadneck and Rainbow (Broadneck Swamp) Tracts. Beyond the floodplain, there has been little new development for residential, commercial, or industrial development. Historic development has occurred in larger towns such as the county seats of Windsor (Bertie County), Williamston (Martin County), and Plymouth (Washington County). New development is occurring along existing highways.

The Roanoke River was once the major transportation avenue in the area. As the area grew and the railroad arrived, river traffic declined. In the twentieth century with the popularity of automobiles, the state developed a network of highways connecting the county to all areas of the eastern United States. The state replaced a drawbridge across the Roanoke River on U.S. Highway 17 at Williamston in 1991-92 with a high-rise bridge. The state is widening U.S. Highway 64 to four lanes in Martin County that will connect the area to Interstate 95 and the Outer Banks. There are small local airports in Windsor, Williamston, Plymouth, and Edenton; and regional airports in Greenville. Amtrak provides passenger rail service as far east as Rocky Mount.

Martin County

Tuscarora Indians lived in Martin County until English settlers pushed them south and north. The first settlers moved from Bertie County to the site of a Tuscarora Indian village on the south side of the Roanoke River in 1730.

The Indians knew the site as "Squhawky," but settlers called it "The Landing." It gradually became the principal shipping point for the tar, pitch, turpentine, and other forest products and meat produced in the area.

The settlement prospered and was designated the county seat when it was chartered in 1774. In 1779, it became the first incorporated town in the county and was named Williamston.

The state created Martin County when officials in Halifax and Tyrrell Counties decided their counties were too large. It formed the new county from parts of those two counties in 1774 and originally named for Josiah Martin, the last Royal Governor of North Carolina.

After the Revolutionary War, the people wanted to change the name of the county because of bitterness towards Martin. They decided to keep the name in honor of Alexander Martin, a state representative to the Philadelphia Constitutional Convention. He was also Governor of North Carolina from 1789 to 1792 (Tetterton 1998).

Williamston's importance as a town and its growth and development immediately before and after its incorporation was largely based on two factors. The first was its location on the banks of a navigable river; and second, its designation as the county seat. The Roanoke River enabled ships of considerable size to navigate its waters as far upstream as Williamston before there were any roads other than the few that followed Indian trails. The presence of a public landing automatically made the town an important shipping point for river freight traffic. The arrival of the railroad increased commerce in Williamston even more.

In 1862, the county was the site of the Battle of Fort Branch along the Roanoke River. Fort Branch was built on a high bluff on the southern bank of the Roanoke River near Hamilton. It prevented Union gunboats from navigating upriver to the Wilmington-Weldon Bridge. The state began to restore the site of the fort in the 1970s and re-enactors recreate the battle every year.

In 1880, settlers established an inland community at Goose Nest as a small, rural trading center. In 1905, the General Assembly changed the town's name to Oak City. The town grew steadily through the early twentieth century when the popularity of the automobile and the end of passenger rail service to Oak City diverted commercial activity to larger towns in the area.

In the twentieth century, the bridging of the Roanoke River in 1922 made Williamston the hub of a system of major highways and roads upon which businesses and commercial life grew. Jamesville and Hamilton were the two other major river towns along the Roanoke River.

Washington County

The first settlers in Washington County were Indian tribes, who lived in the area as early as 10,000 years ago. The plentiful game and fish were their main food supplies, along with a few cultivated crops, such as maize.

Two small tribes, the Moratucs and the Secotans, of the Algonquin Nation were the main inhabitants of Washington County before the arrival of the first European settlers. By 1755, less than 100 years after settlement, the total Indian population in the northeastern part of North Carolina was less than 365 (Lee 1963).

Trapping, logging, and farming were the main sources of livelihood in the early years of the colony. Trade was begun with the West Indies and the northern colonies. The main exports were tar, pitch, turpentine, lumber, corn, and tobacco.

In 1702, a gristmill and sawmill were built in an area that was known as Lee's Mill. By 1799, Washington County had become established and the town known as Lee's Mill became the first county seat. The name Lee's Mill was changed to Roper in 1890.

Several large estates were built in the county, chiefly Buncombe Hall, built in Roper, and Josiah Collins' Somerset Place on Lake Phelps. Corn produced on Collins' plantation was shipped worldwide. Collins attempted to drain Lake Phelps into the Scuppernong River by way of a 6-mile-long by 20-feet-wide canal dug by 80 slaves imported directly from Africa. The canal helped with drainage, irrigation, and shipping. The plantation eventually grew to 100 buildings and 300 slaves (Tetterton 1998).

Plymouth, which was an important seaport until the Civil War, was laid out in 1785. It became the first incorporated town in the county in 1807 and is the present county seat. It was named for Plymouth, Massachusetts, from which the early settlers came (USDA Soil Conservation Service 1981).

During the Civil War, Union forces occupied the town from May 1862 to April 1864. Between April 17 and 20, 1864, 15,000 Confederate soldiers under the command of General Robert Hoke retook the town with the assistance of the ironclad ship C.S.S. Ram Albemarle. The Albemarle held the Union Navy on the Roanoke River. Three days later the Union Army and Navy retook Plymouth (Tetterton 1998).

Northampton County

The early settlers of Northampton County were principally Scotch and Scotch-Irish immigrants from the British Isles. Later settlers included English and French immigrants from Virginia and other northern colonies (USDA Soil Conservation Service 1925).

Northampton County was formed in 1741 from a part of Bertie County after settlers migrated to the area of the Albemarle precinct in the early eighteenth century. It is named for James Crompton, Earl of Northampton, an English nobleman. In 1806, Atherton was established as the county courthouse. The present county seat was named Northampton Courthouse and was renamed Jackson in 1823 for Andrew Jackson (Northampton County Chamber of Commerce 2002b).

Horse racing and especially horse breeding brought Northampton County national attention. In 1816, the famous Sir Archie "foundation sire of the American turf" was brought to Mowfield Plantation just west of Northampton Courthouse. By 1833, the year Sir Archie died, Jackson had an active Jockey Club that meets south of town at Silver Hill Plantation (Albemarle Region Chamber of Commerce 2002).

In the early nineteenth century, members of the Occaneechi Band of the Saponi Nation settled in Northampton County. By 1830, the population of their community known as Little Texas was 250 to 300 (Occaneechi Band of Saponi Nation 2002). In July 1863, the Union Troops occupied Jackson during the Civil War. Following the war, Jackson settled into its role as a small, county seat town.

Halifax County

Scots settled the county first in Scotland Neck in the early eighteenth century, but they moved to a Scottish stronghold along the Cape Fear River.

Halifax County was formed in 1758 from Edgecombe County and named for Charles Montague Dunk, second Earl of Halifax, president of the English Board of Trade and Plantations, English Secretary of State, and Lord Lieutenant of Ireland.

The town of Halifax was founded on the south bank of the Roanoke River and quickly became the focal point for the entire valley. It was a river port, county seat, crossroads, and social center. It was authorized as the county seat in 1757 and incorporated in 1760. By 1769 Halifax had 60 houses and public buildings.

Halifax was the site of several major events of the Revolutionary War. The Fourth North Carolina Provincial congress met in Halifax and passed the "Halifax Resolves" on April 12, 1776. The "Resolves" were the first resolution by any American colony instructing the State's delegates to the Constitutional Congress to vote for independence from Great Britain. The North Carolina General Assembly met in Halifax from 1776 until 1782 (North Carolina Office of Archives and History 2002).

The Roanoke Canal and Locke was completed around the rapids of the river in 1834. The 161.5-mile Wilmington and Weldon Railroad was completed in 1840. It was the world's longest railroad at the time. The railroad was a benefit to the county, but brought an end to the dominance of the town of Halifax in the area economy. The Confederate ironclad ship, Albemarle, was built in Scotland Neck in 1863-1864. The first kraft pulp in the United States was manufactured in Halifax County in 1863-1864 (Tetterton 1998). Since that time, the county's economy has centered on the forest products industry.

VII. Agricultural and Demographic Statistics

Bertie County Agricultural Statistics from the 2002 USDA Census of Agriculture	
Number of Farms	330
Acres in Farms	142,552
Average Size of Farms (Acres)	432
Market Value of Land Per Farm	$877,015
Market Value of Land Per Acre	$2,014
Market Value of Equipment Per Farm	$150,526
Total Cropland (Acres)	92,982
Market Value of All Products Sold	$85,948,000
Market Value of Products Sold Per Farm	$257,652
Market Value of Crops Sold	$29,414,000
Market Value of Livestock Sold	$55,611,000
Operators with Farm as Principal Occupation	247
Operators with Another Occupation as Principal Occupation	83
Broilers	24,399,848
Hogs in Inventory	49,360
Hogs Sold	219,877
Beef Cows in Inventory	845
Beef Cows Sold	274
Land in Cotton (Acres)	36,145
Land in Corn (Acres)	16,797
Land in Peanuts (Acres)	13,563
Land in Soybeans (Acres)	15,104
Land in Tobacco (Acres)	2,286
Land in Wheat (Acres)	1,412

Commodity Production in Bertie County in 2002 and 1997, from the 2002 and 1997 USDA Census of Agriculture			
Commodity	2002 Production	1997 Production	1997-2002 Change
Cotton (Acres)	26,145	34,319	Decreased 24%
Corn (acres)	16,797	21,279	Decreased 21%
Peanuts (acres)	13,563	16,738	Decreased 19%
Soybeans (acres)	15,104	10,677	Increased 41%
Tobacco (acres)	2,286	4,162	Decreased 45%
Wheat (acres)	1,412	2,581	Decreased 45%
Broilers	24,399,848	18,372,040	Increased 33%
Hog Inventory	49,360	45,351	Increased 9%
Hogs Sold	219,877	121,355	Increased 81%
Cattle Sold	274	615	Decreased 55%

Martin County Agricultural Statistics from the 2002 USDA Census of Agriculture	
Number of Farms	305
Acres in Farms	110,677
Average Size of Farms (Acres)	363
Market Value of Land Per Farm	$781,589
Market Value of Land Per Acre	$2,128
Market Value of Equipment Per Farm	$139,267
Total Cropland (Acres)	77,823
Market Value of All Products Sold	$39,891,000
Market Value of Products Sold Per Farm	$130,792
Market Value of Crops Sold	$25,160,000
Market Value of Livestock Sold	$14,732,000
Operators with Farm as Principal Occupation	224
Operators with Another Occupation as Principal Occupation	81
Broilers	4,815,000
Hogs in Inventory	17,717
Hogs Sold	0
Beef Cows in Inventory	1,122
Beef Cows Sold	674
Land in Cotton (Acres)	37,609
Land in Peanuts (Acres)	10,193
Land in Soybeans (Acres)	9,051
Land in Corn (Acres)	3,452
Land in Tobacco (Acres)	3,373
Land in Wheat (Acres)	2,793

Commodity Production in Martin County in 2002 and 1997, from the 2002 and 1997 USDA Census of Agriculture			
Commodity	**2002 production**	**1997 Production**	**1997-2002 Change**
Cotton (acres)	37,609	37,139	Increased 1%
Peanuts (acres)	10,193	12,757	Decreased 20%
Soybeans (acres)	9,051	9,162	Decreased 1%
Corn (acres)	3,452	8,817	Decreased 61%
Wheat (acres)	2,793	5,402	Decreased 49%
Tobacco (acres)	3,373	4,162	Decreased 19%
Broilers	4,815,000	3,219,500	Increased 50%
Hog Inventory	17,717	10,583	Increased 67%
Hogs Sold	0	22,857	N/A
Cattle Sold	674	732	Decreased 8%

Washington County Agricultural Statistics from the 2002 USDA Census of Agriculture	
Number of Farms	193
Acres in Farms	114,423
Average Size of Farms (Acres)	593
Market Value of Land Per Farm	$1,124,786
Market Value of Land Per Acre	$1,954
Market Value of Equipment Per Farm	$157,276
Total Cropland (Acres)	100,388
Market Value of All Products Sold	$46,149,000
Market Value of Products Sold Per Farm	$239,113
Market Value of Crops Sold	$34,027,000
Market Value of Livestock Sold	$12,122,000
Operators with Farm as Principal Occupation	143
Operators with Another Occupation as Principal Occupation	50
Broilers	6,051,300
Hogs in Inventory	0
Hogs Sold	9,090
Beef Cows in Inventory	637
Beef Cows Sold	643
Land in Soybeans (Acres)	33,365
Land in Corn (Acres)	28,346
Land in Cotton (Acres)	26,901
Land in Wheat (Acres)	15,727
Land in Peanuts (Acres)	3,016
Land in Tobacco (Acres)	311

Commodity Production in Washington County in 2002 and 1997, from the 2002 and 1997 USDA Census of Agriculture			
Commodity	2002 Production	1997 Production	1997-2002 Change
Soybeans (acres)	33,365	40,792	Decreased 18%
Corn (acres)	28,346	30,734	Decreased 7%
Cotton (acres)	26,901	7,692	Increased 250%
Wheat (acres)	15,727	25,381	Decreased 38%
Peanuts (acres)	3,016	2,785	Increased 8%
Tobacco (acres)	311	449	Decreased 31%
Broilers	6,051,300	4,868,100	Increased 24%
Hog Inventory	0	72,730	N/A
Hogs Sold	9,090	201,676	Decreased 95%
Cattle Sold	643	607	Increased 6%

Northampton County Agricultural Statistics from the 2002 USDA Census of Agriculture	
Number of Farms	328
Acres in Farms	150,666
Average Size of Farms (Acres)	459
Market Value of Land Per Farm	$858,573
Market Value of Land Per Acre	$2,011
Market Value of Equipment Per Farm	$120,728
Total Cropland (Acres)	95,809
Market Value of All Products Sold	$61,365,000
Market Value of Products Sold Per Farm	$187,090
Market Value of Crops Sold	$17,800,000
Market Value of Livestock Sold	$43,565,000
Operators with Farm as Principal Occupation	247
Operators with Another Occupation as Principal Occupation	81
Broilers	9,300,056
Hogs in Inventory	129,277
Hogs Sold	544,529
Beef Cows in Inventory	1,226
Beef Cows Sold	0
Land in Cotton (Acres)	63,045
Land in Peanuts (Acres)	12,922
Land in Soybeans (Acres)	6,044
Land in Wheat (Acres)	2,071
Land in Corn (Acres)	1,640
Land in Tobacco (Acres)	127

Commodity Production in Northampton County in 2002 and 1997, from the 2002 and 1997 USDA Census of Agriculture			
Commodity	2002 Production	1997 Production	1997–2002 Change
Cotton (acres)	63,929	54,929	Increased 16%
Peanuts (acres)	12,922	22,514	Decreased 43%
Soybeans (acres)	6,044	8,165	Decreased 26%
Wheat (acres)	2,071	2,690	Decreased 23%
Corn (acres)	1,640	5,615	Decreased 71%
Tobacco (acres)	127	318	Decreased 60%
Broilers	9,300,056	8,657,500	Increased 7%
Hog Inventory	129,277	135,931	Decreased 5%
Hogs Sold	544,529	361,215	Increased 51%
Cattle Sold	0	1,237	N/A

Halifax County Agricultural Statistics from the 2002 USDA Census of Agriculture	
Number of Farms	380
Acres in Farms	194,651
Average Size of Farms (Acres)	512
Market Value of Land Per Farm	$886,263
Market Value of Land Per Acre	$1,810
Market Value of Equipment Per Farm	$129,783
Total Cropland (Acres)	103,929
Market Value of All Products Sold	$64,470,000
Market Value of Products Sold Per Farm	$169,659
Market Value of Crops Sold	$29,346,000
Market Value of Livestock Sold	$35,125,000
Operators with Farm as Principal Occupation	222
Operators with Another Occupation as Principal Occupation	158
Broilers	4,531,138
Hogs in Inventory	59,522
Hogs Sold	229,357
Beef Cows in Inventory	3,092
Beef Cows Sold	4,386
Land in Cotton (Acres)	61,933
Land in Peanuts (Acres)	14,784
Land in Soybeans (Acres)	14,407
Land in Corn (Acres)	4,377
Land in Wheat (Acres)	4,202
Land in Tobacco (Acres)	2,136

Commodity Production in Halifax County in 2002 and 1997, from the 2002 and 1997 USDA Census of Agriculture			
Commodity	2002 Production	1997 Production	1997-2002 Change
Cotton (acres)	61,933	56,876	Increased 9%
Peanuts (acres)	14,784	19,587	Decreased 25%
Soybeans (acres)	14,407	8,613	Increased 67%
Corn (acres)	4,377	8,105	Decreased 46%
Wheat (acres)	4,202	3,445	Increased 22%
Tobacco (acres)	2,136	3,849	Decreased 45%
Broilers	4,531,138	4,283,528	Increased 6%
Hog Inventory	59,522	88,875	Decreased 33%
Hogs Sold	229,357	308,693	Decreased 26%
Cattle Sold	4,386	5,913	Decreased 25%

Economic and Population Data for Northeastern North Carolina Counties					
County	Average Income[1]	Poverty Rate (%)[1]	Average 2003 Unemployment Rate (%)[2]	2000 Population[1]	Population Trend[1]
N. Carolina	$35,320	12.6	6.5		+21% since 1990
Counties in the Vicinity of the Roanoke River National Wildlife Refuge					
Bertie	$22,816	12.6	7.7	19,773	Same as 1990
Halifax	$24,471	23.6	9.5	57,370	Same as 1950
Martin	$26,058	20.1	8.4	25,593	Same as 1940
Northampton	$24,218	23.1	8.5	22,086	Same as 1980
Washington	$27,726	20.5	8.9	13,723	Same as 1960
Other Northeastern North Carolina Counties					
Beaufort	$28,614	17.4	9.7	44,958	+6% since 1990
Camden	$35,423	12.2	2.9	6,885	+16% since 1990
Carteret	$34,348	11.8	5.1	59,383	+13% since 1990
Chowan	$27,900	18.7	4.6	14,526	+7% since 1990
Craven	$33,214	13.8	5.5	91,436	+12% since 1990
Currituck	$36,287	10.8	2.8	18,190	+32% since 1990
Dare	$35,258	8.1	5.1	29,967	+32% since 1990
Gates	$30,087	15.4	2.9	10,516	Same as 1900
Hertford	$23,724	23.1	4.5	22,601	Same as 1960
Hyde	$23,568	24.8	7.4	5,826	-37% since 1900
Pamlico	$28,629	16.8	4.5	12,934	+14% since 1990
Pasquotank	$29,305	19.0	4.4	34,897	+11% since 1990
Perquimens	$26,489	19.5	4.2	11,368	Same as 1920
Tyrrell	$21,616	25.7	9.3	4,149	-17% since 1900
[1] U.S. Census Bureau, 2000 Census of the United States					
[2] North Carolina Economic Security Commission, December, 2003					

VIII. Public Participation

At initial planning meetings, the refuge and planning staff discussed strategies for completing the plan, identified their issues and concerns, and compiled a mailing list of likely interested government agencies, nongovernmental organizations, businesses, and individual citizens. The Service invited these agencies, organizations, businesses, and citizens to participate in two public scoping meetings on May 22 and 24, 2001 in Windsor and Halifax, North Carolina. The staff introduced them to the refuge and its planning process and asked them to identify their issues and concerns. The staff published announcements giving the location, date, and time for the public meeting in the *Federal Register* and legal notices in local newspapers. The staff also sent the announcements as press releases to local newspapers and as public service announcements to television and radio stations. The planning staff placed 50 posters announcing the meeting in local post offices, local government buildings, and stores.

The Service expanded the planning team's identified issues and concerns to include those generated by the agencies, organizations, businesses, and citizens from the local community. These issues and concerns formed the basis for the development and comparison of the objectives in the different alternatives described in this environmental assessment.

The alternatives were subjects of discussion at a second round of two public meetings on April 9 and 11, 2002 in Windsor and Halifax, North Carolina. The planning staff again published announcements giving the location, date, and time for the public meeting as legal notices in local newspapers. Press releases were sent to local newspapers and as public service announcements to television and radio stations. The staff placed 75 posters announcing the meeting in local post offices, local government buildings, and stores.

After considering and evaluating the issues, concerns, and suggestions received from the above public meetings, the planning staff developed the Draft Comprehensive Conservation Plan and Environmental Impact Statement. This draft was completed and distributed to the public for review and comment from March 30 to July 18, 2005. A Notice of Availability for public review of the Draft Comprehensive Conservation Plan and Environmental Impact Statement was published in the *Federal Register* on March 30, 2005. Press releases and public service announcements were also sent to local newspapers and television and radio stations to inform the public of the availability of the draft for review and comment.

During this public review period, the refuge and planning staffs hosted two public forums on May 15 and 16, 2005. One was held at the Windsor, North Carolina, community building (the town in which the refuge headquarters is located); and the other was held at the Halifax County Agricultural Center (located near the northern end of the refuge's approved acquisition boundary). Each forum was held from 6:00 p.m. until 9:00 p.m. The forums started as an open house with the refuge staff available to discuss the draft plan and refuge operations with the audience. A 30-minute formal presentation on the draft plan was then made, followed by a facilitated discussion to solicit open-floor comments on the plan. A recorder wrote the comments on a flip chart, and the comments were then transcribed after the forums.

A total of 15 individuals submitted comments on the Draft Comprehensive Conservation Plan and Environmental Impact Statement, either in writing or at the two public forums. Some of these comments have been incorporated in this Comprehensive Conservation Plan and Final Environmental Impact Statement. A summary of the comments and the Service's responses to them are provided in Appendix XIII.

ROANOKE RIVER NATIONAL WILDLIFE REFUGE PLANNING ISSUES WORKSHEET

ACTIVITY	WHAT WOULD YOU LIKE US TO DO? (8 Responses)			
	Keep the Same	Eliminate	Increase	Decrease

WILDLIFE SURVEYS AND MANAGEMENT

	Keep the Same	Eliminate	Increase	Decrease
Waterfowl Survey and Management	0%	0%	100%	0%
Marshbird Survey and Management	22%	0%	78%	0%
Landbird Survey and Management	25%	0%	75%	0%
Reptile / Amphibian Management	25%	0%	75%	0%
Fish Survey and Management	11%	11%	78%	0%
Endangered Species Management	14%	0%	86%	0%
Black Bear Management	0%	17%	83%	0%
White-tailed Deer Management	20%	0%	80%	0%
Water Quality Surveys	25%	0%	75%	0%

HABITAT MANAGEMENT ACTIVITIES

	Keep the Same	Eliminate	Increase	Decrease
Prescribed Burning	33%	0%	67%	0%
Water Management	20%	0%	80%	0%
Mechanical Vegetation Management	50%	0%	50%	0%
Chemical Vegetation Management	0%	0%	50%	50%
Streambank Maintenance	25%	0%	75%	0%
Planting, Seeding, Clearing for Habitat	0%	0%	100%	0%
Habitat Restoration	0%	0%	100%	0%
Management for Wildlife	0%	0%	100%	0%
Insect and Disease Management	0%	0%	100%	0%
Exotic Species Eradication	0%	0%	100%	0%
Special Protection Status	0%	25%	75%	0%

PUBLIC USE ACTIVITIES

	Keep the Same	Eliminate	Increase	Decrease
Hunting	100%	0%	0%	0%
Wildlife Education (School Students)	50%	50%	0%	0%
Wildlife Education (School Teachers)	50%	50%	0%	0%
Wildlife Interpretation (Formal Programs)	50%	50%	0%	0%
Wildlife Interpretation (Printed Material)	50%	50%	0%	0%
Wildlife Interpretation (Facilities)	50%	50%	0%	0%
Wildlife Photography Opportunities	50%	50%	0%	0%
Wildlife Observation Opportunities	75%	25%	0%	0%
Vehicle Parking Lots	75%	25%	0%	0%
Access for Boating, Canoeing	50%	50%	0%	0%

RESOURCE AND VISITOR PROTECTION ACTIVITIES

Visitor Protection	0%	0%	100%	0%
Wildlife Protection	0%	0%	100%	0%
Trespass Violations	25%	0%	75%	0%
Littering/Dumping Violations	14%	0%	86%	0%
Hunting and Fishing Compliance	29%	0%	71%	0%
Land Acquisition	0%	0%	100%	0%
Wilderness Designation	0%	0%	100%	0%
Wildlife Protection	33%	0%	67%	0%

OPERATION AND MAINTENANCE

Road and Trail Restoration	0%	0%	100%	0%
Road and Firebreak Maintenance	33%	0%	67%	0%
Trail Maintenance	20%	0%	80%	0%
Facilities Maintenance (Signs, Buildings)	20%	0%	80%	0%
Boundary Posting	25%	0%	75%	0%

ACTIVITY   WHICH ALTERNATIVE WOULD YOU LIKE US TO DO
(CAN MIX AND MATCH DIFFERENT ALTERNATIVES FOR DIFFERENT ACTIVITIES)
(5 Responses)

	Alternative 1	Alternative 2	Alternative 3
WILDLIFE MANAGEMENT ACTIVITIES			
Colonial Nesting Birds	20%	40%	40%
Fish	20%	40%	40%
Invertebrates	40%	40%	20%
Mammals	40%	40%	20%
Land Birds	20%	40%	40%
Raptors	20%	60%	20%
Reptiles and Amphibians	20%	60%	20%
Shorebirds	20%	20%	60%
Waterfowl	20%	20%	60%
HABITAT MANAGEMENT ACTIVITIES			
Bottomland Hardwoods (On Refuge)	20%	60%	20%
Bottomland Hardwoods (Nash County)	20%	20%	60%
Bottomland Hardwoods (Sampson County)	20%	20%	60%
Cypress – Tupelo Swamp	20%	20%	60%
Freshwater Marsh	20%	20%	60%
Easements	60%	20%	20%
Wood Duck Boxes	20%	40%	40%
PUBLIC USE ALTERNATIVES			
Hunting	50%	25%	25%
Fishing	50%	25%	25%
Environmental Education	0%	50%	50%
Environmental Interpretation	0%	67%	33%
Wildlife Observation	0%	50%	50%
Wildlife Photography	0%	50%	50%
Outreach	25%	25%	50%
Refuge Support	67%	0%	33%

RESOURCE PROTECTION ACTIVITIES

Cultural Resources	25%	25%	50%
Interagency Coordination	0%	100%	0%
Law Enforcement	33%	0%	67%
Pest Animals	33%	33%	33%
Pest Plants	33%	33%	33%
Wilderness Areas	33%	33%	33%
Permits	17%	17%	66%
State Natural Heritage Areas	67%	0%	33%
Wildlife Disease	20%	60%	20%

Issues Raised at the May 2001 Public Forums.

Area of Concern	Issue	Disposition
Wildlife – General	Conduct surveys to evaluate long term population trends.	In plan.
	Base all management on surveys.	In plan.
Wildlife – Fish	Conduct surveys.	In plan.
	Maintain fish populations.	Principle behind management in plan.
	Conduct sturgeon viability surveys.	In plan.
	Consider shortnose and Atlantic sturgeon reintroduction.	Function of fisheries program.
	Evaluate hatchery capacity relative to needs.	Function of fisheries program.
Wildlife – Mammals	Conduct surveys on which to base management.	In plan.
	Study the potential impact of top predators on beaver and nutria.	In plan.
	Identify animal travel corridors considering safety on roads and opportunities for crossings.	Survey of animals killed along the road in plan.
Wildlife – Pest Animals	Manage pest animals.	In plan.
	Manage beaver populations but do not completely eradicate them.	In plan.
Habitat – General	Maintain flexibility in habitat management tools.	In plan.
Habitat – Bottomland Hardwood Forests	Develop forest management step-down plan.	In plan.
	Evaluate the use of beaver management devices.	In plan.
Habitat – Impoundments	Construct impoundments to flood lowlands.	Only legal on prior converted cropland, land protection plan will consider acquiring prior converted cropland.
Habitat – Pest Plants	Manage pest plants.	In plan.

Area of Concern	Issue	Disposition
Habitat - River	Address the impact of the manipulation of water on river on habitat.	In plan.
	Address the impact of water withdrawals on habitat.	In plan.
	Conduct study to define the water flows that will maintain refuge ecosystem health.	Studies of ecosystem health in plan.
	Hire a hydrologist for the northeastern North Carolina refuges.	In plan.
	Maintain participation in water management issues.	In plan.
	Encourage maintenance of year round river flow adequate for refuge habitat.	In plan.
	Encourage the maintenance of river flows to sustain industries downstream.	Not in plan. Industrial interests will have to solicit that maintenance.
	Ensure the rights of riparian landowners.	Not in plan. Landowner interests will have to solicit those rights.
	Designate habitat affected by flood control versus other water regulation.	Studies in plan to assess the impacts of managed flows.
Public Use - General	Monitor the impact of increased public use.	In plan
Public Use - Access	Consider allowing camping to facilitate refuge being part of Roanoke River Canoe Trail (become part of partnership).	In plan.
	Design canoe platforms for people with disabilities (multiple steps for access at different water levels).	Not in plan (refuge not building canoe platforms, Roanoke Partners is building platforms).
	Investigate canoe platforms to facilitate overnight camping on refuge by canoeists.	In plan.

Area of Concern	Issue	Disposition
Public Use - Access	Evaluate parking on and access to refuge.	In plan.
	Develop trails accessible by bicycles.	In plan (refuge roads being surfaced with gravel).
	Do not impose restrictions on motorized boats.	Plan addressed potential co-management of state waters within the refuge.
	Examine existing perimeter roads for safety and access.	Not in plan. The refuge only owns interior roads. The plan provides for maintenance of all refuge roads.
	Provide trails with good access.	Kuralt interpretive trail is the only planned trail. The interior roads are available, but legal access to public roads must be purchased.
	Integrate CCP with transportation plans (TIP=Transportation Improvement Project).	Interagency cooperation is in plan.
Public Use – Environmental Education	Educate public on the water management of the river.	In plan and currently being done.
	Increase public education programs.	In plan.
Public Use – Fishing	Increase fishing.	In plan. Access is the limiting factor to fishing. As interior roads are improved, access will increase.
Public Use - Hunting	Increase hunting.	Not in plan. Hunting is at a maximum now on the land the refuge owns. As the refuge buys more land, more hunting will be allowed.
	Restrict non-toxic shot when possible (rifle shot still lead).	The refuge will coordinate lead shot issues with the NCWRC.
Public Use - Interpretation	Develop an interpretative center.	Not in plan (refuge will cooperate with Cashie / Roanoke River Center).

Area of Concern	Issue	Disposition
Public Use – Wildlife Observation	Consider building a wildlife observation tower to see rookery or canopy of forest.	Remote camera is in plan.
	Design canoe platforms for people with disabilities (multiple steps for access at different water levels).	Not in plan (refuge not building canoe platforms, Roanoke Partners is building platforms).
	Extend access at the Kuralt Trail.	Not in plan. The parking lot is in a wetland and cannot be extended. The trail will be extended.
Resource Protection – Land Protection	Acquire more land.	Land protection step-down plan in plan.
	Consider easements and cooperative management agreements in protection strategies.	Land protection step-down plan in plan.
	Set priorities in land protection plan.	Land protection step-down plan in plan.
	Consider establishing corridors towards Great Dismal Swamp NWR and Pocosin Lakes NWR.	Land protection step-down plan in plan.
Resource Protection – Law Enforcement	Consider law enforcement on non-refuge land.	Not in plan. Refuge officers have no jurisdiction off the Refuge.
	Hire a law enforcement officer.	In plan.
Resource Protection – Pest Animals	Manage beaver and nutria populations.	In plan.
Resource Protection – Water Quality	Conduct water quality surveys every year.	In plan.
	Maintain USGS water quality surveys.	Resumption of surveys in plan.
	Cooperate with other agencies in water quality surveys.	Resumption of surveys in plan.
Resource Protection – Wilderness	Consider Goodman and Great Island for wilderness.	No wilderness in plan. USFWS does not own mineral rights on islands.
	Do not designate wilderness, but designate areas for no management.	Habitat management step-down plan in plan.
	Designate some wilderness.	No wilderness in plan. Tracts are small and bisected by roads and ditches.

IX. Decisions and Approvals

INTRA-SERVICE SECTION 7 BIOLOGICAL EVALUATION

Originating Person: Harvey Hill
Telephone Number: 252-794-3808
E-Mail: harvey_hill@fws.gov
Date: July 26, 2004

Project Name: Roanoke River National Wildlife Refuge Comprehensive Conservation Plan

I.   **Service Program:**
___ Ecological Services
___ Federal Aid
___ Clean Vessel Act
___ Coastal Wetlands
___ Endangered Species Section 6
___ Partners for Fish and Wildlife
___ Sport Fish Restoration
___ Wildlife Restoration
___ Fisheries
_x_ Refuges/Wildlife

II.   **State/Agency:** North Carolina/ U.S. Fish and Wildlife Service

III.   **Station Name:** Roanoke River National Wildlife Refuge

IV.   **Description of Proposed Action (attach additional pages as needed):** Implementation of the Comprehensive Conservation Plan for Roanoke River National Wildlife Refuge by adopting the preferred alternative that will provide guidance, management direction, and operation plans for the next 15 years.

V.   **Pertinent Species and Habitat:**

     A.   **Include species/habitat occurrence map:**

Bald eagles are commonly seen during winter months and occasionally seen during the summer months on the refuge.

Shortnose sturgeon have been documented in the Roanoke River near Plymouth at the downstream end of the refuge.

     B.   **Complete the following table:**

SPECIES/CRITICAL HABITAT	STATUS[1]
Bald Eagle	Threatened
Shortnose Sturgeon	Endangered

[1]STATUS: E=endangered, T=threatened, PE=proposed endangered, PT=proposed threatened, CH=critical habitat, PCH=proposed critical habitat, C=candidate species

VI.   Location (attach map):

    A.   **Ecoregion Number and Name:** Roanoke-Tar-Neuse-Cape Fear No. 34

    B.   **County and State:** Bertie, Martin, Halifax, Northhampton, North Carolina

    C.   **Section, township, and range (or latitude and longitude):**

    D.   **Distance (miles) and direction to nearest town:** 10 miles southwest of Windsor, North Carolina; just northeast of Williamston, North Carolina; downstream end just northeast of Plymouth, North Carolina

    E.   **Species/habitat occurrence:**

    Bald Eagle- occasionally observed during winter. No active nest.

    Shortnose Sturgeon- known to occur in the Roanoke River at the downstream end of the refuge.

VII.   **Determination of Effects:**

    A.   **Explanation of effects of the action on species and critical habitats in item V. B (attach additional pages as needed).**

SPECIES/CRITICAL HABITAT	IMPACTS TO SPECIES/CRITICAL HABITAT
Bald Eagle	Disturbance to nesting habitat by refuge visitors.
Shortnose Sturgeon	Degradation of habitat by construction on the refuge.

    B.   **Explanation of actions to be implemented to reduce adverse effects.**

SPECIES/CRITICAL HABITAT	ACTIONS TO MITIGATE/MINIMIZE IMPACTS
Bald Eagle	Monitor for active nests; limit access to nesting sites.
Shortnose Sturgeon	Follow best management practices when grading roads, installing water control structures, building structures.

VIII.   **Effect Determination and Response Requested:**

SPECIES/ CRITICAL HABITAT	DETERMINATION			RESPONSE REQUESTED[1]
	NE	NA	AA	
Bald Eagle		X		Concurrence
Shortnose Sturgeon		X		Concurrence

[1]DETERMINATION/RESPONSE REQUESTED:
NE = no effect. This determination is appropriate when the proposed action will not directly, indirectly, or cumulatively impact, either positively or negatively, any listed, proposed, candidate species or designated/proposed critical habitat. Response Requested is optional but a "Concurrence" is recommended for a complete Administrative Record.

NA = not likely to adversely affect. This determination is appropriate when the proposed action is not likely to adversely impact any listed, proposed, candidate species or designated/proposed critical habitat or there may be beneficial effects to these resources. Response Requested is a "Concurrence."

AA = likely to adversely affect. This determination is appropriate when the proposed action is likely to adversely impact any listed, proposed, or candidate species or designated/proposed critical habitat. Response requested for listed species is "Formal Consultation." Response requested for proposed or candidate species is "Conference."

_____   _____
Signature (originating station)   Date

_____
Title

IX. Reviewing Ecological Services Office Evaluation:

      A. Concurrence _____   Nonconcurrence _____

      B. Formal consultation required _____

      C. Conference required _____

      D. Informal conference required _____

      E. Remarks (attach additional pages as needed):

_____   _____
Signature   Date

_____   _____
Title   Office

United States Department of the Interior

FISH AND WILDLIFE SERVICE
Raleigh Field Office
Post Office Box 33726
Raleigh, North Carolina 27636-3726

December 10, 2004

Memorandum

To: Natural Resource Planner, Ecosystem Planning Office

From: Acting Ecological Services Supervisor, FWS, Raleigh, NC   *John S. Hammond*

Subject: Draft Comprehensive Conservation Plan and Environmental Impact Statement
(CCP/WIS) and Intra-service Section 7 Consultation for Roanoke River National
Wildlife Refuge

This follows our review of the August 2, 2004 memorandum of the Chief, Division of Planning.
Southeastern Region and accompanying Intra-service Section 7 Biological Evaluation Form (BE
Form), Draft Comprehensive Conservation Plan (CCP) and Environmental Impact Statement
(EIS) for the Roanoke River National Wildlife Refuge, Bertie County, North Carolina. The CCP
is being developed to provide refuge staff with strategic guidance for management of Roanoke
River National Wildlife Refuge. The plan will direct Refuge programs and actions over the next
15 years. The CCP was developed in compliance with the National Wildlife Refuge System
Improvement Act of 1997 and Part 602 of the Fish and Wildlife Service Manual. Our comments
are provided in accordance with section 7 of the Endangered Species Act of 1973, as amended
(16 USC 1531 *et seq.*).

The CCP/EIS describes the location of the Roanoke River NWR within the South Atlantic
Coastal Plain and identifies specific issues/threats affecting trust resources in this physiographic
region including forest loss/fragmentation, alteration of hydrology, siltation of aquatic
ecosystems and proliferation of invasive aquatic plants. A major function of the CCP, in
compliance with the purposes of the National Wildlife Refuge System, is to establish
conservation priorities and outline the steps needed to protect trust species and their habitats.
The means for achieving the Refuges goals are step-down management plans to be updated or
developed.

Step Down Management Plans for Implementing the CCP

Step-down Plan	*Status*
Land Protection Plan	To be developed; draft completion 2007
Habitat Management Plan	To be developed; draft completion 2008
Moist Soil/Water Management Plan	To be updated; draft completion 2007
Forest Management Plan	To be developed; draft completion 2007
Fire Management Plan	To be updated; draft completion 2006
Road Plan	To be developed; draft completion 2007

Step Down Management Plans for implementing the CCP

Step-down Plan	*Status*
Integrated Pest Management Plan	To be developed; draft completion 2009
Nuisance Animal Management Plan	To be updated; draft completion 2009
Exotic Plant Control Plan	To be developed; draft completion 2009
Visitor Services Plan	To be developed; draft completion 2007
Environmental Education Plan	To be developed; draft completion 2007
Fishing Plan	To be updated; draft completion 2006
Hunting and Trapping	To be updated; draft completion 2006
Sign Plan	To be updated; draft completion 2006
Biological Inventory/Monitoring Plan	To be developed; draft completion 2008
Law Enforcement Plan	To be up dated; draft completion date 2006

The CCP states that as these plans are developed, they will be evaluated as appropriate through the National Environmental Policy Act. To ensure compliance with section 7 of the Endangered Species Act, refuge staff should coordinate with the Raleigh Ecological Services Office as these step-down plans are developed so that the latest information regarding the status and distribution of listed and candidate species is considered.

The planning area for the CCP/EIS extends beyond the refuge boundaries to include properties that may be acquired, and/or where the Service's refuge staff may be involved in partnerships/ collaborative planning efforts. Presently, Roanoke River NWR contains and manages 20,978 acres. The acquisition boundary includes an additional 9,000+ acres. While the current extent of Roanoke River NWR is contained in Bertie County, the acquisition area for the refuge also includes Halifax and Martin counties.

A list of federally protected and federal species of concern occurring within Bertie, Halifax and Martin counties is included below. It is unlikely that suitable habitat for all of these species is present within the CCP study area. However, suitable roosting/hibernating habitat and maternity colony sites Rafinesque's big-eared bat (*Corynorhinus rafinesquii*), a federal species of concern, may exist on the refuge. Such habitat may occur in forested regions of the refuge where large, hollow trees or abandoned buildings exist. Where conservation of trust resources is considered in the CCP, we recommend the biological needs of this species be included as well.

The BE Form evaluates the potential for actions outlined in the CCP to affect the federally listed, threatened bald eagle (*Haliaeetus leucocephalus*) and endangered shortnose sturgeon (*Acipenser brevirostrum*). Bald eagle nesting habitat may be affected by frequent access by refuge visitors. Bald eagles are known to nest near the refuge but no nests have been documented on the refuge or in the acquisition area. Surveys should be conducted prior to the creation of new access trails into the refuge to ensure nesting habitat is not affected. Roanoke River NWR will monitor for active nests and will limit access to sensitive bald eagle habitat where necessary. Details for protecting nesting habitat can be further provided as the step-down plans are drafted.

Construction of facilities on the refuge could contribute to the degradation of shortnose sturgeon habitat within the River. The Refuge will follow best management practices when grading roads and installing water control structures and buildings to ensure these effects are effectively minimized.

Based on the information contained in the August 2, 2004 memorandum and accompanying BE Form, we concur with the determination that implementation of the Roanoke River CCP is not likely to adversely affect the bald eagle, shortnose sturgeon or any other federally listed endangered or threatened species, their formally designated critical habitat, or species currently proposed for federal listing under the Endangered Species Act, as amended.

We believe that the requirements of section 7 of the Act have been satisfied. We remind you that obligations under section 7 consultation must be reconsidered if: (1) new information reveals impacts of this identified action that may affect listed species or critical habitat in a manner not previously considered; (2) this action is subsequently modified in a manner that was not considered in this review; or, (3) a new species is listed or critical habitat determined that may be affected by the identified action.

If you have questions concerning this response please call me at (919) 856-4520 Ext 28.

CC: Kevin Moody
      Harvey Hall

ROANOKE RIVER NATIONAL WILDLIFE REFUGE COMPATIBILITY DETERMINATION

Uses: The following uses were considered for compatibility determination reviews: hunting, fishing, wildlife observation, photography, environmental education, interpretation, trapping of selected furbearers for nuisance animal management, forest management program, and refuge resource research studies. A description and anticipated biological impacts for each use are addressed separately in this Compatibility Determination.

Refuge Name: Roanoke River National Wildlife Refuge.

Date Established: August 14, 1989.

Establishing and Acquisition Authority(ies): 16 U.S.C., Sec. 3901(b), 100 Stat. 3583 (Emergency Wetlands Resources Act of 1986) and 16 U.S.C. Sec. 664 (Migratory Bird Conservation Act of 1929).

Refuge Purpose: The purpose of Roanoke River National Wildlife Refuge, as reflected in the refuge's authorizing legislation, is to protect and conserve migratory birds, and other wildlife resources through the protection of wetlands, in accordance with the following laws:

> ...the conservation of wetlands of the Nation in order to maintain the public benefits they provide and to help fulfill international obligations contained in various migratory bird treaties and conventions... 16 U.S.C., Sec. 3901(b), 100 Stat. 3583 (Emergency Wetlands Resources Act of 1986);

> ...for use as an inviolate sanctuary, or for any other management purpose, for migratory birds... 16 U.S.C. Sec. 664 (Migratory Bird Conservation Act of 1929);

> ...for the development, advancement, management, conservation, and protection of fish and wildlife resources... 16 U.S.C. Sec 742f(a)4; and

> ...for the benefit of the United States Fish and Wildlife Service, in performing its activities and services... 16 U.S.C. Sec. 742f(b)1 (Fish and Wildlife Act of 1956).

The refuge's purpose and importance to migratory birds, particularly waterfowl, are further described in the Service's Environmental Assessment for the proposed establishment of the refuge (1989): *To preserve wintering habitat for mallards, American black ducks, and wood ducks and production habitat for wood ducks to meet the habitat goals presented in the Ten-Year Waterfowl Habitat Acquisition Plan and the North American Waterfowl Management Plan.*

The refuge purpose was further described in the Approval Memorandum for the purchase of lands for the establishment of Roanoke River National Wildlife Refuge, which stated the primary reason for acquisition and inclusion of the area into the National Wildlife Refuge System was to preserve wintering habitat for mallards, American black ducks, wood ducks, and production habitat for wood ducks (USFWS Southeast Region Approval Memorandum 1989). Three objectives for which the area would be managed were identified in the Approval Memorandum: to preserve an area which has traditional high use for wintering waterfowl; to provide additional waterfowl habitat through refuge management; and to establish a waterfowl sanctuary.

National Wildlife Refuge System Mission:

The mission of the System, as defined by the National Wildlife Refuge System Improvement Act of 1997, is:

... to administer a national network of lands and waters for the conservation, management, and where appropriate, restoration of the fish, wildlife and plant resources and their habitats within the United States for the benefit of present and future generations of Americans.

Other Applicable Laws, Regulations, and Policies:

Antiquities Act of 1906 (34 Stat. 225)
Migratory Bird Treaty Act of 1918 (15 U.S.C. 703-711; 40 Stat. 755)
Migratory Bird Conservation Act of 1929 (16 U.S.C. 715r; 45 Stat. 1222)
Migratory Bird Hunting Stamp Act of 1934 (16 U.S.C. 718-178h; 48 Stat. 451)
Criminal Code Provisions of 1940 (18 U.S.C. 41)
Bald and Golden Eagle Protection Act (16 U.S.C. 668-668d; 54 Stat. 250)
Refuge Trespass Act of June 25, 1948 (18 U.S.C. 41; 62 Stat. 686)
Fish and Wildlife Act of 1956 (16 U.S.C. 742a-742j; 70 Stat.1119)
Refuge Recreation Act of 1962 (16 U.S.C. 460k-460k-4; 76 Stat. 653)
Wilderness Act (16 U.S.C. 1131; 78 Stat. 890)
Land and Water Conservation Fund Act of 1965
National Historic Preservation Act of 1966, as amended (16 U.S.C. 470, et seq.; 80 Stat. 915)
National Wildlife Refuge System Administration Act of 1966 (16 U.S.C. 668dd, 668ee; 80 Stat. 927)
National Environmental Policy Act of 1969, NEPA (42 U.S.C. 4321, et seq; 83 Stat. 852)
Use of Off-Road Vehicles on Public Lands (Executive Order 11644, as amended by Executive Order 10989)
Endangered Species Act of 1973 (16 U.S.C. 1531 et. seq; 87 Stat. 884)
Refuge Revenue Sharing Act of 1935, as amended in 1978 (16 U.S.C. 715s; 92 Stat. 1319)
National Wildlife Refuge Regulations for the Most Recent Fiscal Year (50 CFR Subchapter C; 43 CFR 3101.3-3)
Emergency Wetlands Resources Act of 1986 (S.B. 740)
North American Wetlands Conservation Act of 1990
Food Security Act (Farm Bill) of 1990 as amended (HR 2100)
The Property Clause of the U.S. Constitution Article IV 3, Clause 2
The Commerce Clause of the U.S. Constitution Article 1, Section 8
The National Wildlife Refuge System Improvement Act of 1997 (Public Law 105-57, USC668dd)
Executive Order 12996, Management and General Public Use of the National Wildlife Refuge System. March 25, 1996
Title 50, Code of Federal Regulations, Parts 25-33
Archaeological Resources Protection Act of 1979
Native American Graves Protection and Repatriation Act of 1990

Compatibility determinations for each description listed were considered separately. Although for brevity, the preceding sections from "Uses" through "Other Applicable Laws, Regulations and Policies" are only written once within the plan, they are part of each descriptive use and become part of that compatibility determination if considered outside of the comprehensive conservation plan.

Description of Use: Most of the refuge area is a mosaic of forest blocks of mid-succession bottomland hardwoods, and interconnected streams, ditches, and backswamps. There is a great variety of tree species on the refuge that includes baldcypress, tupelo gum, oak, sugarberry, black gum, hickory, elm, green ash, bitter pecan, and willow. This rich forested wetland provides good habitat for a number of game species including white-tailed deer, turkey, squirrel, raccoon, woodcock, and waterfowl.

Many of the local residents enjoy an informal, rural lifestyle that includes frequent recreational use of the area's natural resources. Hunting and fishing have been, and continue to be, popular uses of refuge lands. Hunting has been permitted since 1990, when the refuge was first approved to offer hunting of big game, small game, and waterfowl. The administration, as well as special regulations for hunting, has changed over time but the majority of the program has remained unchanged.

The comprehensive conservation plan calls for the continued hunting of deer, small game, waterfowl, and turkey. All hunts fall within the framework of the State's open seasons and follow state regulations. There are additional refuge-specific regulations to supplement state regulations. These refuge-specific regulations are reviewed annually and incorporated into the refuge hunting and fishing brochure and permit that hunters are required to have before hunting on the refuge. The comprehensive conservation plan would increase law enforcement presence during hunting seasons; would evaluate the hunt program annually and modify seasons, hunt areas or regulations if necessary; and additional non-hunting areas could be added as the refuge expands through an active land acquisition program. Implementation of the proposed alternative, as described in the comprehensive conservation plan, would ensure that opportunities for various types of wildlife-dependent recreation would continue for future generations.

Availability of Resources: Based on a review of the refuge's budget allocated for this activity, there is adequate funding to ensure compatibility and to administer this use at its current level. Additional fiscal resources are needed to conduct this use as proposed. A permanent, full-time law enforcement officer and public use specialist are needed to assist with hunting program administration and visitor service. Upgrading and expanding the current radio system to Department of the Interior standards is needed to improve emergency response and ensure the safety of officers in the field.

Anticipated Impacts of the Use: The deer herd has expanded and increased significantly since the Service established the refuge. Prior to refuge establishment, this portion of Bertie County was subject to excessive deer poaching that maintained the deer herd at low levels. Following refuge establishment and initiation of an effective wildlife law enforcement program, the deer herd has increased significantly in and around the refuge. The refuge's forested habitat, combined with commercially harvested forests and agricultural fields adjacent to the refuge, provides ideal habitat conditions for white-tailed deer.

Turkey populations on the refuge have fluctuated since refuge establishment due to the impacts of spring flooding on nest success. Recent gobbler surveys indicated an expanding turkey population and the Service held the first spring gobbler-only turkey season on the refuge in spring 2001. Two 2-day quota turkey hunts were conducted in 2001 resulting in the harvest of two gobblers, although several other gobblers were heard and worked.

The flood plain hardwood forests of the area support high squirrel populations and have for several years. As a result, fall squirrel hunting is one of the most popular activities on the refuge. Squirrel dogs are occasionally used in late winter following leaf fall.

The raccoon population appears to be increasing throughout the area, and in the absence of predators, raccoon populations rapidly build to levels resulting in disease problems and impacts to the reproduction of non-game forest breeding birds and wild turkeys. Therefore, in addition to providing hunting opportunities, an effective hunting program for raccoons is particularly important to keep the raccoon population at a level that does not negatively affect non-game forest-breeding birds and wild turkeys.

The traditional method for hunting raccoons is the use of dogs at night to tree raccoons. The use of dogs typically occurs with a single, well-trained dog under a high level of control by the hunter and rarely, if ever, results in unacceptable levels of disturbance to other wildlife. Many years of experience, on multiple refuges and national recreation areas across the Southeast Region, indicate that traditional methods of take for these species, conducted under controlled conditions of carefully regulated and enforced seasons on large forested land areas, do not negatively or cumulatively affect other wildlife or other users. As with all hunts on the refuge, results would be carefully monitored and changes implemented as needed across time to minimize the impacts and maintain compatibility.

Duck hunting occurs in a number of creeks and backswamps throughout the refuge. Dabbler species such as mallard, American black duck, and wood duck are the most abundant species by number and thus are the most commonly harvested species.

Harvest management of big game (white-tailed deer and turkey) is the art of combining wildlife science and landowner objectives for the attainment of a specific management goal. Harvest management strategies should be based on objectives established as part of hunting plans developed for the area. The objective-setting process must be based on a complete analysis of biological data. Specific harvest objectives allow the setting of hunting regulations. Results of each hunting season would be thoroughly evaluated to ensure that the harvest management program remains dynamic and responsive to an evolving management environment (Bookhout 1994).

Harvest management of upland game and furbearers (e.g., squirrel, rabbit, raccoon, opossum, beaver) is considerably different from that of both big game and migratory birds. Current literature suggests that user take (<50 percent of total mortality) of most upland game is compensatory; that factors such as immigration from adjacent areas and density-dependent production operate in most upland game populations; and that hunting does not significantly impact populations. Hunting is substituted for natural mortality. Production of large, annual surpluses of young allows for lengthy seasons and generous bag limits with little concern for over-harvest and minimal chance of population impacts in most areas (Bookhout 1994).

Harvest management of migratory birds (e.g., ducks and woodcock) is more difficult to assess. Migratory bird regulations are established at the federal level each year following a series of meetings involving both state and federal biologists. Harvest guidelines are based on population survey data with regulations that are subject to change each year, including bag limits, season lengths, and framework dates (Bookhout 1994). Schimidt (1993) states, "In general, all studies have demonstrated a high degree of compensation of hunting mortality by other 'natural' mortality factors for harvest levels experienced to date." He also reports, "The proportion of waterfowl populations subject to hunting on refuges is very low, thus hunting is not likely to have an adverse impact on the status of any recognized waterfowl population in North America."

The refuge's great variety and abundance of high quality wetland areas provide outstanding habitat for a variety of wading birds. Wading birds frequent these wetlands and two known rookeries are present on the property. Primary species include the great blue heron, little blue heron, green heron, cattle egret, snowy egret, great egret, anhinga, and night herons (Fish and Wildlife Service 1989). The potential of disturbance, especially during the nesting season, does exist for these rookeries; however, this potential would be virtually nonexistent due to no overlap of hunting seasons with nesting season.

Similar to wading birds, the area's habitat for neotropical migratory birds is outstanding (Fish and Wildlife Service 1998). Neotropical migrants use the interior hardwood forested areas and edges. Disturbance to neotropicals would be minimal and temporary as the habitat would be slightly altered for the betterment of these species.

Based on available information, no threatened or endangered species, other than the bald eagle and shortnose sturgeon, have been documented on Roanoke River National Wildlife Refuge. It is anticipated that the current levels and expected future levels of hunting or other wildlife-dependent recreation activities would not directly, indirectly, or cumulatively impact any listed, proposed, or candidate species or designated/proposed critical habitat. Data gathered from future biological surveys regarding the importance or potential importance of the refuge to threatened or endangered species or critical habitat (or proposed threatened, endangered, or critical habitat), could result in changes to public use activities across time; however, these changes would have no effect on listed species.

Incidental take of other wildlife species, either illegally or unintentionally, may occur with any consumptive use program. At current and anticipated public use levels, incidental take would be very small and would not directly or cumulatively impact current or future populations of wildlife either on this refuge or in the surrounding areas. Implementation of an effective law enforcement program and development of site specific refuge regulations/special conditions would eliminate most incidental take problems.

Public Review and Comment: The period of public review and comment began March 30, 2005 and ended July 18, 2005. Methods used to solicit public review and comment included posted notices at refuge headquarters and area locations, copies of the draft comprehensive conservation plant distributed to adjacent landowners, the public, and local, State, and Federal agencies, two public forums, press releases and public service announcements to area newspapers, and local radio announcements. Appendix XIII summarizes the public comments.

Determination (check one below):

_____ Use is Not Compatible

__X__ Use is Compatible With Following Stipulations

Stipulations Necessary to Ensure Compatibility: Hunting is permitted in accordance with State of North Carolina regulations and licensing requirements. An Environmental Assessment is on file at the refuge headquarters as part of the Hunting Plan. Following completion of the comprehensive conservation plan, the staff will revise the Hunting Plan. The following stipulations would help ensure the refuge hunting program is compatible with refuge purposes.

- Vehicles are restricted to parking lots. Travel is limited to foot travel only.

- Firearms, bows, and other weapons are prohibited except during designated hunting seasons.

- Hunting deer with dogs is not allowed on the refuge. Use of dogs for hunting rabbit, squirrel, raccoon, waterfowl, and woodcock is allowed during designated seasons only.

- Camping overnight on the refuge is allowed only to facilitate hunting.

- All hunts are designed to provide quality user opportunities based upon known wildlife population levels and biological parameters. Hunt season dates and bag limits will be adjusted as needed to achieve balanced wildlife population levels within carrying capacities, regardless of impacts to user opportunities.

- As additional data is collected and a long-range hunt plan developed, additional refuge-specific regulations could be implemented. These regulations could include, but may not be limited to, season dates that differ from those in surrounding state zones, refuge permit requirements, and closed areas on a permanent or seasonal basis (to reduce disturbance to specific wildlife species or habitats, such as bird rookeries, wintering waterfowl or threatened/endangered species, or to provide for public safety).

Justification: Hunting is compatible with the purposes for which the refuge was established and the mission of the National Wildlife Refuge System. It is one of the public use recreational activities that the 1997 National Wildlife Refuge System Improvement Act specifically identifies as one to be allowed where possible on refuges. The refuge uses deer and raccoon hunts as management tools to protect the diverse ecosystem. It has been well documented that hunting mortality from small game and spring gobbler harvests is incidental to overall mortality. Waterfowl hunting mortality has been documented as being compensatory to natural mortality factors and the number or waterfowl hunted on refuges is insignificant in terms of the overall continental population.

Mandatory 15-year Re-evaluation Date: _____9/26/2020_____

FISHING

Description of Use: Sport fishing is a common public use on the state waters of the Roanoke River from the banks located on the Roanoke River National Wildlife Refuge. Fish creel limits, boating safety, and license requirements are in accordance with State of North Carolina regulations. A public boat ramp is located on the Roanoke River across the river from the refuge at U.S. Route 17. Development of public access to the Roanoke River on the refuge would allow the public to utilize these important fishery resources. As identified in the comprehensive conservation plan, additional access to the banks will be provided, creel surveys conducted, and water quality analysis performed in order to provide a high quality fishing experience.

Availability of Resources: Based on a review of the refuge's budget allocated for this activity, there is adequate funding to ensure compatibility and to administer the use at its current level. Additional fiscal resources are needed to conduct this use as proposed. To improve sport-fishing opportunities, the plan includes proposals for additional access and water quality analyses.

Anticipated Impacts of the Use: Recreational fishing should not adversely affect the fisheries resource, wildlife resource, endangered species, or any other natural resource of the refuge. There may be some limited disturbance to certain species of wildlife and some trampling of vegetation; however, this should be short-lived and relatively minor and would not negatively impact wetland values of the refuge. Known bird rookery sites do not occur at locations currently popular for fishing activities; therefore, disturbance should not be a problem. If disturbance at these sites is identified as a problem in future years, closed areas would be established during nesting season to eliminate this concern.

Improvement of access would create some disturbance to the natural environment during construction and lead to increased public use on the Roanoke River. All construction activities would be carried out with appropriate permits under Section 404 of the Clean Water Act and State Historic Preservation Officer review of cultural resources. Sediment retention barriers would be utilized during access improvement and soil stabilization features would be incorporated in to design of access points to minimize any future soil erosion potential. Public use of the Roanoke River would be expected to increase as a result of improved access, but the level of use is not expected to cause detrimental wildlife disturbance. Problems associated with littering and illegal take of fish would be controlled through law enforcement activities. Providing information to refuge visitors about rules and regulations, along with increased law enforcement patrol, would keep these negative impacts to a minimum.

Public Review and Comment: The period of public review and comment began March 30, 2005 and ended July 18, 2005. Methods used to solicit public review and comment included posted notices at refuge headquarters and area locations, copies of the draft comprehensive conservation plant distributed to adjacent landowners, the public, and local, State, and Federal agencies, two public forums, press releases and public service announcements to area newspapers, and local radio announcements. Appendix XIII summarizes the public comments.

Determination (check one below):

_____ Use is Not Compatible

__X__ Use is Compatible with Following Stipulations

Stipulations Necessary to Ensure Compatibility: Conflicts between fishermen and hunters or other visitors using the refuge for non-consumptive wildlife recreation have not been a problem in the past and are not expected to be a problem in the future. Associated violations such as taking undersize fish, open fires, and littering can be minimized by a continued law enforcement presence. Following completion of the comprehensive conservation plan, the Fishing Plan will be developed. The following stipulations will help ensure the refuge fishing program is compatible with refuge purposes.

> All fishing tackle must be attended at all times.

> Leaving boats on the refuge overnight is prohibited.

> Fishing allowed during daylight hours only.

Justification: Refuge regulations permit fishing of state waters from banks on the refuge under state regulations whenever there is no hunting on the refuge. Recreational fishing is providing a quality fishing experience on a sustainable basis. Fishing is a public use activity that, according to the 1997 National Wildlife Refuge System Improvement Act, should be provided and expanded where possible. Improved access facilities would reduce bank erosion and habitat disturbance, while providing additional quality fishing opportunities.

Mandatory 15-year Re-evaluation Date:_____9/26/2020_____

WILDLIFE OBSERVATION AND PHOTOGRAPHY

Description of Use: Non-consumptive wildlife observation uses such as bird watching, auto tour routes, hiking, and nature photography are minimal at this time due to the area's distance from large metropolitan areas and the general lack of access and facilities. It is estimated that 5,000 visits per year are attributed to wildlife observation and related activities.

It is anticipated that an increase in non-consumptive wildlife-dependent uses would occur over the next few years as facilities and access are provided, and especially as the public and conservation groups become aware of the excellent birding/wildlife viewing opportunities on the refuge. This anticipated increase would be slow in developing and due to the remoteness of the area high numbers of users are not expected.

Refuge roads are not maintained for public vehicle travel. The Service has upgraded 3 miles of refuge roads and maintains them for administrative purposes, while another 12 miles of old logging roads are available for pedestrian use. If the Service enacts the comprehensive conservation plan, the refuge will upgrade 12 additional miles of refuge roads to national refuge road standards and extend the Kuralt Trail.

Availability of Resources: Based on a review of the refuge's budget allocated for this activity, there is adequate funding to ensure compatibility and to administer the use at its current level. Additional fiscal resources are needed to provide this use as proposed. To provide safe, high quality wildlife observation and photography opportunities, vehicular road access must be improved, wildlife observation points developed, and directional/interpretive signage provided.

Anticipated Impacts of the Use: Wildlife observation and photography activities might result in some disturbance to wildlife, especially if visitors venture too close to one of the bird rookeries. Refuge road systems, foot trails, boardwalks and wildlife observation platforms opened to pedestrian use by the public will be located to minimize disturbance that could occur in these sensitive areas. If unacceptable levels of disturbance are identified at any time, sensitive sites will be closed to public entry. Some minimal trampling of vegetation also may occur.

Construction of foot trails, boardwalks, observation platforms, upgrading refuge roads, and converting all-terrain vehicle trails to vehicular traffic will alter small portions of the natural environment. Proper planning prior to construction, sediment retention and grade stabilization features will reduce negative impacts to wetlands, threatened and endangered species, and species of special concern. Impacts such as trampling vegetation and wildlife disturbance by refuge visitors do occur, but is presently not significant. Upgrading refuge roads would reduce soil erosion associated with the current dirt roads and trails. Visitors cause other potential negative impacts, such as littering or illegally taking plants or animals, or violating refuge regulations. Refuge roads are maintained for habitat and biological management programs and law enforcement. Use of the roads by the public does incur added maintenance costs.

Public Review and Comment: The period of public review and comment began March 30, 2005 and ended July 18, 2005. Methods used to solicit public review and comment included posted notices at refuge headquarters and area locations, copies of the draft comprehensive conservation plant distributed to adjacent landowners, the public, and local, State, and Federal agencies, two public forums, press releases and public service announcements to area newspapers, and local radio announcements. Appendix XIII summarizes the public comments.

Determination (check one below):

_____ Use is Not Compatible

__X__ Use is Compatible with Following Stipulations

Stipulations Necessary to Ensure Compatibility: Prior to construction, the refuge staff would obtain permits from local, state, and federal regulatory agencies to reduce the possibility of negatively impacting wetlands, cultural resources, or protected species. Law enforcement patrol of public use areas would continue to minimize violations of refuge regulations. The staff will close refuge roads to the public during extremely wet periods such as flooding to prevent road damage and for visitor safety. The staff will monitor public use for wildlife observation and photography to document any negative impacts. If any negative impacts become noticeable, the Service will take corrective action to reduce or eliminate the effects on wildlife.

Justification: Wildlife observation and photography are an important and preferred public uses on Roanoke River National Wildlife Refuge and the National Wildlife Refuge System. The 1997 National Wildlife Refuge System Improvement Act identified wildlife observation as a priority pubic recreational use to be facilitated on refuges. It is through permitted, compatible public uses such as this, that the public becomes aware of and provides support for our national wildlife refuges.

Mandatory 15-year Re-evaluation Date:_____9/26/2020_____

ENVIRONMENTAL EDUCATION AND INTERPRETATION

Description of Use: Environmental education and interpretation are those activities that seek to increase the public's knowledge and understanding of wildlife, national wildlife refuges, ecology and land management, as well as contribute to the conservation of natural resources. If the comprehensive conservation plan is enacted, the refuge will develop interpretation and environmental education programs. Environmental education/interpretation activities have been largely nonexistent in prior years. Efforts to develop this program are planned and will usually be associated with structured activities conducted by refuge staff or trained volunteers. Refuge staff will develop and provide curriculum and support materials to area teachers for use both on and off the refuge. Informational kiosks and interpretive panels will be developed at key refuge entrance points, and wildlife observation platforms constructed as part of the environmental education/interpretation program.

Availability of Resources: Based on a review of the refuge's budget allocated for these activities, funding is inadequate to ensure compatibility and to administer these uses at current or proposed levels. Current staffing is extremely limited with no public use staff. The management of a volunteer program will be essential to successfully implement the education and visitor use program. The refuge staff will recruit and train volunteers to assist in developing and implementing environmental education and interpretive programs. The addition of a permanent public use specialist and facilities, including access roads, boardwalks, signs, parking and trail head development, kiosks, and environmental education materials, are needed to provide and conduct wildlife observation, wildlife photography, and environmental education and interpretation activities.

Anticipated Impacts of the Use: Construction of facilities such as boardwalks, kiosks, and observation platforms will alter small portions of the natural environment on the refuge. Proper planning and placement of facilities will ensure that wetlands, threatened or endangered species, or species of special concern are not negatively impacted. The refuge staff will obtain proper permits through the county, state, and federal regulatory agencies prior to construction to ensure resource protection. The use of on-site, hands-on, action-oriented activities to accomplish environmental education and interpretive tours may impose a low-level impact on the sites used for these activities. These low-level impacts may include trampling of vegetation and temporary disturbance to wildlife species in the immediate area. Educational activities held off-refuge will not create any biological impacts on the resource.

Public Review and Comment: The period of public review and comment began March 30, 2005 and ended July 18, 2005. Methods used to solicit public review and comment included posted notices at refuge headquarters and area locations, copies of the draft comprehensive conservation plant distributed to adjacent landowners, the public, and local, State, and Federal agencies, two public forums, press releases and public service announcements to area newspapers, and local radio announcements. Appendix XIII summarizes the public comments.

Determination (check one below):

_____ Use is Not Compatible

__X__ Use is Compatible with Following Stipulations

Stipulations Necessary to Ensure Compatibility: Zoning of visitor activities by time and space, clustering public use facilities, proper monitoring, educating visitors, and enforcement will ensure compatibility with the purposes of the refuge and mission of the National Wildlife Refuge System. Through periodic evaluation of trails and visitor contact points, the visitor services program will assess resource impacts. If future human impacts are determined through evaluation to be detrimental to important natural resources, actions will be taken to reduce or eliminate those impacts. Major portions of the refuge will remain undeveloped, without public interpretive facilities.

Justification: Interpretation and environmental education are identified in the 1997 National Wildlife Refuge System Improvement Act as activities that the Service should provide and expand on refuges. Educating and informing the public through structured environmental education courses, interpretive materials, and guided tours about migratory birds, endangered species, wildlife management, and ecosystems will lead to improved support of the Service's mission to protect our natural resources.

Mandatory 15-year Re-evaluation Date:_____9/26/2020_____

TRAPPING OF SELECTED FURBEARERS FOR MANAGEMENT

Description of Use: The staff may direct management through trapping on raccoon and beaver. Both species are at a sufficiently high level on the refuge to adversely affect ecosystem functions. As indicated in the comprehensive conservation plan, beaver activities have caused significant deterioration and loss of bottomland hardwoods throughout the refuge, and excessive numbers of raccoons can have negative effects on the reproduction of forest breeding birds and wild turkeys. Protection and restoration of bottomland hardwoods and improvements in game and nongame populations are central components of the plan. To this end, trapping and/or hunting remain the only viable methods to reduce population levels of beaver and raccoon. The Service would issue special use permits to administer a trapping program consistent with sound biology, refuge purposes, and conservation of ecosystem functions.

Availability of Resources: No additional fiscal resources are needed to conduct this use. The existing staff can administer permits and monitor this use as part of routine management duties.

Anticipated Impacts of the Use: Targeted removal of beaver and raccoon from portions of the refuge will reduce the negative impacts these species are having on ecosystem functions. Control of beaver populations will help ensure the protection of important bottomland hardwood forests. Regulated trapping of raccoon populations will reduce the nest predation this species causes to neotropical birds and wild turkeys. However, no trapping program, regardless of how well it is designed, can prevent the possible take of other species. Trappers will be required to report the incidental take of other species. A negligible impact on other wildlife species is expected in both the short and long term.

Public Review and Comment: The period of public review and comment began March 30, 2005 and ended July 18, 2005. Methods used to solicit public review and comment included posted notices at refuge headquarters and area locations, copies of the draft comprehensive conservation plan distributed to adjacent landowners, the public, and local, State, and Federal agencies, two public forums, press releases and public service announcements to area newspapers, and local radio announcements. Appendix XIII summarizes the public comments.

Determination (check one below):

_____ Use is Not Compatible

__X__ Use is Compatible with Following Stipulations

Stipulations Necessary to Ensure Compatibility: As a trapping program is implemented on the refuge, the staff will monitor it closely to assess the potential adverse effects on other wildlife, as well as the benefits to game and nongame species and their habitats. The staff will modify the program as needed to maintain compatibility. Trappers will carry out all trapping activities under a refuge special use permit. The staff will limit trappers by number, area, and season in order to target problem areas and minimize any negative impacts. The staff will require each trapper to report the number and location of all traps and all wildlife taken. The implementation of a trapping program, under controlled conditions, provides an essential population control management tool and is compatible with the purposes of the refuge.

Justification: The purposes of Roanoke River National Wildlife Refuge emphasize conservation of wetlands and migratory birds. Trapping is a wildlife population management tool used to regulate the population of certain wildlife species when those species are disrupting ecosystem functions. There is documentation that beavers and raccoons cause negative impacts to forested wetlands and nesting birds. When these negative impacts become significant on the refuge, wildlife managers need trapping as a management tool to control the level on damage. Certainly, beavers and raccoons are important components of the ecosystem, but when their populations and negative impacts become significant, wildlife managers need a regulated trapping program to reduce their populations to acceptable levels.

Mandatory 10-year Re-evaluation Date:_____9/26/2015_____

FOREST MANAGEMENT - TIMBER HARVEST

Description of Use: Roanoke River National Wildlife Refuge will initiate a forest management program in accordance with an approved forest management plan targeted for completion in 2007. The staff will direct forest management, as described in the comprehensive conservation plan, towards protecting, restoring, and managing the functions and values of the refuge forest to support viable populations of native flora and fauna consistent with sound biological principles.

The refuge staff will inventory and map the entire refuge forest habitat as part of the development of a forest management plan. This plan will provide a comprehensive forest management prescription to achieve forest habitat objectives over a 15-year planning cycle. Forest management prescriptions will include timber stand improvement, commercial timber harvest, and reforestation.

The staff will manipulate forest habitat by commercial timber harvests. Contractors will conduct all harvesting by special use permit and carry it out in accordance with the Refuge Manual. The staff will carry out the sale and disposition of forest products by open market rules and formal bid solicitations.

Availability of Resources: Based on a review of the refuge's budget allocated for this activity, there is adequate funding to ensure compatibility and to administer the current forest management program, which consists of thinning, water management, and fire protection. The comprehensive conservation plan proposes a forest management program that will utilize timber harvest to promote the enhancement of habitats for both threatened and endangered species, migratory birds, and resident wildlife; promote habitat restoration; protect cultural resources; and provide opportunities for public recreation and environmental education. Managing the forest will require additional funding and staffing to inventory forest stands, prepare a forest management plan, develop forest prescriptions, and administer timber harvest.

Anticipated Impacts of the Use: It is anticipated that forest habitat management will enhance the existing forest and help restore the functions and values typically associated with bottomland hardwood forest. Forest management operations will be directed at providing more vertical diversity (i.e., understory, midstory, canopy and superemergent trees) within each forest block in support of the habitat requirements of forest dwelling birds, black bears and other resident wildlife. The large forest block will support area-sensitive species such as the Mississippi kite; prothonotary, Swainson's, and Cerulean warblers; and black bears.

Forest management will include the use of commercial timber harvest operations that, if not tightly controlled and supervised, have the potential to cause adverse impacts on environmental quality. The controls placed on harvesting operations minimize possible adverse effects caused by logging equipment, such as excessive defacement and negative impacts on surface water quality. However, minimum short-term impacts do occur from harvesting operations such as actual mechanized operation disturbance to wildlife and trampling of the understory vegetation by equipment. The understory vegetation usually recovers in one growing season and usually is more beneficial to wildlife due to increased density and palatability caused by harvest operations (i.e., decreased competition and increased sunlight reaching the forest floor).

Public Review and Comment: The period of public review and comment began March 30, 2005 and ended July 18, 2005. Methods used to solicit public review and comment included posted notices at refuge headquarters and area locations, copies of the draft comprehensive conservation plant distributed to adjacent landowners, the public, and local, State, and Federal agencies, two public forums, press releases and public service announcements to area newspapers, and local radio announcements. Appendix XIII summarizes the public comments.

Determination (check one below):

_____ Use is Not Compatible

_X_ Use is Compatible with Following Stipulations

Stipulations Necessary to Ensure Compatibility: The refuge will carry out commercial timber harvest operations only after the staff has completed a comprehensive forest inventory and prepared a Forest Habitat Management Plan. The staff will direct forest management operations at providing a desired future condition for the overall refuge forest. They will inventory individual forest stands, develop timber harvest prescriptions, and carry out timber harvest operations in a manner that will accomplish the refuge's forest habitat management objectives for migratory birds, threatened and endangered species, and resident wildlife. Timber harvest operations will target select trees to be sold, and then commercial timber and pulpwood operators will remove the timber. Those same operators may also remove trees through a timber stand improvement operation or permittees can harvest the trees when commercial sales are not feasible. Only trees needing to be removed in order to improve the forest habitat for wildlife or to restore the integrity of the forested wetlands ecosystem will be taken. The staff may conduct forest management operations throughout the year, but only according to the guidelines detailed in a Forest Habitat Management Plan.

Justification: The forest management actions proposed in the Comprehensive Conservation Plan for Roanoke River National Wildlife Refuge are in accordance with Service guidelines for the protection, management, and enhancement of habitats for wildlife populations on the refuge. Adherence to a Forest Habitat Management Plan promotes the enhancement of habitats for both threatened and endangered species, migratory birds, and resident wildlife species; promotes habitat restoration; protects cultural resources; and provides opportunities for public recreation and environmental education.

Mandatory 10 year Re-evaluation Date:_____9/26/2015_____

REFUGE RESOURCE RESEARCH STUDIES

Description of Use: This activity will allow university students and professors, nongovernmental researchers, and governmental scientists access to the refuge's natural environment to conduct both short-term and long-term research projects. The outcome of this research will result in better knowledge of our natural resources and improved methods to manage, monitor, and protect refuge resources. The refuge will support Fish and Wildlife Service and U.S. Geological Survey research of neotropical migratory birds, waterfowl, bottomland hardwood restoration, amphibians and reptiles, forest bats, and yellow-crowned night herons. Efforts would be made to expand partnerships with North Carolina State University and other area universities to conduct research on the refuge associated with neotropical migratory songbirds.

Availability of Resources: The refuge needs no additional fiscal resources to conduct this use if the university or agency conducting the research initiates the request. Existing staff can administer permits and monitor use as part of routine management duties.

Anticipated Impacts of the Use: There should be no significant negative impacts from scientific research on the refuge. The knowledge gained from the research would provide information to improve management techniques and better meet the needs of trust resource species. Impacts such as trampling vegetation and temporary disturbance to wildlife will occur, but should not be significant. Researchers may collect a small number of individual plants or animals for further study. These collections would have an insignificant effect on refuge plant and animal populations.

Public Review and Comment: The period of public review and comment began March 30, 2005 and ended July 18, 2005. Methods used to solicit public review and comment included posted notices at refuge headquarters and area locations, copies of the draft comprehensive conservation plan distributed to adjacent landowners, the public, and local, State, and Federal agencies, two public forums, press releases and public service announcements to area newspapers, and local radio announcements. Appendix XIII summarizes the public comments.

Determination (check one below):

_____ Use is Not Compatible

__X__ Use is Compatible with Following Stipulations

Stipulations Necessary to Ensure Compatibility: The staff will examine each request for use of the refuge for research on its individual merit. They will ask questions of who, what, when, where, and why to determine if the requested research will contribute to the refuge purposes and if the research can be conducted on the refuge without significantly affecting the resources. If so, the refuge will issue a special use permit to the researcher. The staff will monitor the progress and require the researcher to submit annual progress reports and copies of all publications derived from the research.

Justification: The benefits derived from sound research provide a better understanding of species and the environmental communities present on the refuge. These benefits far outweigh any short-term disturbance or loss of individual plant and animals that might occur.

Mandatory 10 year Re-evaluation Date:_____9/26/2015_____

Literature Cited

Bookhout, T.A.. 1994. Research and management techniques for wildlife and habitats. Fifth edition. The Wildlife Society, Bethesda, MD 740pp.

Schmidt, P.R. 1993. Memorandum - Information request regarding impacts of hunting on national wildlife refuges. U.S. Department of the Interior, Fish and Wildlife Service, Office of Migratory Bird Management, Washington, D.C. 7pp.

Approval of Compatibility Determination

The signature of approval is for all compatibility determinations considered within the Comprehensive Conservation Plan for Roanoke River National Wildlife Refuge. If one of the descriptive uses is considered for compatibility outside of the plan, the approval signature becomes part of that determination.

Refuge Manager: //S// **Harvey Hill** 9/14/05
(Signature/Date)

Regional Compatibility Coordinator: //S// **Steve Johnson** 26 Sep 2005
(Signature/Date)

Refuge Supervisor: //S// **Pete Jerome**
(Signature/Date)

Regional Chief, National Wildlife Refuge System, Southeast Region: //S// **Jon Andrew** 9-28-05
(Signature/Date)

X. Management Methods and Priorities

PARTNERSHIPS

The National Wildlife Refuge System of the U.S. Fish and Wildlife Service cooperates with other programs within the Service, state and federal agencies, nongovernmental organizations, and private landowners to provide and manage habitat for wildlife. Within the Service, the refuge staff works with the migratory bird program on waterfowl and migratory songbird issues, the fisheries program on anadromous fish issues, the ecological services office on endangered species and Federal Energy Regulatory Commission issues, and law enforcement personnel on regulatory issues.

The United States Department of Agriculture, Natural Resources Conservation Service, assists landowners to conserve natural resources and to restore habitat converted to agricultural uses. The Service provides input to the Natural Resources Conservation Service's program priorities and ranking factors for the various programs: the Conservation Reserve Program, the Wetland Reserve Program, the Environmental Quality Incentives Program, the Wildlife Habitat Incentives Program, and the Grassland Reserve Program. In the Roanoke River Valley, the Service works with the United States Army Corps of Engineers and Federal Energy Regulatory Commission on their management of water on the Roanoke River for flood control and hydroelectric power generation.

In North Carolina, the Service cooperates with the North Carolina Wildlife Resources Commission and several divisions in the North Carolina Department of Environment and Natural Resources to protect and manage existing habitat and restore habitats converted to other uses. The North Carolina Wildlife Resources Commission assists landowners to manage their habitats, manages its own game lands, and provides specialists to consult with Service personnel. The Division of Soil and Water Conservation administers an agricultural conservation cost share program that complements the efforts of the Natural Resources Conservation Service. The Division also administers the Conservation Reserve Enhancement Program that restores environmentally sensitive habitats. The Division of Forest Resources assists forest landowners in managing their timber. The Natural Heritage Program identifies sensitive animals, plants, and ecological communities and encourages landowners to protect them.

Nationwide, the Service cooperates with The Nature Conservancy on land protection initiatives. In the Roanoke River Valley, The Nature Conservancy has helped the Service acquire land, has acquired and manages its own land, and offers suggestions on the management of refuge lands.

The Service's Partners for Fish and Wildlife program helps accomplish its mission by offering technical and financial assistance to private landowners to voluntarily restore wetlands and other fish and wildlife habitats on their land. The program emphasizes the reestablishment of native vegetation and ecological communities for the benefit of fish and wildlife in concert with the needs and desires of private landowners.

The Service also enlists the assistance of a wide variety of other partners to help restore wildlife habitat on private lands. These partners include other federal agencies, Native American tribes, state and local governments, conservation organizations, academic institutions, businesses and industries, school groups, and private individuals. While not a program requirement, a dollar-for-dollar cost share is usually sought on a project-by-project basis.

Since the Partner for Fish and Wildlife Program's inception in 1987, these partnerships have generated significant habitat restoration accomplishments on private lands, primarily focused on the restoration of wetlands, native grasslands, stream banks, riparian areas, and in-stream aquatic habitats. These restored habitats now provide important food, cover, and water for federal trust species including migratory birds (e.g., waterfowl, shore and wading birds, songbirds, and birds of prey) and anadromous fish, threatened and endangered species, as well as other fish, wildlife and plant species that have experienced population declines in the recent past. Many of these projects are located near existing National Wildlife Refuge System lands, or State Wildlife Management Areas, providing increased benefits to fish and wildlife that rely on these lands for survival.

The assistance that the Service offers to private landowners may take the form of informal advice on the design and location of potential restoration projects, or it may consist of designing and funding restoration projects under a voluntary cooperative agreement with the landowner. Under the cooperative agreements, the landowner agrees to maintain the restoration project as specified in the agreement for a minimum of 10 years.

Typical restoration projects may include, but are not limited to:

- Restoring wetland hydrology by plugging drainage ditches, breaking tile drainage systems, installing water control structures, dike construction, or re-establishing old connections with waterways.

- Installing fencing and off-stream livestock watering facilities to allow for restoration of stream and riparian areas.

- Removal of exotic plants and animals that compete with native fish and wildlife and alter their natural habitats.

- Prescribed burning as a method of removing exotic species and to restore natural disturbance regimes necessary for some species survival.

- Reconstruction of in-stream aquatic habitat through bioengineering techniques.

In addition to providing restoration assistance to private landowners, the Service also provides biological technical assistance to U.S. Department of Agriculture agencies implementing key conservation programs of the Farm Bill. The Service's assistance helps the Department of Agriculture meet the technical challenges presented by these programs while maximizing benefits to fish and wildlife resources. The Service also assists in on-the-ground habitat restoration actions associated with several of these programs.

Under the Wetlands Reserve Program, conservation easements are required to protect and restore formerly degraded agricultural wetlands. The Service provides technical assistance to Department of Agriculture agencies and to private landowners on site selection, restoration planning, and compatible uses for easements offered voluntarily by interested landowners.

Forest Breeding Birds. The goal for forest breeding birds in the South Atlantic Coastal Plain was to establish self-sustaining populations for all of the roughly 70 species that breed in the coastal plain. Although habitat objectives must ultimately address both quality and quantity, the Service initially concentrated on the size and number of forest patches in this highly fragmented landscape. A 6-step process was established to set habitat objectives and population goals. The Partners-in-Flight prioritization process (Hunter et al., 1993) was utilized to set breeding bird species priorities in the coastal plain. Seven of the highest priority species breeding in the coastal plain nest in bottomland hardwood forests: Swainson's warbler, prothonotary warbler, northern parula, hooded warbler, wood thrush, worm-eating warbler, and chuck-will's- widow. Based on this and the historical ecosystem structure of the valley, bottomland hardwood forests were selected as the highest priority habitat type for breeding bird conservation. To determine forest patch sizes, two sources of information were used: empirical studies and a mathematically derived theoretical genetically viable population. Empirical studies were used primarily for the swallow-tailed kite and the Cerulean warbler.

To determine the forest patch size requirements for the theoretical genetically viable populations the following formula was used:

$$A = (N \times D) + B$$

A = Area of forest patch required to support a source population
N = number reproductive units (usually breeding pairs) required for a source population
D = Breeding density (usually expressed as hectares/breeding pair)
B = The area of a one kilometer forested buffer around the forest core (N*D).

For each of several populations, the Service adopted a proposed minimum effective population size of 500 breeding adults in the recovery plan for the Red-cockaded woodpecker. For monogamous species this constitutes 250 breeding pairs. However, establishing conservation goals at the minimum threshold seems fraught with peril. Thus, to buffer breeding populations within forest patches, a goal of 500 breeding pairs per forest patch (N=500) was adopted.

For the value of D, average breeding densities from Breeding Bird Censuses conducted in the Southeastern United States was used. Even under optimal conditions, bird density in bottomland hardwoods is determined by the frequency of occurrence of patchily distributed microhabitat features (e.g., thickets for Swainson's warblers, cypress brakes for yellow-throated warblers, etc.). To account for these habitat quality factors, it was assumed that birds rarely occur in the valley at densities as high as reported in the literature, which is an additional reason for the adoption of 500 breeding pairs per forest patch as a target population.

The agricultural matrix that dominates the valley is generally considered hostile to birds breeding within forest patches. Researchers working in fragmented landscapes have found that nest predation and parasitism were high even in large forest patches (5,000 acres) in landscapes with a low percentage of forest cover. They also have found that female Brown-headed cowbirds travel an average of 2 miles between feeding and breeding sites. One researcher has found that male Ovenbirds singing on territories less than 900 feet from the edge of the forest were more likely to be unpaired than males from the interior of the forest. For planning purposes, it is assumed that a 0.6-mile forest buffer surrounding an interior forest core will reduce these negative impacts. Only those pairs within the forest core are assumed to reproduce at a rate sufficient to serve as a source population. Because the area of a 0.6-mile buffer will vary with the geometric configuration of each forest patch, the area requirements of each will differ. For planning purposes, until the actual areas of interior forest within each forest patch are determined, doubling the core forest area (B=2) will generally result in forest patch requirements that approximate or exceed a 0.6-mile buffer around the desired interior forest area.

As an example, Swainson's warblers have been noted to occur at densities generally ranging of one pair per 6 to 11 acres. Taking the average of one pair per 9 acres, if Swainson's warblers occur over a large area at this density, 500 pairs would require 4500 acres. Applying the doubling factor as a surrogate for the 0.6-mile buffer produces a desired forest patch size of 9,000 acres. The Service made this calculation for all valley forest breeding species. For planning purposes, the Service placed species into 3 forest patch size groups designed to meet their specific area requirements: 10,000-20,000, 20,000-100,000, and >100,000 acres.

Having determined the aerial habitat requirements of the high priority species and measured the existing habitat using 1992 thematic mapper images, specific locations across the valley were identified for habitat protection/restoration. In addition to habitat requirements and existing forest locations, several other factors such as flooding frequency, current land use, adjacent land use, ownership, and reforestation potential were used to identify proposed habitat protection/restoration sites. Where possible, restoration sites were centered on existing public land. Where linkages could logically be created, existing forest patches were combined to reach target sizes. This sometimes resulted in several existing 10,000- or 20,000-acre patches being combined into a proposed 100,000-acre patch.

Ultimately 101 proposed Breeding Bird Forest Patches were identified for the valley, but the number and location of these sites are not final, and probably never will be. A massive reforestation effort will be necessary to meet these objectives and their achievement often will be opportunity driven. As new opportunities arise and old objectives become unattainable, the locations of the Breeding Bird Forest Patches will change.

A prioritized species list was developed for Roanoke River National Wildlife Refuge, based on present and potential habitat (Table II-1, p. 41). The Refuge is part of the South Atlantic Coastal Plain Physiographic Region, and is one of the most extensive alluvial bottomland hardwood stands in the region. High priority species for this forest patch include: Mississippi kite, Swainson's warbler, prothonotary warbler, and cerulean warbler. For Roanoke River National Wildlife Refuge a target density for Swainson's warblers would be approximately one nesting pair per 9 acres. To support 4,000 pairs, assuming all acreage is suitable or optimal habitat, about 36,000 acres (without the buffer included) will be needed. However, as stated above it is risky to accept the assumption that all habitat is suitable or optimal for any priority species within a discrete habitat patch. A better assumption is that no more than half of all forested acreage is optimal or suitable (e.g., ridges, within a ridge and swale topography) for this species and therefore 72,000 acres (with buffer included) may be necessary to support the population target of 4,000 pairs. This acreage requirement is well above that suggested for this species elsewhere in the valley, but where there are already larger existing forest patches Swainson's warblers occur in higher densities.

The American Bird Conservancy has made an acreage target for bottomland hardwoods in the South Atlantic Coastal Plain Physiographic Region and Roanoke River National Wildlife Refuge in the hope that Swainson's, prothonotary, and Cerulean warblers and Mississippi kites may nest at optimum densities. As efforts continue to expand forested acreage, increasing densities from 6 to 9 pairs/100 acres may be an appropriate population objective. The staff will collect reproductive data collection to measure whether nesting success and fledgling survival changes accordingly for this and other species on the above list.

Food is assumed to be the limiting factor for both southbound migrating shorebirds and wintering waterfowl. Following this assumption, the amount of energy required to support one bird for one day, the length of each bird's stay in the valley (wintering or transient), was calculated along with the amount of energy available from potential food sources.

$$H = \frac{P \times S \times E}{K \times F}$$

H = Amount of habitat (hectares)
P = Population goal (number of birds)
S = Length of stay in the South Atlantic Coastal Plain (days)
E = Energetic requirement of one bird for one day (kilojoules [kj])
K = Energetic value of food source (kj/gram)
F = Available food (grams/ha)

With some adjustments, this formula was used to calculate the amount of habitat needed to support the target populations of shorebirds and waterfowl.

Wintering Waterfowl. The flyway goal for waterfowl is to provide enough habitat to support 4.3 million wintering ducks and 1.0 million wintering geese. The duck goal was derived from goals of the North American Waterfowl Management Plan by determining the proportion of the continental wintering population found in the valley and then multiplying the continental breeding population goal by this proportion. Duck population levels from the 1970s were used as the basis for this goal because those levels are believed to be high enough to maintain huntable populations yet attainable in today's social and economic environment. The goose population goal was derived from the number of geese observed in the valley during the mid-winter waterfowl inventories in the mid-1980s, a period when most goose populations in the Atlantic Flyway were at or near historic high levels.

As with shorebirds, it is assumed that food is the limiting factor on wintering populations. The energy value and availability of various foods (soybean, rice, corn, moist soil, and bottomland hardwood forest) were calculated, and the daily energy requirement of a female mallard (292 kilocalories/day) was used. The wintering period for waterfowl is 120 days.

Approximately 650,000 acres of foraging habitat and an additional 625,000 acres of naturally flooded habitat are needed to support the wintering waterfowl population goal. Within each state habitat objectives are divided between public and private ownership, managed and unmanaged lands, and three foraging habitats: bottomland hardwood forests, moist soil, and agricultural fields. The availability of naturally flooded habitat depends on adequate precipitation and the resultant ponding or overbank flooding.

ARCHAEOLOGICAL AND HISTORIC RESOURCE PROTECTION

With the enactment of the Antiquities Act of 1906, the Federal Government recognized the importance of cultural resources to the national identity and sought to protect archaeological sites and historic structures on those lands either owned, managed, or controlled by the United States. The body of historic preservation laws has grown dramatically since 1906. Several themes are consistently present in the laws and the promulgating regulations. They include: 1) each agency to systematically inventory the "historic sites" on their holdings and to scientifically assess each site's eligibility for the National Register of Historic Places; 2) consideration of impacts to cultural resources during the agency's management activities and seek to avoid or mitigate adverse impacts; 3) protection of cultural resources from looting and vandalism to be accomplished through a mix of informed management, law enforcement efforts, and public education; and 4) the increasing role of consultation with groups, such as Native American tribes and African American communities, to address how a project or management activity may impact specific archaeological sites and landscapes deemed important to those groups. The objectives and strategies below outline the Service's attempt to achieve mandated historic preservation responsibilities in a manner consistent with its mission and the refuge's mission.

The Fish and Wildlife Service Regional Archaeologist coordinates a Memorandum of Understanding with pertinent federal and state agencies, such as the North Carolina State Historic Preservation Office, to enhance law enforcement of the Archaeological Resources Protection Act, the Native American Grave Protection and Repatriation Act, and Section 50 of the Code of Federal Regulations as well as to facilitate investigations of the Archaeological Resources Protection Act violations and unpermitted artifact collection on the refuge.

A review of the State Site Files located at the North Carolina State Historic Preservation Office has provided preliminary information on the known or potential archaeological sites and historic structures within and near the refuge. Such information will aid the Service in the development of a long-term management plan for cultural resources. A comprehensive refuge-wide archaeological survey is recommended so that the Service's management options can be fully realized in a cost-effective manner. The survey will provide a site predictive model based upon the region's cultural history, known site distribution, oral history interviews, historic documents, historic land use patterns, topography, geomorphology, soils, hydrology, and vegetative patterns.

ECOSYSTEM MANAGEMENT

Healthy habitats are necessary to sustain fish, wildlife, and plants on lands in the system. In the past, the administrative boundaries of national wildlife refuges have often bounded the scope of planning and policy decisions. The Service develops conservation strategies at two spatial levels in a collaborative process to solve broad scale ecological problems. Within a large spatial level, the Service has developed a cross-program approach for the Roanoke-Tar- Neuse-Cape Fear Ecosystem considering issues within the ecological, political, and social boundaries. The Roanoke-Tar-Neuse-Cape Fear Ecosystem Team focuses on landscape problems affecting fish and wildlife resources and provides specific guidance that will best serve trust species and species of concern and reduce impacts associated with forest fragmentation. At a smaller spatial level, the comprehensive conservation planning team reflects the conservation strategies for national wildlife refuges within the ecosystem and identifies select area species on which to focus management efforts.

Ecosystems are communities of living organisms interacting among themselves and with the physical component of their environment. Ecosystems are experiencing increasing impacts from human activities, the threat of which will require extraordinary flexibility and innovation to successfully conserve and manage them. In recent years conservationists have fostered the idea that resource conservation can best be achieved by taking a holistic approach to management. The Service is working with divergent interests on ecosystem-based approaches to conserve the variety of life and its processes in the Nation's diverse ecosystem.

The Service's mission is to conserve, protect, and enhance the Nation's fish and wildlife and their habitats for the continuing benefit of the American people. The Service has adopted an ecosystem approach to more effectively achieve this mission. Our objective is to implement consistent policies and procedures that will embrace the ecosystem approach in a "management environment" which considers the needs of all our resources in decision-making. This holistic approach to fish and wildlife conservation will enable the Service to more efficiently and effectively maintain healthy ecosystems on a long-term basis and to conserve the Nation's rich biological heritage.

An ecosystem approach to fish and wildlife conservation means protecting or restoring the function, structure, and species composition of an ecosystem while providing for its sustainable socioeconomic use. It involves recognizing that, in some way, all things are connected. The ecosystem approach emphasizes conservation and management of discrete land units, watersheds, or ecosystems and requires the identification of ecosystem goals that represent resource priorities on which all programs of the Service will collectively focus their efforts. The Service must work closely and consistently with external partners, public and private, who share responsibility for ecosystem health and biological diversity. This approach will enable the Service to fulfill its fish and wildlife trust responsibilities with greater efficiency and effectiveness.

In the Southeast Region, we are approaching our nationally mandated leadership role for fish and wildlife conservation on an ecosystem basis, partnering with other Service regions, with other Federal agencies, with States and their local governments and citizenry, and with non- governmental organizations. Together, we are working to achieve healthy, sustainable ecosystems that ensure a continuing legacy of abundant fish and wildlife resources for all Americans to use and enjoy.

XI. Refuge Operation Needs System (RONS) Projects

Projects are ordered by first two digits of the project number which stand for the fiscal year the project was developed to facilitate finding the projects listed in the management alternatives.

Projects are listed as tier 1 projects that support approved critical mission or approved minimum staff or tier 2 projects that do not.

Project 90008 Enhance Visitor Services (Radio System)
Tier 2 Project
First Year Request $60,000, Recurring Request $10,000
Station Rank - 14
This project will provide a critical visitor service with the installation of a new radio system that meets Service Standards and provides communications with other northeastern North Carolina field stations, local cooperating law enforcement agencies and medical establishments. The Service's communications coordinator and contractors will install and secure equipment and repeater space on existing tower(s). Following completion, communications and cooperation necessary to respond to visitor's needs will equip the refuge staff with the ability to facilitate development of the six priority public uses, especially youth and physically challenged hunting, bird watching, environmental education, and photography. This is not an upgrade of current radio equipment.

Project 90011 Implement Forest Insect Pest Survey Program
Tier 2
First Year Request $30,000, Recurring Request $10,000
Station Rank - 15
This project will provide the funding to develop a comprehensive biological survey and monitoring program to determine the presence and status of gypsy moth infestations on refuge property. Recent discoveries of the exotic gypsy moth on Devil's Gut Island (a refuge inholding) resulted in 3,500 acres adjacent to refuge lands undergoing chemical treatment in 1999. Gypsy moths defoliate hardwood trees, targeting primarily oak trees and weakening them, and when combined with other stresses, eventually killing them. Detection of early stage gypsy moth invasions would require specialized attention from refuge staff unavailable at this time. In coordination with North Carolina Division of Forestry and the U.S. Department of Agriculture, this project will develop a strategy to address and monitor infestations. The expertise of other agencies through partnerships will be essential to controlling the gypsy moth on the Roanoke River floodplain in an effort to protect forest health and integrity.

Project 90016 Habitat Management Capabilities (Heavy Equipment)
Tier 2 Project
First Year Request $250,000, Recurring Request $20,000
Station Rank - 2
This project will provide the funding to purchase and maintain a truck, equipment transport trailer, and a bulldozer. This equipment is necessary to accomplish annual maintenance of the road system and structures needed to accomplish refuge goals. Provide and maintain necessary equipment to accomplish annual maintenance and rehabilitation of refuge road system and structures. Rehabilitating refuge roads historically used in silviculture practices prior to refuge acquisition will restore the natural hydrology of the floodplain and contribute to improved water management. This will provide protection for many wetland habitats important to migratory birds (e.g., waterfowl, songbirds, and wading birds). Maintaining refuge infrastructure on an annual basis to Fish and Wildlife Service standards will reduce the necessity of periodic, expensive rehabilitation projects and continually enhance wetland habitat.

Project 91022 Manage Wetland Easement Habitats (Biological Technician)
Tier1
First Year Request $65,000, Recurring Request $53,000
Station Rank - 6
This project will provide funding to employ a biological technician to protect, manage, and enhance habitat on 98 easements in 19 counties of the Roanoke-Tar-Neuse-Cape Fear Ecosystem. The wetland easements, which are located on former Farm Service Agency inventory lands, protect a variety of natural resources ranging from groundwater recharge to endangered freshwater mussels. This project will increase the Service presence needed to develop private partnerships while decreasing boundary marker destruction, timber trespass, and degradation due to illegal dumping. A biological technician will be dedicated to administering the wetland easement program and will allow other refuge staff to spend more time on other partnerships and resource management programs.

Project 93028 Improve Environmental Education and Outreach (Park Ranger)
Tier1
First Year Request $65,000, Recurring Request $63,000
Station Rank 5
This project will provide funding to employ a park ranger to create, coordinate, and implement a formal environmental education and interpretation program for local students, refuge visitors, and the community. Great potential exists to attract visitors to the refuge from U.S. Highway 64, a travel corridor 5 miles from refuge property that brings 2-3 million tourists per year to the area. In addition, vast opportunities exist to educate students in the surrounding school systems of the importance of the Roanoke River bottomland hardwood forest and its associated floodplain and enhance critical thinking and decision-making skills in a low income area. An outreach specialist will communicate the value of the refuge's forested wetlands, which provide important habitat for migratory waterfowl, songbirds, and commercially important fish, and the mission and objectives of the Service and the refuge by developing a formal, curriculum-based environmental education program through partnerships with the local school system and developing outreach strategies to attract and educate visitors. Partnerships with the refuge's cooperating association (Roanax Sponsas), and the adjacent Roanoke-Cashie River Center will provide additional opportunities to enhance education and interpretation efforts.

Project 97032 Preserve Cultural Resources
Tier 2 Project
One Time Request $35,000
Station Rank - 16
This project will provide the funding to implement a contract for a survey of cultural resources on the refuge. The contracted archaeological survey will be conducted to locate and identify sites and determine potential impacts from proposed road rehabilitation projects. The survey results will assist the refuge staff to preserve cultural resources associated with refuge property formerly occupied by Tuscarora Indians. The refuge contains one known site listed on North Carolina's list of Historical Sites. This survey could reveal other undiscovered cultural sites that could otherwise be damaged or destroyed in the rehabilitation process. The State Historical Preservation Officer will verify other sites that the staff believes to have been previously surveyed. This survey will also provide a condition assessment of the one known site, as damage due to managed river flows could be occurring.

Project 97033 Document Impacts of Growing Season Flooding due to Managed River Flows
Tier 2 Project
One Time Request $60,000
Station Rank - 18
This project will provide funding to study the relationship between unnatural growing season floodplain inundation on the nesting and foraging of wading birds. The relationship between growing season floodplain flows and crustaceans (especially crayfish) is largely unknown. These crayfish are a primary food source for wading birds such as herons, egrets, and cormorants. The refuge contains the largest inland heron rookery in North Carolina. Understanding the relationship between floodplain inundation and the wading bird's prey will provide refuge staff with the information necessary for managing habitat to support natural populations of wading birds. The project will provide information critical to the comprehensive conservation plan.

Project 97035 Improve and Manage Habitat for Migratory Birds
Tier 2 Project
One Time Request $30,000
Station Rank - 17
This project will provide the funding to conduct a graduate-level study to determine the effects of the altered flow regime of the Roanoke River on wildlife habitat and productivity. Upstream flood control releases often top natural river levees during the habitat's growing season and are believed to negatively impact crucial nesting and foraging habitat for 35 species of migratory birds. The study will focus on the regime's effects on vertebrates, the staple food source of many migratory birds, and refuge river cane, a primary nesting habitat for many of these species, represented in this study by the Swainson's warbler. Results are needed for comprehensive conservation planning.

Project 97037 Improve Wetland Habitat Management (Heavy Equipment Operator)
Tier 1
First Year Request $65,000, Recurring Request $51,000
Station Rank - 2
This project will provide funding to employ an equipment operator to initiate active habitat management and increase facility maintenance. The project will enhance wetland management on the 21,000-acre river refuge. Flood control and hydropower dams located upstream of the refuge have altered the hydrology on the lower Roanoke River and associated refuge lands by more frequent and prolonged flooding than the river's natural flow regime. When these floods occur during growing season, it can have a significant impact on plant diversity by drowning overcup oaks and other floodplain trees. It also restricts management of moist-soil units and damages refuge roads.

The refuge currently employs one heavy equipment operator who is alone in remote conditions loading, unloading, and operating heavy equipment with no assistance. The addition of another heavy equipment operator will drastically improve safety for the current employee. This position will also provide the staff support needed to monitor, maintain, and regulate water flows in refuge wetlands in a timely manner and maintain water control levels and roads to improve water management capabilities.

Project 99002 Improve Forest Health (Forest Technician)
Tier 2 Project
First Year Request $65,000, Recurring Request $59,000
Station Rank - 6
This project will provide funding to employ a forest technician to initiate resource management of the refuge's bottomland hardwoods. Forest health and diversity maintenance is necessary to maintain habitat for approximately 200 species of birds, including 35 migratory species. This project will also help protect riparian zones that provide spawning, nursery, and foraging habitat for alewife, blueback herring, hickory shad and striped bass (all leave marine habitats to ascend rivers to spawn). Maintenance will be conducted to enhance riverine habitat critical to the endangered short-nosed sturgeon and rookery habitat for the state's largest wood duck nesting population and state's largest inland colonial bird rookery. The technician will perform studies, collect data, and provide habitat management to improve conditions for many migratory species.

Project 99003 Reinitiate Water Quality Monitoring
Tier 1
Recurring Request $65,000
Station Rank - 7
This project will provide funding to reinitiate the water quality monitoring program on the Roanoke River, which supplies water to the wetland units of the 21,000-acre refuge. The Service began water quality monitoring at five stations along the river in 1998 with contaminants funding. This funding expired in 2001. New partners were found to fund the program on an annual basis, but permanent funding is needed to continue to collect essential data for sound management. Good science, of which water quality monitoring provides important data, is required to support and corroborate Service concerns related to upstream operations of hydropower dams; protection of a river corridor critical to endangered short nose sturgeon, migratory birds, and recently recovered populations of recreationally and commercially important striped bass and herring; and maintenance of the state's largest inland heron rookery, largest wood duck nesting population, and the only known yellow-crowned night heron rookery in the lower sections of the Roanoke River basin.

Project 00001 Increase Public Awareness of Importance of Roanoke River Basin's Wetlands
Tier 2 Project
First Year Request $155,000, Recurring Request $5,000
Station Rank - 10
This project will provide funding to install and maintain forested wetlands exhibits in the refuge's visitor contact station within its administrative offices that depict the relationships between managed river flows, wildlife, and refuge habitat. The refuge's contact station is located on the grounds of the Roanoke-Cashie River Center, an environmental education facility operated by the Partnership for the Sounds. This project will be developed in cooperation with the local county and city governments and non-profit organizations, which will contribute an additional 30 percent to offset initial costs. This project will complement the Bottomland Hardwood Exhibit placed in the Roanoke-Cashie River Center as an earlier partner's project (97039). The exhibits will be designed for the contact station's unique location adjacent to major federal highway corridors accommodating 2-3 million travelers annually.

Project 00002 Visitor Receptionist/Clerical Assistance (Office Assistant)
Tier 2 Project
First Year Request $45,500, Recurring Request $34,000
Station Rank - 24
This project will provide funding to employ an office assistant to relieve refuge staff involved in the production of planning documents and respond to visitors and written and oral inquiries. The project will increase visitor awareness of missions, goals, issues, and recreational opportunities of the Fish and Wildlife Service and the Roanoke River National Wildlife Refuge. The seasonal administrative staff person will provide clerical and visitor service assistance during peak visitation to the refuge. The assistant will be responsible for the daily operation of the visitor contact station and administrative offices building, including greeting and assisting visitors, answering phones, mailing information packets, stocking refuge publications, and performing clerical activities. The project will greatly enhance services to refuge visitors and the local community.

Project 00003 Enhance Basic Refuge Operations and Maintenance
Tier 1
Recurring Request $85,000
Station Rank - 1
This project will provide additional base funding to restore capabilities to enhance partnerships initiated for wetland restoration and improve resource maintenance, management, and outreach on the 21,000-acre river refuge. The project is needed to support refuge programs and operations such as hiring a contract aircraft for annual aerial biological surveys, accomplishing minimal boundary maintenance, fostering success of a new cooperating association, improving the use of volunteers and interns, replacing small maintenance equipment and interpretive leaflets in a timely manner, securing equipment and supplies for outreach booths and career fairs, developing and securing interpretive signs, and acquiring control devices to manage beaver ponds. The project will enhance partnership efforts, improve visitor use facilities and programs, and enhance resource management programs.

Project 00004 Wildlife and Habitat Monitoring Program (Biological Technician)
Tier 2 Project
First Year Request $85,000, Recurring Request $59,000
Station Rank - 4
This project will provide funding to employ a biological technician to perform surveys of wildlife and habitat. It will increase habitat and wildlife surveys to monitor wildlife populations, habitat conditions, and relationships to provide sound science required to manage refuge properties. Good science is required to protect migratory songbirds, wood ducks, hooded mergansers, wading birds, wintering waterfowl, and furbearers and their associated habitats. The addition of a biological technician will ensure the continuation of sound science in the Roanoke River floodplain. Surveys of wood duck and hooded merganser broods, furbearers, gypsy moth egg cases, the endangered shortnose sturgeon, and wading bird rookeries will be initiated. Current surveys to be expanded include point counts, colonial bird production on Conine Island, and wood duck nest box surveys.

Project 00005 Initiate Management of Forested Wetland Habitat (Forester)
Tier1
First Year Request $65,000, Recurring Request $87,000
Station Rank - 4
This project will provide funding to employ a resource specialist (forester, ecologist) to develop and implement habitat management plans. It will enhance management of the refuge's seasonally flooded forest habitat to improve plant and wildlife diversity, especially for migratory birds. The

development and management of a comprehensive forest management program on this 21,000-acre refuge will be conducted. The refuge provides prime bottomland hardwood forest habitat for 350 species of birds, mammals, fish, reptiles, and amphibians. A forester will enhance management of the refuge's seasonally flooded forest habitat (which is complicated by an unnatural water regime caused by upstream dams) for forest diversity, quality, health, and sustainability. A model will also be developed that can be used by private landowners, local governments, and others to manage their bottomland hardwood forest habitat along the 400-mile Roanoke River watershed.

Project 00006 Protect Refuge Water Rights (Hydrologist)
Tier 2
First Year Request $95,000, Recurring Request $96,000
Station Rank - 9
This project will provide funding to employ a hydrologist to gather and distribute data on the impact of inter-basin water diversion on refuge resources. It will protect refuge water rights that will preserve refuge integrity. Flood control and hydropower dams located upstream of the refuge have altered the hydrology on the lower Roanoke River and associated refuge lands by more frequent and prolonged flooding than the river's natural flow regime. Water is the driving force on the refuge and significantly altering its behavior can have detrimental consequences to the plants and wildlife that evolved with an unmanaged flow regime. Ensuring the protection and sustainability of refuge natural resources and surrounding 200,000 acres of bottomland hardwood floodplain resources, a hydrologist is needed to quantify hydrological concerns. This project is for a staff hydrologist who can provide the necessary expertise to formulate a hydrological regime that protects refuge resources and that also meets the objectives of dam operators.

Project 00007 Improve Media Relations and Outreach (Park Ranger - Media Specialist)
Tier 2 Project
First Year Request $65,000, Recurring Request $82,000
Station Rank 8
This project will provide funding to employ a park ranger (media specialist) to communicate the Fish and Wildlife Service and Roanoke River National Wildlife Refuge missions, goals, management practices, and current issues to the public. This function is essential to enhancing awareness of and leveraging support for the agency and the refuge. This staff member will develop and implement a communications strategy involving printed media (e.g., brochures, fliers, etc.), and presentation materials (e.g., audio-visual talks, off-site displays, etc.), to provide information to the public and local communities in a timely and professional manner. This staff member will also form relationships with local news and entertainment media to communicate Service and refuge information to a wide audience. Involvement in off-site events and in local school systems will improve outreach and develop relations with the local community. Partnerships with local non-profits, government agencies, and school systems will allow additional outreach opportunities.

Project 00008 Support Forested Habitat Management (Equipment Operator)
Tier 2 Project
First Year Request $195,000, Recurring Request $59,000
Station Rank - 3
This project will provide funding to employ an equipment operator to implement the forest management plan and purchase the equipment to operate. It will provide ground support for 21,000-acre refuge that continually requires road, trail, and habitat maintenance due to unnatural flooding from upstream dam. A heavy equipment operator will maintain and enhance roads and trails for staff and public access to refuge lands that experience damage from prolonged flooding events. Habitat maintenance will restore historic migratory fish passages, provide habitat for migratory waterfowl, protect the bottomland hardwood forest ecosystem, and support overall forest health. This project will

also provide support to implement a prescribed fire program and support to maintain refuge equipment. Operator projects will support a Forest Habitat Management Plan and comprehensive conservation plan objectives.

Project 00009 Support Forest Habitat Management (Heavy Equipment Operator)
Tier 2 Project
First Year Request $35,000, Recurring Request $56,000
Station Rank - 21
This project will provide funding to employ an equipment operator to implement the forest management plan and to purchase the equipment needed to implement the plan. It will provide ground support for the 21,000-acre refuge that continually requires road, trail, and habitat maintenance due to unnatural flooding from upstream dam. A heavy equipment operator will maintain and enhance roads and trails for staff and public access to refuge lands that experience damage from prolonged flooding events. Habitat maintenance will restore historic migratory fish passages, provide habitat for migratory waterfowl, protect the bottomland hardwood forest ecosystem, and support overall forest health. This project will also provide support to implement a prescribed fire program and support to maintain refuge equipment. Operator projects will support a Forest Habitat Management Plan and comprehensive conservation plan objectives.

Project 00010 Support Forested Wetland Habitat Management (Administrative Assistant)
Tier 2 Project
First Year Request $65,000, Recurring Request $69,000
Station Rank - 11
This project will provide funding to employ an administrative assistant to handle multiple accounts, contract documents, fund accountability, and budget planning for the administrative forester (RONS 00005). Bottomland hardwoods intensively managed for multiple objectives and landscape goals will also involve multiple and complex partnerships, methods, and communications that will require a level of skill beyond traditional clerical assistance. Completion of the comprehensive conservation plan will elevate refuge habitat management, and multiple additional talents will be required of administrative positions. The administrative forester must have on-the-ground assistance and access to staff that focus on accounting, accountability, and budget planning.

Project 00011 implement Integrated Pest Management (Entomologist)
Tier 2 Project
First Year Request $65,000, Recurring Request $96,000
Station Rank - 13
This project will provide funding to employ an entomologist to detect insect invasions, explore biological controls, and cooperate with other agencies and organizations. The entomologist will institute an integrated pest management program in coordination with the North Carolina Department of Agriculture, the U.S. Department of Agriculture, and the North Carolina Division of Forestry. Indications are that three consecutive years of water tupelo defoliation by the forest tent caterpillar will begin to cause tree mortality. Water tupelo constitutes approximately 50 percent of the refuge's tree canopy and provides all the nesting and most of the foraging habitat for the refuge's 4,000 - 5,000 colonial nesting birds. Focused efforts by a staff entomologist are necessary to check the pest that has implications for 75,000 acres of floodplain habitat. A separate forest health survey will be conducted to determine if a relationship exists between unnatural growing season floodplain inundation and the forest tent caterpillars that have defoliated thousands of acres of tupelo for four consecutive years. These contracted surveys will be an important step in maintaining a major element of the refuge's essential migratory bird habitat.

Project 00012 Provide Custodial Maintenance of Buildings (Maintenance Mechanic)
Tier 2 Project
First Year Request $5,000, Recurring Request $46,000
Station Rank - 22
This project will provide funding to employ a maintenance mechanic to maintain the refuge equipment and provide support for refuge maintenance projects. Upon completion of comprehensive conservation planning and construction of modern maintenance and equipment storage facilities, custodial maintenance will be required to ensure refuge equipment is maintained in a safe and operable condition. This maintenance mechanic will also assist heavy equipment operators with habitat management projects, maintenance of refuge roads, trails and public use facilities, and provide assistance with biological surveys.

Project 00013 Supervising Maintenance Staff (Wage Grade Leader)
Tier 2 Project
First Year Request $65,000, Recurring Request $66,000
Station Rank - 12
This project will provide funding to employ a wage grade leader to manage a large maintenance program and staff. Upon implementation of the refuge's comprehensive conservation plan, forest habitat management will have risen to a higher level providing for up to seven maintenance staff positions. These positions will need focused supervision. Maintenance expertise, coupled with an understanding of the refuge's mission and goals, will provide leadership, guidance, oversight, and direction.

Project 00014 Facility Support (Maintenance Mechanic)
Tier 2 Project
First Year Request $5,000, Recurring Request $46,000
Station Rank - 5
This project will provide funds to employ a maintenance mechanic to maintain visitor facilities. Operations and maintenance of facilities will approximately double upon completion of a combination visitor center and administrative office complex. A maintenance mechanic will ensure that all public facilities are maintained to safety standards and are in working order. The mechanic will also maintain and ensure safety of other public facilities such as trails, signs, and kiosks and assist maintenance staff with other refuge projects to provide a safe learning environment for refuge visitors.

Project 00015 Interpretive Trail Support (Maintenance Worker)
Tier 2 Project
First Year Request $26,000, Recurring Request $17,000
Station Rank - 19
This project will provide funding to employ a maintenance worker to provide resources for annual maintenance and sanitation of the Kuralt Trail, the refuge's first and only interpretive facility. The trail is located near a major travel corridor that supports 2-3 million visitors a year. Increased visitation will require additional maintenance of the trail, its interpretive panel, signs, and parking lot. A minimal public toilet will allow visitors to spend additional time in the area participating in refuge recreational opportunities. The aesthetics of the trail will greatly improve with the implementation of this project. The Kuralt Trail is a unit of the northeastern North Carolina Kuralt Trail, a memorial to the late Charles Kuralt. The addition of a one-half mile handicap-accessible wetland walk (MMS# 99001) will provide a comprehensive interpretive facility for a refuge that is otherwise boat accessible only.

Project 00016 Getting Back to Standards with Seasonal Focus (Post Boundaries)
Tier 2 Project
One Time Request $30,000
Station Rank - 20
This project will provide funding to restore refuge and easement boundaries. Seasonal staff and volunteers will be trained to Fish and Wildlife Service standards to conduct boundary maintenance to replace worn, faded, or missing signs on refuge and easement properties. Many signs were destroyed by wind throw in storm events and hurricanes in the last few years. The refuge boundary spans 70 miles of the Roanoke River along five separate refuge units. Boundary posting requires boat access and traversing difficult conditions in the bottomland hardwood swamp. In addition, the refuge manages 98 conservation easements in 19 counties covering 2,870 acres and involving 75 landowners. Law enforcement and public access will be greatly improved with this project.

Project 00017 Assess Implications of Wide Spread Dioxin
Tier 2 Project
One Time Request $40,000
Station Rank - 23
This project will provide funding for a study to assess the Environmental Protection Agency's delineation of lower Roanoke River dioxin contamination. Recent sediment sampling found these wide spread toxic, cancer-causing agents contaminating the lower Roanoke River. Dioxin contamination has serious implications for refuge integrity. Dioxin is known to be in the Eastmost River, a Roanoke River tributary and eastern boundary of the refuge's Goodman Island unit. Dioxin may also be in the Middle River, the eastern boundary of the refuge's Great Island unit. Sediment sampling within the refuge boundary will be conducted and data will be analyzed to create two Risk Assessments, Ecological and Human Health. The Environmental Protection Agency will then decide

if risks should generate a response. Determination of the total extent of resource impacts cannot be made until additional work is completed.

Project 02001 Improve Safety, Environmental Compliance, and Asset Management (Assistant Manager - Facilities)
Tier 2 Project
First Year Request $65,000, Recurring Request $69,000
Station Rank - 1
This project will provide funding to employ an assistant refuge manager for facilities to provide a safety, environmental compliance, and asset manager to meet ever-increasing demands for environmental protection and ensure a safe visitation experience and employee work environment. This position will serve as the station's safety officer and be responsible for conducting periodic safety inspections, identifying safety issues, managing all safety documentation, and conducting safety meetings. Refuge environmental audits and compliance implementation will be coordinated through this position. The individual will also be responsible for managing real property inventory and personal property databases and managing the station's Service Asset and Maintenance System, a maintenance management software program to track maintenance expenditures, capture maintenance needs, quantify maintenance activities, and report maintenance accomplishments.

Project 05001 Protect Refuge Resources and Visitors (Law Enforcement Officer)
Tier 2 Project
First Year Request $65,000, Recurring Request $64,000
Station Rank - 3
This project will provide funding to employ a full-time refuge law enforcement officer. The position will improve public safety and refuge resource protection at a refuge too small to provide a collateral-duty officer. The area zone officer oversees 10 refuges in North Carolina and can only devote minimal time and resources to the issues faced at this refuge. Refuge tracts span a 70-mile corridor of the Roanoke River floodplain and include 21,000 acres. This officer will provide maintenance on more than 100 miles of refuge boundary to prevent trespass on sensitive lands, ensure that refuge rules and regulations are conveyed and enforced with the visiting public, provide an outreach presence, and become cooperatively involved in striped bass protection with other land management agencies.

Project 05002 Enhance Interpretive Facilities
Tier 2 Project
One Time Request $30,000
Station Rank - 26
This project will provide funding to interpret the regional importance of the Roanoke River's floodplain to the residential and visiting public. Seven interpretive kiosks will be installed at key visitation points throughout the 21,000-acre refuge. The refuge headquarters is located 10 miles from the nearest land tract, so face-to-face contact with visitors is limited. Most visitors access the refuge by boat or foot without knowing they are visiting a national wildlife refuge. These kiosks will interpret the ecology of the Roanoke River and associated floodplain, cultural and natural history of the area, and habitat management strategies.

Project 05003 Restore Floodplain Hydrology
Tier 2 Project
One Time Request $50,000
Station Rank - 7
This project will provide funding to restore floodplain hydrology essential to the overall health of bottomland hardwood forests. Beaver dams create impoundments that flood stands of hardwood trees, creating habitat for wood ducks and hooded mergansers to feed and raise their young. Too many impoundments, however, can flood hardwood stands for many years, killing the trees and altering the habitat beyond use for many species of wildlife. The beaver population along the Roanoke River floodplain has exploded due to ideal habitat conditions and the loss of a top predator in the system to keep the beaver population under control. As a result, the number of beaver impoundments is abnormally high. This project will fund a contract animal pest controller to survey, locate, and eliminate beavers and/or their dams that pose a risk to floodplain hydrology.

Project 05004 Herpetology Impact Study
Tier 2 Project
One Time Request $65,000
Station Rank - 27
This project will provide funding to study the effects of the Roanoke River's altered flow regime on the diversity and abundance of key reptile (e.g., eastern box turtle) and amphibian (e.g., frogs and salamanders) species on the refuge. Flood control and hydropower dams located upstream of the refuge have altered the hydrology on the lower Roanoke River and associated refuge lands by more frequent and prolonged flooding than the river's natural flow regime. Water is the driving force on the refuge and significantly altering its behavior can have detrimental consequences to the plants and wildlife that evolved with an unmanaged flow regime. Reptiles and amphibians are bio-indicator species that can signal the health of an ecosystem. Understanding the characteristics of their populations can indicate the overall health of the bottomland hardwood system of the lower Roanoke River.

Project 05005 Develop Interpretive Materials
Tier 2 Project
One Time Request $12,000
Station Rank - 28
This project will provide funding to develop interpretive materials to encourage refuge visitation and recreational opportunities. This project will develop three interpretive brochures (e.g., hunting, fishing, and wildlife observation) to inform visitors of the available wildlife opportunities on the refuge. These activities are three of the six identified in the National Wildlife Refuge System Improvement Act of 1997 as priority wildlife-dependent recreation that will receive enhanced and priority consideration in refuge planning and management over other public uses. The refuge headquarters is located 10 miles from the nearest land tract, so face-to-face contact with visitors is limited. Most visitors access the refuge by boat or foot without knowing they are visiting a national wildlife refuge. These brochures will provide activity information, access areas, maps, regulations, and contact information for the refuge. These brochures will assist in creating a positive recreational experience for visitors and promote national wildlife refuges as places to enjoy these activities.

Project 05006 Study Migratory Waterfowl Food Resources
Tier 2 Project
One Time Request $65,000
Station Rank - 25
This project will provide funding to conduct a study to determine the impacts of the altered flow regime on the availability of food resources for wintering waterfowl. Flood control and hydropower dams located upstream of the refuge have altered the hydrology on the lower Roanoke River and associated refuge lands by more frequent and prolonged flooding than the river's natural flow regime. Water is the driving force on the refuge and significantly altering its behavior can have detrimental consequences to the plants and wildlife that evolved with an unmanaged flow regime. The North American Waterfowl Management Plan identified the lower Roanoke River as an important wintering area for black duck and other waterfowl. Protecting the bottomland hardwood forest along the lower Roanoke River was one of the primary objectives for creating the refuge.

	Roanoke River Island National Wildlife Refuge			
	Refuge Operation Needs System (RONS) Projects Listed by Project Number			
Station Rank/ Tier	Project Number	Cost (First Year, Recurring)	Positions	Project Title
14/2	90008	$60,000 $10,000	0.0	Enhance Visitor Services (Radio System)
15/2	90011	$30,000 $10,000	0.0	Implement Forest Insect Survey Program
2/2	90016	$250,000 $20,000	0.0	Habitat Management Capabilities (Heavy Equipment)
6/1	91022	$65,000 $53,000	1.0	Manage Wetland Easement Habitats (Biological Technician)
5/1	93028	$65,000 $63,000	1.0	Improve Environmental Education and Outreach (Park Ranger)
16/2	97032	$35,000 $0	0.0	Preserve Cultural Resources (Study)
18/2	97033	$60,000 $0	0.0	Document Impacts of Growing Season Flooding due to Managed River Flows
17/2	97035	$30,000 $0	0.0	Improve and Manage Habitat for Migratory Birds (Study)
2/1	97037	$65,000 $51,000	1.0	Improve Wetland Habitat Management (Heavy Equipment Operator)
6/2	99002	$65,000 $59,000	1.0	Improve Forest Health (Forest Technician)
7/1	99003	$0 $65,000	0.0	Reinitiate Water Quality Monitoring
10/2	00001	$155,000 $5,000	0.0	Increase Public Awareness of Importance of Roanoke River Basin's Wetlands (Forested wetland Exhibit)
24/2	00002	$45,500 $34,000	0.7	Provide Clerical Assistance and Visitor Receptionist (Office Assistant)
1/1	00003	$0 $85,000	0.0	Enhance Basic Refuge Operations and Maintenance
4/2	00004	$85,000 $59,000	1.0	Wildlife and Habitat Monitoring Program (Biological Technician)
4/1	00005	$65,000 $87,000	1.0	Initiate Management of Forested Wetland Habitat (Forester)
9/2	00006	$95,000 $96,000	1.0	Protect Refuge Water Rights (Hydrologist)
8/2	00007	$65,000 $82,000	1.0	Maximize Outreach and Education (Media Specialist)

Roanoke River Island National Wildlife Refuge Refuge Operation Needs System (RONS) Projects Listed by Project Number				
Station Rank/ Tier	Project Number	Cost (First Year, Recurring)	Positions	Project Title
3/2	00008	$195,000 $59,000	1.0	Support Forested Habitat Management (Equipment Operator)
21/2	00009	$35,000 $56,000	1.0	Support Forested Habitat Management (Equipment Operator)
11/2	00010	$65,000 $69,000	1.0	Support Forested Wetland Habitat Management (Administrative Assistant)
13/2	00011	$65,000 $96,000	1.0	Implement Integrated Pest Management (Entomologist)
22/2	00012	$5,000 $46,000	1.0	Provide Custodial Maintenance of Buildings (Maintenance Mechanic)
12/2	00013	$65,000 $66,000	1.0	Supervising Maintenance Staff (Wage Grade Supervisor)
5/2	00014	$5,000 $46,000	1.0	Facility Support (Maintenance Mechanic)
19/2	00015	$26,000 $17,000	.4	Interpretive Trail Support (Maintenance Worker)
20/2	00016	$30,000 $0	0.0	Getting Back to Standards With Seasonal Focus (Boundary Posting)
23/2	00017	$40,000 $0	0.0	Assess Implications of Wide Spread Dioxin
1/2	02001	$65,000 $69,000	1.0	Improve Safety, Environmental Compliance, and Asset Management (Assistant Manager – Facilities)
3/1	05001	$65,000 $64,000	1.0	Protecting Your National Wildlife Refuge (Law Enforcement Officer)
26/2	05002	$30,000 $0	0.0	Enhance Interpretive Facilities (Seven Kiosks)
7/2	05003	$50,000 $0	0.0	Restore Floodplain Hydrology (Beaver Exclusion Devices)
27/2	05004	$65,000 $0	0.0	Herpetology Impact Study
28/2	05005	$12,000 $0	0.0	Develop Interpretive Materials (Three Brochures)
25/2	05006	$65,000 $0	0.0	Study Migratory Waterfowl Food Resources

Roanoke River Island National Wildlife Refuge Refuge Operation Needs System (RONS) Projects Listed by Tier and Station Rank				
Station Rank/	Project Number	Cost (First Year, Recurring)	Positions	Project Title
Tier 1				
1	00003	$0 $85,000	0.0	Enhance Basic Refuge Operations and Maintenance
2	97037	$65,000 $51,000	1.0	Improve Wetland Habitat Management (Heavy Equipment Operator)
3	05001	$65,000 $64,000	1.0	Protecting Your National Wildlife Refuge (Law Enforcement Officer)
4	00005	$65,000 $87,000	1.0	Initiate Management of Forested Wetland Habitat (Forester)
5	93028	$65,000 $63,000	1.0	Improve Environmental Education and Outreach (Park Ranger)
6	91022	$65,000 $53,000	1.0	Manage Wetland Easement Habitats (Biological Technician)
7	99003	$0 $65,000	0.0	Reinitiate Water Quality Monitoring
Tier 2				
1	02001	$65,000 $69,000	1.0	Improve Safety, Environmental Compliance, and Asset Management (Assistant Manager – Facilities)
2	90016	$250,000 $20,000	0.0	Habitat Management Capabilities (Heavy Equipment)
3	00008	$195,000 $59,000	1.0	Support Forested Habitat Management (Equipment Operator)
4	00004	$85,000 $59,000	1.0	Wildlife and Habitat Monitoring Program (Biological Technician)
5	00014	$5,000 $46,000	1.0	Facility Support (Maintenance Mechanic)
6	99002	$65,000 $59,000	1.0	Improve Forest Health (Forest Technician)
7	05003	$50,000 $0	0.0	Restore Floodplain Hydrology (Beaver Exclusion Devices)
8	00007	$65,000 $82,000	1.0	Maximize Outreach and Education (Park Ranger)
9	00006	$95,000 $96,000	1.0	Protect Refuge Water Rights (Hydrologist)
10	00001	$155,000 $5,000	0.0	Increase Public Awareness of Importance of Roanoke River Basin's Wetlands (Forested Wetland Exhibit)

Station Rank	Project Number	Cost (First Year, Recurring)	Positions	Project Title
		Roanoke River Island National Wildlife Refuge Refuge Operation Needs System (RONS) Projects Listed by Project Number		
11	00010	$65,000 $69,000	1.0	Support Forested Wetland Habitat Management (Administrative Assistant)
12	00013	$65,000 $66,000	1.0	Supervising Maintenance Staff (Wage Grade Supervisor)
13	00011	$65,000 $96,000	1.0	Implement Integrated Pest Management (Entomologist)
14	90008	$60,000 $10,000	0.0	Enhance Visitor Services (Radio System)
15	90011	$30,000 $10,000	0.0	Implement Forest Insect Survey Program
16	97032	$35,000 $0	0.0	Preserve Cultural Resources (Study)
17	97035	$30,000 $0	0.0	Improve and Manage Habitat for Migratory Birds (Study)
18	97033	$60,000 $0	0.0	Document Impacts of Growing Season Flooding due to Managed River Flows
19	00015	$26,000 $17,000	0.4	Interpretive Trail Support (Maintenance Worker)
20	00016	$30,000 $0	0.0	Getting Back to Standards With Seasonal Focus (Boundary Posting)
21	00009	$35,000 $56,000	1.0	Support Forested Habitat Management (Equipment Operator)
22	00012	$5,000 $46,000	1.0	Provide Custodial Maintenance of Buildings (Maintenance Mechanic)
23	00017	$40,000 $0	0.0	Assess Implications of Wide Spread Dioxin
24	00002	$45,500 $34,000	0.7	Provide Clerical Assistance and Visitor Receptionist (Office Assistant)
25	05006	$65,000 $0	0.0	Study Migratory Waterfowl Food Resources
26	05002	$30,000 $0	0.0	Enhance Interpretive Facilities (Seven Kiosks)
27	05004	$65,000 $0	0.0	Herpetology Impact Study
28	05005	$12,000 $0	0.0	Develop Interpretive Materials (Three Brochures)

XII. Maintenance Management System (MMS) Projects

(Ordered by Project Number, Tables by Number and Rank Follow Descriptions)

Project 90014 Construct Maintenance Facility Compound
Cost Estimate $1,271,000
Station Rank – 1 (Large Construction)
Currently, the refuge leases equipment storage space. This project involves the construction of a modern maintenance compound. The compound will consist of three maintenance buildings, including a storage building for boats and vehicles, a shop building for repairs and maintenance, and a pole shed for heavy equipment and supplies. The construction of a new maintenance facility will provide the maintenance staff with suitable working and storage space in order to maintain refuge facilities and equipment to Service standards.

Project 99001 Construct Kuralt Trail Interpretive Boardwalk
Cost Estimate $595,000
Station Rank – 3 (Large Construction)
Currently, the refuge does not provide visitors with a handicap-accessible trail. This project will construct a 1/2 mile, handicap accessible, raised boardwalk on the Kuralt Trail, to be equipped with educational signs for interpretation by visitors. This new boardwalk will provide refuge visitors with a unique look at the flora and fauna of the bottomland hardwood forest.

Project 01001 Replace D-6 Crawler Tractor
Cost Estimate $185,000
Station Rank – 5 (Non Construction Heavy Equipment)
An existing, old D-6 Crawler Tractor will be replaced. This relatively new (established 1989) and growing refuge needs equipment dedicated to its fire program. Initial acquisitions (18,000 acres) involved forested wetlands not subject to hazardous fire danger. Recent and future acquisitions involve several thousand acres of uplands that will be subject to wildfire and will require reforestation prescriptions requiring fire program-type equipment. The station's old D-6 Crawler Tractor requires pins, bushings, idlers, and roller replacements. Rather than make expensive repairs to an old item of equipment, it will be upgraded with a D-5, LGP Crawler equipped to respond to fire emergencies, whether on-site or at a nearby refuge. The equipment will complement existing refuge equipment required to manage habitat and maintain its habitat management road system necessary to attain the refuge's goals of protecting habitat for nesting and wintering waterfowl, protecting spawning habitat for migratory fish, and providing wildlife oriented public use opportunities for the American people.

Project 01005 Replace 1999 4x4 Dodge Pickup
Cost Estimate $26,000
Station Rank – 999 (Non-Construction Small Equipment)
This project will provide the funding necessary to replace a 1999 4x4 Dodge Pickup truck.

Project 01007 Replace 1999 4x4 Dodge Service Truck
Cost Estimate $31,000
Station Rank – 999 (Non-Construction Heavy Equipment)
This project will provide the funding necessary to replace a 1999 4x4 Dodge Service truck.

Project 01008 Replace 1992 4x4 Chevrolet Fire Truck
Cost Estimate $31,000
Station Rank – 999 (Non-Construction Small Equipment)
This project will replace an aging 1992 4x4 Chevrolet fire truck used in all aspects of fire management on this growing refuge. Recent and future land acquisitions involve several thousands of acres of uplands that are subject to wildfire and will require prescription burning to maintain habitat and wildlife and protect adjacent communities and structures.

Project 01010 Replace 1998 400 All-Terrain Vehicle (ATV)
Cost Estimate $6,000
Station Rank – 999 (Non-Construction Small Equipment)
This project will provide funding for replacement of an aging 1998 ATV used in all aspects of refuge and habitat management. This ATV is used for biological surveys, access to remote areas of the refuge, and equipment transportation for management purposes.

Project 02001 Replace 2000 4x4 Dodge Pickup Truck
Cost Estimate $26,000
Station Rank – 999 (Non-Construction Small Equipment)
This project will provide funding to replace a 2000 4x4 Dodge pickup truck used in all aspects of refuge management.

Project 04001 Replace 2004 New Holland TS Tractor
Cost Estimate $58,000
Station Rank – 999 (Non-Construction Heavy Equipment)
Replace tractor used for habitat management and maintenance of roads and public use trails. This tractor maintains roads that provide access to remote areas of the refuge otherwise accessible only by boat. Seasonal storms wash out roads that provide access to conduct waterfowl banding, wildlife surveys, managed water flow analysis, law enforcement activities, and fire activities. A safe, dependable road system is critical to accessing wetland units to respond to public emergencies (e.g., accidents, altercations, illegal substances, etc.), and accomplish management, restoration and protection of forest and wetland resources. Road access benefits hunting, wildlife observation, and wildlife photography opportunities. This tractor will need replacement by 2014.

Project 04002 Replace 2004 New Holland Batwing Mower
Cost Estimate $15,000
Station Rank – 999 (Non-Construction Small Equipment)
Replace mower operated to maintain refuge roads and trails for habitat management and public use to a refuge otherwise accessible only by boat. These roads provide access to conduct wildlife surveys and studies, law enforcement activities, fire activities, and public use opportunities. A safe and dependable road system is critical to accessing wetland and forest units to respond to public emergencies (e.g., accidents, altercations, etc.), and accomplish management, restoration, and protection of habitat resources. Maintaining roads benefits several wildlife-dependent recreational priorities set by the National Wildlife Refuge System Improvement Act of 1997 (e.g., hunting, fishing, wildlife observation, and wildlife photography). This mower will need replacement by 2009.

Project 04003 Replace 2004 Caterpillar Bulldozer
Cost Estimate $144,000
Station Rank – 999 (Non-Construction Heavy Equipment)
Replace bulldozer used to maintain refuge roads and trails for habitat management and public use to an otherwise boat-only accessible refuge. These roads provide access to conduct wildlife surveys and studies, law enforcement activities, fire activities, and public use opportunities. A safe and dependable road system is critical to accessing wetland and forest units to respond to public emergencies (e.g., accidents, altercations, etc.), and accomplish management, restoration, and protection of habitat resources. Maintaining roads benefits several wildlife-dependent recreational priorities set by the National Wildlife Refuge System Improvement Act of 1997 (e.g., hunting, fishing, wildlife observation, and wildlife photography). This bulldozer will need replacement by 2014.

Project 04004 Construct 125' x 40' Pole Shed
Cost Estimate $75,000
Station Rank – 2 (Small Construction)
This project involves the plan, design, and construction of a 125'x40' pole shed on the Broadneck Swamp unit to house heavy equipment operated to support habitat management and public recreation opportunities. This management unit is located 30-40 minutes from existing facilities and heavy equipment is needed to enable effective management of wetland and upland habitat stretched along approximately 15 miles of the Roanoke River. This 5,000-square-foot storage building will provide a secure area to store heavy equipment necessary to support operations at this site and improve transportation logistics of heavy equipment from existing storage to the unit. A septic system would be constructed to provide restroom facilities for staff at this remote site. Planning and design and construction contracting can be accomplished in one year.

Project 04005 Replace 2004 Ford F-150 4x4 Pickup Truck
Cost Estimate $25,000
Station Rank – 999 (Non-Construction Heavy Equipment)
Replace Ford F-150 4x4 Supercab truck that transports refuge staff and equipment to and from the refuge to accomplish refuge management of wetland and upland sites. This truck transports personnel to and from refuge lands, training sessions, workshops, meetings, stores, etc. This vehicle will need replacement by 2010.

Project 04006 Rehabilitate Public Use Parking Lots on Roanoke River NWR
Cost Estimate $66,000
Station Rank – 999 (Deferred Maintenance)
Rehabilitate Askew West, Askew East, Conine North, and Conine South Parking Areas. (Rte. 900, 901, 902, 903) These parking areas serve visitors participating in several wildlife-dependent activities, including wildlife observation, wildlife photography, and hunting. It also provides parking space and access for refuge personnel to conduct wildlife and habitat studies and management.

Project 04010 Replace 2004 Chevrolet ¾ Ton Pickup Truck
Cost Estimate $23,000
Station Rank – 999 (Non-Construction Small Equipment)
Replace 2004 Chevrolet 3/4 Ton pickup that transports staff and equipment to and from the refuge to accomplish refuge management of wetland and upland habitat sites. This truck transports personnel to and from refuge lands, training sessions, workshops, meetings, stores, etc.

Project 05001 Construct Photo Blinds
Cost Estimate $ 10,000
Station Rank – 999 (Small Construction)
Construct three photo blinds to facilitate wildlife viewing and photography opportunities in key wildlife viewing locations on the refuge. These activities are two of the six identified in the National Wildlife Refuge System Improvement Act of 1997 as priority wildlife-dependent recreation that will receive enhanced and priority consideration in refuge planning and management over other public uses. Since most of the refuge is accessible only by boat, wildlife observation and photography opportunities are limited. This project will provide a positive recreational experience for visitors and promote the national wildlife refuge system as a place to observe and photograph plants and wildlife.

MMS Projects Organized by Number			
Number	Description	Cost	Rank
90014	Construct Maintenance Facility Compound	$1,271,000	1
99001	Construct Kuralt Trail Interpretive Boardwalk	$595,000	3
01001	Replace D-6 Crawler Tractor	$185,000	5
01005	Replace 1999 4x4 Dodge Pickup	$26,000	N/A
01007	Replace 1999 4x4 Dodge Service Truck	$31,000	N/A
01008	Replace 1992 4x4 Chevrolet Fire Truck	$31,000	N/A
01010	Replace 1998 400 ATV	$6,000	N/A
02001	Replace 2000 4X4 Dodge Pickup Truck	$26,000	N/A
04001	Replace 2004 New Holland TS Tractor	$58,000	N/A
04002	Replace 2004 New Holland Batwing Mower	$19,000	N/A
04003	Replace 2004 Caterpillar Bulldozer	$144,000	N/A
04004	Construct 125' x 40' Pole Shed	$75,000	2
04005	Replace 2004 Ford F-150 4x4 Pickup Truck	$25,000	N/A
04006	Rehabilitate Public Use Parking Lots	$66,000	N/A
04010	Replace 2004 Chevrolet ¾ ton Pickup Truck	$23,000	N/A
05001	Construct Photo Blinds	$10,000	N/A

MMS Projects Organized by Rank			
Rank	Number	Description	Cost
1	90014	Construct Maintenance Facility Compound	$1,271,000
2	04004	Construct 125' x 40' Pole Shed	$75,000
3	99001	Construct Kuralt Trail Interpretive Boardwalk	$595,000
5	01001	Replace D-6 Crawler Tractor	$185,000
N/A	01005	Replace 1999 4x4 Dodge Pickup	$26,000
N/A	01007	Replace 1999 4x4 Dodge Service Truck	$31,000
N/A	01008	Replace 1992 4x4 Chevrolet Fire Truck	$31,000
N/A	01010	Replace 1998 400 ATV	$6,000
N/A	02001	Replace 2000 4X4 Dodge Pickup Truck	$26,000
N/A	04001	Replace 2004 New Holland TS Tractor	$58,000
N/A	04002	Replace 2004 New Holland Batwing Mower	$19,000
N/A	04003	Replace 2004 Caterpillar Bulldozer	$144,000
N/A	04005	Replace 2004 Ford F-150 4x4 Pickup Truck	$25,000
N/A	04006	Rehabilitate Public Use Parking Lots	$66,000
N/A	04010	Replace 2004 Chevrolet ¾ ton Pickup Truck	$23,000
N/A	05001	Construct Photo Blinds	$10,000

XIII. Summary of Public Comments and the Service's Responses

This appendix summarizes all comments that were received on the Draft Comprehensive Conservation Plan and Environmental Impact Statement for Roanoke River National Wildlife Refuge. Public comments on this draft document were accepted from March 30 to July 18, 2005.

A total of 15 individuals submitted comments on the Draft Comprehensive Conservation Plan and Environmental Impact Statement, either in writing or at public forums held on May 15 and 16, 2005. More than one individual represented some agencies or organizations.

PUBLIC FORUMS

During the March 30 – July 18, 2005, public review period, the refuge and planning staffs hosted two public forums, one on May 15 at the Windsor, North Carolina, community building (the town in which the refuge headquarters is located) and one on May 16 at the Halifax County Agricultural Center (near the northern end of the refuge's approved acquisition boundary). Each forum began at 6:00 p.m. and concluded at 9:00 p.m. The forums started as an open house with the refuge staff available to discuss the draft plan and refuge operations with the attendees. A 30-minute formal presentation on the draft plan was then given, followed by a facilitated discussion to solicit open-floor comments on the plan. A recorder wrote the comments on a flip chart, and the comments were then transcribed after the forums. A total of 8 individuals offered comments during these two public forums.

AFFILIATIONS OF RESPONDENTS

The table below identifies the names and affiliations of respondents who commented on the Draft Comprehensive Conservation Plan and Environmental Impact Statement, either in writing or at the two public forums. The State of North Carolina has many agencies with an interest in the Roanoke River floodplain. The refuge has close relationships with those agencies, as well as nongovernmental organizations that have been instrumental in protecting the lands of the Roanoke River Valley and promoting ecotourism in the area.

Name of Respondent	Affiliation
Leslie Catherwood	The Wilderness Society, Washington, DC
Dale Davis	North Carolina Wildlife Resources Commission, Edenton, NC
Michael Hinton	USDA, Natural Resources Conservation Service, Raleigh, North Carolina
Jeff Horton	The Nature Conservancy, Windsor, NC
Boyce Hudson	North Carolina Department of Environment and Natural Resources, Office of Conservation and community Affairs, Raleigh, NC
Tommy Hughes	North Carolina Wildlife Resources Commission, New Bern, NC
Jimmy Johnson	North Carolina Department of Agriculture, Raleigh, NC

Name of Respondent	Affiliation
Rives Manning	Halifax County Commission, Halifax, NC
Wib Owen	North Carolina Wildlife Resources Commission, Raleigh, NC
Christopher Papouchis	Animal Protection Institute
Phil Patrick	Partnership for the Sounds, Windsor, NC
Sam Pearsall	The Nature Conservancy, Durham, NC
B. Sachau	Jean Public.com, Florham Park, NJ
Jim Thornton	Dominion Power, Glen Allen, VA
Garcy Ward	North Carolina Department of Environment and Natural Resources, Division of Water Quality, Washington, NC

The number of affiliations represented in the above table can be summarized as follows: federal agencies, 1; state agencies, 4; local (city and county) agencies, 1; nongovernmental organizations, 5; public citizens (general public), 0; and businesses, 1.

COMMENT MEDIA

The types of media used to deliver the comments received by the refuge and planning staffs are categorized as follows: oral (given at the two public forums), 8; written letter, 6; and e-mail, 1.

GEOGRAPHIC ORIGIN OF RESPONDENTS

The geographic origins of the individual respondents who submitted comments are North Carolina, 12; Virginia, 1; California, 1; and New Jersey, 1.

SUMMARY OF CONCERNS AND THE SERVICE'S RESPONSES

The public comments received address the following concerns. The Fish and Wildlife Service's responses to each concern are also summarized.

FISH AND WILDLIFE POPULATIONS – SPECIES OF CONCERN

Comment: Add the mallard as a wintering waterfowl species.

Service Response: In the Comprehensive Conservation Plan and Final Environmental Impact Statement, the mallard has been added to the discussion of the waterfowl objective as a wintering waterfowl species.

HABITATS - STUDIES

Comment: The estimates of study costs are low and do not reflect recurring costs.

Service Response: The estimates in the Refuge Operation Needs System (RONS) are reviewed, revised, and resubmitted annually. The cost estimates will be reviewed next year and revised as appropriate. For items that are not personnel-related, the Refuge Operation Needs System does not handle recurring costs well. In the past, the refuge has secured recurring funding for studies from the Service's flex funding grants and from U.S. Geological Survey grant programs.

VISITOR SERVICES (PUBLIC USE) – WATERFOWL HUNTING

Comment: Currently all waterfowl hunting terminates on January 1. There is a need to utilize the state's entire waterfowl hunting season.

Service Response: The refuge will be open to waterfowl hunting for the entire state waterfowl hunting season beginning in 2006-2007. After consultation with the public, Service biologists, and the North Carolina Wildlife Resources Commission, it was concluded that hunting in January would not significantly impact the wood duck population.

VISITOR SERVICES (PUBLIC USE) – OPPOSITION TO HUNTING

Comment: Eliminate all hunting on the refuge.

Service Response: Hunting is one of the six priority public uses specified in the National Wildlife Refuge Improvement Act of 1997. The Service allows hunting as long as it is compatible with the mission of the Service, the National Wildlife Refuge System, and the purposes of the refuge.

RESOURCE PROTECTION – FERAL HOGS

Comment: Develop a strategy to monitor and manage feral hog populations on the refuge.

Service Response: Feral hogs have been added to the specified list of pest animals to be monitored in the strategies for pest animals. The pest animal control plan will specify detailed monitoring plans. As the presence of hogs is documented, the Service will implement control measures.

RESOURCE PROTECTION – LAND PROTECTION

Comment: Incorporate the protection of land discussed in the Service's 1994 document, "Preliminary Project Proposal: Proposed Expansion of Eastern North Carolina Refuges."

Service Response: The proposal was approved for detailed planning, but it was deliberately not discussed during this planning process. The staff was advised not to propose any expansion of the refuge during this planning process.

RESOURCE PROTECTION – MANAGED RIVER FLOWS

Comment 1: Articulate a plan of action that will utilize scientific studies and political mechanisms to influence water management decisions. Include a specific strategy to remedy prolonged flooding.

Comment 2: There are no scientific links to the regulation of Roanoke River flows at the dams and their negative effects on the floodplain.

Service Response: The six-member refuge staff has spent and will continue to spend a large proportion of its time attending meetings developing the relicensing agreement for the operation of the hydroelectric power generators regulated by the Federal Energy Regulatory Commission (FERC) and reviewing the operation of the flood control dams under Section 216 of the Flood Control Act.

Both the relicensing agreement and the Section 216 review will result in studies of the effects of water management on the ecosystem. The refuge does not have the lead in these efforts. The Service's Raleigh, North Carolina, Ecological Services Office is the lead office. The refuge staff and the Fisheries Coordination Office support the Ecological Services Office. The refuge has successfully applied for grants from the Service through its flex funding process and from the U.S. Geological Survey through its Science Support Partnership Program. Many other applications have not been funded.

The Introduction on page 1 of the Comprehensive Conservation Plan and Final Environmental Impact Statement has been rewritten to elaborate the efforts of the refuge staff and other Service offices.

Although there is little documentation of the effects of managed river flows on the Roanoke River ecosystem, data from other river ecosystems throughout the United States and elsewhere have documented and demonstrated the effects of managed flows. Please refer to the following references listed from the literature cited in Appendix II: Beasley and Hightower 2000; Boon et al. 1992; Collier et al. 1996; Fontaine and Bartell 1983; Fredrickson and Heitmeyer 1998; Hunt 1988; Jackson and Marmulla 1999; Ligon et al. 1995; Merona et al. 2001; Petts 1984; Poff and Hart 2002; Pringle et al. 2000; Ruane et al. 1986; Trush et al. 2000; and Vaughn and Taylor 1999.

RESOURCE PROTECTION – WATER QUALITY

Comment: Document the water quality in the Roanoke River.

Service Response: Reinitiating water quality monitoring is a high priority on the refuge. The RONS (Refuge Operation Needs System) projects that propose new funding initiatives list water quality monitoring as a Tier 1 Project (Projects to Support Essential Refuge Functions).

ADMINISTRATION – PERSONNEL MANAGEMENT

Comment: The plan gives relatively little staff support to conservation of natural environments and habitats, compared to constructed infrastructure and equipment management.

Service Response: The proposed staffing plan reflects an intention to support the improved biological and public use initiatives and support them with maintenance staff and skilled employees. The total biological or resource conservation staff numbers eight, while the maintenance staff numbers eight. Some of the eight-member maintenance staff will support the biological program directly by conducting precommercial thinning of trees and maintaining water control structures. The remainder of the maintenance staff will support all programs by maintaining access for refuge staff and the public on roads and trails. The priority order of filling the new positions in the plan (RONS projects order of rank) is as follows: (1) an equipment operator to work with the sole equipment operator currently on staff to manage the water control structures; (2) a forester; (3) a park ranger; (4) a second biological technician; and (5) an assistant manager for facilities, before hiring (6) a third equipment operator to support forestry management activities.

The proposed staff – 25 positions, 24.1 Full Time Equivalents (FTEs) – is as follows:

Management Staff: Manager, assistant manager, office assistant, law enforcement officer, assistant manager for facilities, and part-time clerk (0.4 FTE) (6 positions, 5.4 FTEs).

Biological Staff: Wildlife biologist, biological technician, resource specialist (forester/ecologist), biological technician, biological technician, forestry technician, hydrologist, administrative assistant (forestry operations), and entomologist (9 positions, 9 FTEs).

Maintenance Staff: Equipment operator, equipment operator, equipment operator, maintenance mechanic, wage grade supervisor, part-time maintenance worker (0.7 FTE), equipment operator, and maintenance mechanic (8 positions, 7.7 FTEs).

Public Use Staff: Public use specialist and media specialist (2 positions, 2 FTEs).